The Work of Day and Night

THE WORK OF DAY AND NIGHT

Suyūṭī's Collection of Prophetic Practices and Prayers

JALĀL AL-DĪN AL-SUYŪṬĪ

عمل اليوم والليلة

Translated by

RASHAD JAMEER

This edition published 2016 by
THE ISLAMIC TEXTS SOCIETY
MILLER'S HOUSE
KINGS MILL LANE
GREAT SHELFORD
CAMBRIDGE CB22 5EN, UK

British Library Cataloguing-in-Publication Data.
A catalogue record for this book is
available from The British Library.

ISBN 978 1903682 89 0

Reprinted 2018

Front cover Arabic calligraphy by Arabiccalligraphy4you

Typesetting by Martin Humphreys

CONTENTS

Acknowledgements ix
Translator's Introduction xi

THE WORK OF DAY AND NIGHT

The Work of Day and Night 2
Daily Practices upon Awakening 4
Daily Practices upon Entering the Washroom 6
Daily Practices for the Lesser Ablution 10
Daily Practices for the Greater Ablution 16
Daily Practices for the Ritual Prayer 18
Supererogatory Prayers 46
Supplications for the Morning and the Evening 58
Daily Practices for the Day of Jumᶜa 74
Daily Practices during the Ten Days of Dhū'l-Ḥijja 82
Daily Practices for the Day of ᶜArafa 84
Daily Practices for Reciting the Qur'ān 88
Daily Practices for Fasting 98
Daily Practices for Eating and Drinking 104
Daily Practices for Clothing and Adornment 110
Daily Practices for Sitting and Standing 118
Daily Practices upon Sleeping 122
Various Practices during the Night and the Day 138
Invocations during Times of Need 154
Various Reported Supplications 172
Various Reported Expressions of Seeking Refuge in God . . . 194
The Ninety-nine Beautiful Names of God 200

Endnotes 207
Appendix: A Selection of Transliterated Prayers 223
Glossary 229
Bibliography 233

'And God will observe your deeds, and [so will] His Messenger; then you will be taken back to the Knower of the unseen and the witnessed, and He will inform you of what you used to do.'

(Q.IX.94)

Dedication

To my daughter, to my teachers, especially Ustadh Abd al-Hakim al-Asyuti, to all students of knowledge and to you, the reader. May this book be a *wasīla* (means) for us to gain the company of Sayyidunā Muḥammad al-Muṣṭafā ﷺ. Āmīn.

ACKNOWLEDGMENTS

It is rigorously authenticated that the Prophet ﷺ said, 'Whoever does not thank people, has not thanked God.' So in this light, I would like to thank my parents, my wife and daughter, my family, my extended family, and my spiritual family at the *masājid* for all of their love and support. I would also like to thank the Islamic Texts Society for making this work come to life and, especially, Phoebe Luckyn-Malone for her contribution to this work in the editing and in providing the Appendix and Glossary. I would like to thank Shaykh Muhammad Yusuf, Muhammad Heft, Chaplain Rasheed Carter and Ustadh Abdus Shakur Brooks for their advice; and Abu Bakr Tiano, Abdullah Laban, Ali Cubias, Ibrahim Robertson for their good company while we lived in Egypt. I would like to thank Shaykh Faraz Rabbani for directing me to Ibn Ḥajar's addendum of Suyūṭī's *ʿAmal al-yawm wa'l-layla* and Sidi Abdullah Rajih for graciously gifting me his copy. May God reward you all for your care and support.

Rashad Jameer
Toronto, Canada
4 Safar 1437/16 November 2015

TRANSLATOR'S INTRODUCTION

Jalāl al-Dīn al-Suyūṭī, a prominent Egyptian scholar of the ninth/fifteenth century, composed the *Work of Day and Night* (ʿAmal al-yawm wa'l-layla) as a guide to correct conduct and worship in accordance with the example of the Prophet ﷺ and the Pious Predecessors. This book contains some of the most beautiful prayers in Islamic devotional literature and Suyūṭī has provided guidance about nearly every situation that one is likely to encounter day-to-day. It is hoped that this bilingual volume will enable a wider English-speaking audience to access one of the treasures of traditional Islamic knowledge and practice, and that it will provide Muslim readers with a source of inspiration in everyday life.

ʿABD AL-RAḤMĀN JALĀL AL-DĪN AL-SUYŪṬĪ

Abū al-Faḍl ʿAbd al-Raḥmān Jalāl al-Dīn al-Suyūṭī (AH 849–911/1445–1505 CE) was one of the most prolific authors of all time writing in Arabic. An outstanding scholar and polymath, Suyūṭī touched on almost every aspect of Islamic learning in his writings. Much is known about his life and works thanks to the biographies written by his students,[1] and from his own autobiography, *al-Taḥadduth bi-niʿmat Allāh*.[2] He was born in Cairo to a Circassian mother in 849/1445. His father was of Persian ancestry and worked as a teacher of Shāfiʿī jurisprudence at the mosque of Shaykhū. Tragically, he died when Suyūṭī was only six years old. Yet this did not hinder Suyūṭī from learning and

[1] For instance, see the biography written by his student ʿAbd al-Qādir al-Shādhilī, *Bahjat al-ʿābidīn bi-tarjamat Ḥāfiẓ al-ʿAṣr Jalāl al-Dīn al-Suyūṭī*, ed. ʿAbd Allāh Nabhān, Damascus: Majmaʿ al-Lugha al-ʿArabiyya, 1998. For further biographical sources, see J. H. Kramers et al., *Encyclopaedia of Islam*, 11 vols., new edn. (*EI²*), Leiden: E. J. Brill, 1954–2002, s.v. '*al-Suyūṭī*.'
[2] E. M. Sartain, *Jalāl al-Dīn al-Suyūṭī*, University of Cambridge Oriental Publications, nos. 23–24, Cambridge: Cambridge University Press, 1975.

excelling in the traditional religious sciences, beginning with the memorization of the Qur'ān and followed by Qur'ānic exegesis, *Ḥadīth* science, Shāfiʿī jurisprudence, Arabic grammar and *adab* ('literature' or 'belles-lettres').

Suyūṭī was a prodigious student and was educated by some of the best teachers of his day, including Jalāl al-Dīn al-Maḥallī (d. 864/1459), Ṣāliḥ b. ʿUmar ʿAlam al-Dīn al-Bulqīnī (d. 868/1464), Sharaf al-Dīn al-Munāwī (d. 871/1467) and Muḥyī al-Dīn al-Kafyājī (d. 879/1474). At the age of sixteen, he was granted a license (*ijāza*) to teach *adab* and grammar; at seventeen, his teacher Bulqīnī, the chief judge of Cairo, granted him permission to teach Shāfiʿī jurisprudence and to issue *fatwās*; and at eighteen, he inherited his father's former position at the mosque of Shaykhū. In the decades that followed, Suyūṭī was appointed to various posts; one was at the Shaykhūniyya, where he taught *Ḥadīth*, and two others were administrative positions at the Baybarsiyya *khānaqā* and the mausoleum of Barqūq al-Nāṣirī. These roles left him with ample time to devote to studying and writing.

He is said to have memorised 200,000 *ḥadīth*s and he considered himself to be especially skilled in seven scholarly disciplines: Qur'ānic exegesis, *Ḥadīth* science, jurisprudence, Arabic grammar and three further disciplines relating to rhetoric.[3] He is also reported to have excelled in the fields of the recitation of the Qur'ān, accounting, the division of inheritances, medicine, Arabic morphology, polemics, principles of jurisprudence, prose and letter writing.[4] When it came to jurisprudence, Suyūṭī was a staunch Shāfiʿī; his theological position was that of a conventional Ashʿarī and he appears to have been a follower of the Shādhilī Sufi order.[5]

[3] M. J. Saleh, 'Al-Suyūṭī and his work: their place in Islamic scholarship from Mamluk times to the present,' *Mamlūk Studies Review*, vol. v, 2000, pp. 75–76.
[4] Ibid., p. 76.
[5] Sartain, *Jalāl al-Dīn al-Suyūṭī*, vol. 1, pp. 35–36. For Suyūṭī's own views on the Shādhilī order, see Suyūṭī, *Ta'yīd al-ḥaqīqa al-ʿaliyya wa-tashyīd al-ṭarīqa al-Shādhiliyya*, ed. ʿAbd Allāh al-Ghumārī, Cairo: al-Maṭbaʿa al-Islāmiyya, 1352/1934.

One of the most remarkable aspects of his career was that he professed to have the ability to exercise independent judgment (*ijtihād*) on questions relating to the *Sharīʿa*, *Ḥadīth* and the Arabic language, albeit as a *mujtahid muntasab* ('an affiliated *mujtahid*'), which he was careful to explain meant that he would never contravene the rulings of the Shāfiʿī school of jurisprudence.[6] He also hoped that that his fellow scholars would come to recognise him as the tenth/sixteenth century's 'renewer of religion' (*mujaddid al-dīn*).[7] Unfortunately, the antagonistic response of many of his contemporaries in Cairo disappointed these hopes, but scholars outside of Egypt (especially in West Africa) held him in high esteem.[8]

Due in part to ongoing disputes with his rivals and conflicts with the authorities, Suyūṭī gradually withdrew from public life when he was around forty years old. In 906/1501, he retreated completely and remained at his house on the island of Rawḍa in the middle of the Nile. He declared that he intended to devote himself to God and occupied himself with editing and revising his works. He remained in seclusion until he died in 911/1505. After his death, he became particularly revered; reports surfaced that he had performed miracles during his lifetime and had witnessed visions of the Prophet ﷺ while awake and asleep.[9]

There is no question that Suyūṭī's literary output was tremendous. His own students drew up lists of between 200 and 600 titles that were approved by him, and one of them reported that he was

[6] Sartain, *Jalāl al-Dīn al-Suyūṭī*, vol. II, pp. 205–214. On the response of Suyūṭī's contemporaries to his declaration, see Saleh, 'Al-Suyūṭī and his work,' p. 77.

[7] See *EI*², s.v. '*Mudjaddid*.'

[8] His most vociferous critic was Shams al-Dīn al-Sakhāwī (d. 902/1497). On Suyūṭī's connections abroad, see for instance, E. M. Sartain, 'Jalal ad-Din as-Suyuti's relations with the people of Takrur,' *Journal of Semitic Studies*, vol. XVI, no. 2, 1971, pp. 193–198.

[9] See Muḥammad b. Aḥmad Ibn Iyās, *Badāʾiʿ al-zuhūr fī waqāʾiʿ al-duhūr*, ed. Paul Kahle and Muṣṭafā Muḥammad, Istanbul: Staatsdruckerei, 1931, vol. IV, p. 83 and ʿAbd al-Wahhāb al-Shaʿrānī, *al-Ṭabaqāt al-ṣughrā*, ed. ʿAbd al-Qādir Aḥmad ʿAṭā, Cairo: Maktabat al-Qāhira, 1970, p. 30.

able to work on multiple compositions simultaneously.[10] A list drawn up in the year 904/1498–99 recorded his works on the following general subjects: exegesis of the Qurʾān, *Ḥadīth* science, jurisprudence, principles of jurisprudence, principles of religion, Sufism, Arabic language, history, literature and poetry.[11] His most famous books were those concerning the Qurʾān (*al-Itqān fī ʿulūm al-Qurʾān*, *al-Durr al-manthūr fī al-tafsīr al-maʾthūr* and *Tafsīr al-Jalālayn*), but also *Ḥadīth* (*Jāmʿ al-jawāmiʿ* and *Tadrīb al-rāwī fī sharḥ Taqrīb al-Nawawī*) and history (*Taʾrīkh al-khulafāʾ*). An enormous number of his writings have been published in modern times, and many of these exist in English translation; however, until now, his *Work of Day and Night* has been unjustly neglected. The bilingual volume presented here is intended to remedy this oversight and to expand the range of traditional books of Muslim piety available in English.

THE WORK OF DAY AND NIGHT

The most important form of prayer in Islam is the *ṣalāt*, the ritual prayer, but there are innumerable other invocations and supplications appropriate for every occasion. While an individual may offer personal prayers at any time, the observant Muslim may also turn to the formal expressions of petition and praise that derive from the Qurʾān, the Prophet Muḥammad ﷺ and his Companions. These set prayers have been gathered and transmitted by Muslims from generation to generation in devotional texts, of which Suyūṭī's *Work of Day and Night* is a celebrated example.

In this book of devotion, Suyūṭī has provided his readers with a comprehensive collection of prayers for reciting on a daily basis. A special section is dedicated to prayers that are recommended

[10] Suyūṭī's student, Dāwūdī, is reported to have said, 'I have seen the shaykh write three quires in one day, both composing and writing down, as well as dictate *ḥadīth* and answer opponents.' Quotation from Saleh, 'Al-Suyūṭī and his work,' p. 75.

[11] Ibid., pp. 85–86.

for reading at times of need due to their widely recognised protective qualities. Suyūṭī took great care to explain precisely how to perform each of these daily practices (*waẓāʾif*, sing. *waẓīfa*) in accordance with the *Sunna* of the Prophet Muḥammad ﷺ, since they must be conducted in a particular way to be accepted by God Most High. Collectively, these acts of devotion—whether in word or deed—comprise the external works (*aʿmāl*, sing. *ʿamal*) prescribed by the *Sharīʿa*.

Suyūṭī's *Work of Day and Night*, which was completed in Rajab 892/June or July 1487,[12] was one of a number of similar texts composed during the pre-modern era, such as those with the same title by Nasāʾī (d. 303/915) and his student Ibn Sunnī (d. 364/974), and *al-Tahajjud wa-qiyām al-layl* by Ibn Abī al-Dunyā (d. 281/894).[13] Suyūṭī's *Work of Day and Night* complements his own other writings on similar themes, such as *Dāʿī al-falāḥ fī adhkār al-masāʾ wa'l-ṣabāḥ*[14] and *Adhkār al-adhkār*, but it is notable for its comprehensive subject matter and accessible arrangement. The work is also found in several manuscript copies with the variant title, *Waẓāʾif al-yawm wa'l-layla*, and this version has been published in at least one edition.[15]

Suyūṭī's *Work of Day and Night* was itself the subject of a later commentary by the celebrated Shāfiʿī scholar Aḥmad b. Muḥammad Ibn Ḥajar al-Haytamī (d. 974/1567). This commentary

[12] This date comes from the colophon found at the end of the original Arabic text.

[13] See Aḥmad b. Shuʿayb al-Nasāʾī, *ʿAmal al-yawm wa'l-layla*, ed. Fārūq Hamāda, Beirut: Muʾassasat al-Risāla, 1987; Aḥmad b. Muḥammad Ibn al-Sunnī, *ʿAmal al-yawm wa'l-layla*, Medina: Maktabat Dār al-Zamān, 2009; and ʿAbd Allāh b. Muḥammad Ibn Abī al-Dunyā, *al-Tahajjud wa-qiyām al-layl*, ed. Masʿad ʿAbd al-Ḥamīd al-Saʿdanī, Cairo: Maktabat al-Qurʾān, 1994.

[14] Suyūṭī, *Dāʿī al-falāḥ fī adhkār al-masāʾ wa'l-ṣabāḥ*, ed. Aḥmad ʿAbd Allāh Bājūr, Cairo: Dār al-Miṣriyya al-Lubnāniyya, 1994.

[15] Suyūṭī, *Waẓāʾif al-yawm wa'l-layla*, ed. Muṣṭafā ʿAbd al-Qādir ʿAṭā, Beirut: Dār al-Kutub al-ʿIlmiyya, 1407/1987. There are minor variations in wording between the two versions of the text, but not in terms of the overall structure or contents.

of Ibn Ḥajar's, entitled *Tanbīh al-akhyār ʿalā muʿḍilāt waqaʿat fī kitābay al-Waẓāʾif wa-Adhkār al-adhkār*, was a valuable supplement to Suyūṭī's *Work of Day and Night* because it provided explanations and additional authentications of Suyūṭī's opinions, all in the context of the Shāfiʿī school of jurisprudence (*madhhab*).[16] Ibn Ḥajar also clarified for his readers precisely where Suyūṭī's opinions departed from the Shāfiʿī consensus, making his comments indispensable for fully understanding the *Work of Day and Night*.

THE TRANSLATION

The Arabic text presented here, and the English translation that accompanies it, are derived from the Arabic edition published in Cairo by Maktabat wa-Maṭbaʿat Muṣṭafā al-Bābī al-Ḥalabī wa-Awlādihi in 1946. That edition was prepared from a manuscript copied for the Egyptian publisher in 1364/1945 at the request of Shaykh ʿAbbās Qaṭṭān, Mayor of Mecca.

The present translation was prepared with extensive reference to Ibn Ḥajar's commentary, *Tanbīh al-akhyār*, which was mentioned above. Where Ibn Ḥajar's remarks are of particular significance to the understanding of Suyūṭī's text, and when they help to clarify the status of his opinions within the wider Shāfiʿī *madhhab*, they have been quoted or summarised in the footnotes that accompany the translation.

A glossary has been included in the present volume and the Arabic text has been fully vocalised to aid those readers who are studying the Arabic language and the traditional Islamic sciences. In addition, a selection of some of the most beautiful and useful prayers from each chapter has been supplied in the appendix; they are in transliterated form so that all worshippers may benefit by reciting them—regardless of Arabic ability. Prayers that have been transliterated and included in the appendix are indicated by a superscript letter at the end of the prayer.

[16] Ibn Ḥajar al-Haytamī, *Tanbīh al-akhyār*, Amman: Arwiqa li'l-Dirāsāt wa'l-Nashr, 2013.

NOTE FROM THE ISLAMIC TEXTS SOCIETY

In order to facilitate the recitation of the prayers, which can be long, and because it is not always clear from the Arabic whether prayers that extend over a number of paragraphs are intended to be recited together or as alternative prayers from which the reader can choose, the publishers have inserted line breaks in between some of the prayers. This has also been adopted in the case of *ḥadīth* and other reports, and to divide the different instructions from each other.

Readers will appreciate that—given the very different natures of Arabic and English—aligning the text on facing pages is highly problematic. In order to do so, we have not been able to maintain equal spacing between sentences and paragraphs. Facing pages have therefore been adjusted individually, in order to ensure, as much as possible, that the prayers are on facing pages.

THE WORK OF DAY AND NIGHT

عَمَلُ الْيَوْمِ وَاللَّيْلَةِ

THE WORK OF DAY AND NIGHT

In the name of God, Most Compassionate and Merciful

Praise be to God, Lord of the worlds, and may God's blessings and peace be upon our Master Muḥammad and upon his family and his Companions. Praise be to God and may peace be upon His servants, whom He has selected. This is a small treatise entitled *The Work of Day and Night* (ʿAmal al-yawm wa'l-layla), which is a selection of clear and reliable *ḥadīths* that I have excerpted from the two books [by Ibn Taymiyya], *The Way of the Sunna* (Minhāj al-Sunna) and *The Goodly Word* (al-Kalim al-ṭayyib);[1] and God is the Guardian of success.

عَمَلُ الْيَوْمِ وَاللَّيْلَةِ

بِسْمِ اللهِ الرَّحْمٰنِ الرَّحِيم

اَلْحَمْدُ لِلّٰهِ رَبِّ الْعَالَمِينَ، وَصَلَّى اللهُ عَلَى سَيِّدِنَا مُحَمَّدٍ وَآلِهِ وَصَحْبِهِ وَسَلَّمَ.

اَلْحَمْدُ لِلّٰهِ وَسَلَامٌ عَلَى عِبَادِهِ الَّذِينَ اصْطَفَى، هٰذَا جُزْءٌ لَطِيفٌ فِي عَمَلِ الْيَوْمِ وَاللَّيْلَةِ مُنْتَخَبٌ مِنَ الْأَحَادِيثِ وَالْآثَارِ مُحَرَّرٌ مُعْتَبَرٌ لَخَّصْتُهُ مِنْ كِتَابَيْ مِنْهَاجِ السُّنَّةِ وَالْكَلِمِ الطَّيِّبِ، وَاللهُ وَلِيُّ التَّوْفِيقِ.

DAILY PRACTICES UPON AWAKENING

When awakening from sleep one should say, *Praise be to God who has given us life after causing us to die,*[2] *and to Him is the return. Praise be to God who has returned my spirit to me, Who has given health to my body and Who has allowed me to remember Him. There is no god but God alone; He has no partner. To Him is the dominion, to Him is all praise and He has power over all things.*[A] Whoever says this will have their sins forgiven, even if [those sins] are like the foam of the sea.

Praise be to God Who created sleep and wakefulness. Praise be to God Who awakened me in good health. I bear witness there is no god but God, He gives life to the dead and truly He has power over all things.

One should begin by using a tooth-cleaning stick (*siwāk*)[3] because there is a *ḥadīth* which says that, 'The Messenger of God ﷺ would not sleep without a *miswāk* beside him, so when he awoke he would begin [his day] by using the *miswāk*.' Aḥmad [Ibn Ḥanbal] narrated this.[4]

When lifting one's head [from the pillow] one should say, *Glory be to You, O God, and praise be to You. I seek Your forgiveness and turn to You in repentance.*

When leaving the house and looking up at the sky one should say, '*Our Lord, you have not created this in vain...,*' [and continue reciting to the end of] the Qur'ānic verse (*āya*).[5]

وَظَائِفُ الإِسْتِيقَاظِ

إِذَا اسْتَيْقَظَ الْإِنْسَانُ مِنْ نَوْمِهِ قَالَ: اَلْحَمْدُ لِلّٰهِ الَّذِي أَحْيَانَا بَعْدَ مَا أَمَاتَنَا وَإِلَيْهِ النُّشُورُ. اَلْحَمْدُ لِلّٰهِ الَّذِي رَدَّ عَلَيَّ رُوحِي وَعَافَانِي فِي جَسَدِي، وَأَذِنَ لِي بِذِكْرِهِ. لَا إِلٰهَ إِلَّا اللهُ وَحْدَهُ لَا شَرِيكَ لَهُ. لَهُ الْمُلْكُ وَلَهُ الْحَمْدُ وَهُوَ عَلَى كُلِّ شَيْءٍ قَدِيرٌ. مَنْ قَالَهَا غُفِرَتْ ذُنُوبُهُ وَإِنْ كَانَتْ مِثْلَ زَبَدِ الْبَحْرِ.

اَلْحَمْدُ لِلّٰهِ الَّذِي خَلَقَ النَّوْمَ وَالْيَقْظَةَ. اَلْحَمْدُ لِلّٰهِ الَّذِي بَعَثَنِي سَالِماً. أَشْهَدُ أَنْ لَا إِلٰهَ إِلَّا اللهُ يُحْيِي الْمَوْتَى وَأَنَّهُ عَلَى كُلِّ شَيْءٍ قَدِيرٌ.

وَيَبْدَأُ بِالسِّوَاكِ فَفِي الْحَدِيثِ: «أَنَّ رَسُولَ اللهِ ﷺ كَانَ لَا يَنَامُ إِلَّا وَالسِّوَاكُ عِنْدَهُ فَإِذَا اسْتَيْقَظَ بَدَأَ بِالسِّوَاكِ.» رَوَاهُ أَحْمَدُ.

فَإِذَا رَفَعَ رَأْسَهُ إِلَى سَقْفِ الْبَيْتِ قَالَ: سُبْحَانَكَ اللّٰهُمَّ وَبِحَمْدِكَ. أَسْتَغْفِرُكَ وَأَتُوبُ إِلَيْكَ.

فَإِذَا خَرَجَ مِنَ الْبَيْتِ وَنَظَرَ إِلَى السَّمَاءِ قَالَ: ﴿رَبَّنَا مَا خَلَقْتَ هٰذَا بَاطِلاً...﴾ اَلْآيَة.

DAILY PRACTICES UPON ENTERING THE WASHROOM

The *Sunna* is to enter [the washroom] with the left foot and say, *In the name of God. O God, I seek refuge in you from the male and female devils. O God, I seek refuge in You from filth and dirt that is foul and makes one filthy, and from Satan the accursed.*[B]

One should exit with the right foot and say, *Your forgiveness! Praise be to God Who has removed harm from me and Who has given health to me. Praise be to God Who has given me the pleasure of its [the food's] deliciousness, Who has made its nourishment remain in me and has pushed its harm away from me. Praise be to God Who has expelled from me what harms me and Who has retained for me what benefits me.*

[When entering the washroom] one should not wear anything that has the name of God or His Messenger ﷺ upon it, such as a ring or a coin. Nor should one face the *qibla* or turn one's back on it,[6] for whoever avoids doing so will have a good deed recorded and a bad deed erased. One should not face the *Bayt al-Maqdis*,[7] the sun, the moon, or [towards] the wind or turn one's back to it. One should go far away into the desert so one cannot be seen.

When relieving himself, what the Prophet ﷺ preferred was to conceal himself behind a raised building or a palm tree.

However, if one can find nothing but sand nearby to heap up and turn one's back to, then one should do that.

وَظَائِفُ دُخُولِ الْخَلَاءِ

اَلسُّنَّةُ أَنْ يُقَدِّمَ الْيُسْرَى فِي الدُّخُولِ وَيَقُولُ: بِسْمِ اللهِ اَللّٰهُمَّ إِنِّي أَعُوذُ بِكَ مِنَ الْخُبُثِ وَالْخَبَائِثِ. اَللّٰهُمَّ إِنِّي أَعُوذُ بِكَ مِنَ الرِّجْسِ وَالنَّجَسِ، اَلْخَبِيثِ الْمُخْبِثِ الشَّيْطَانِ الرَّجِيمِ.

وَالْيُمْنَى عِنْدَ خُرُوجِهِ وَيَقُولُ: غُفْرَانَكَ اَلْحَمْدُ لِلّٰهِ الَّذِي أَذْهَبَ عَنِّي الْأَذَى وَعَافَانِي. اَلْحَمْدُ لِلّٰهِ الَّذِي أَذَاقَنِي لَذَّتَهُ وَأَبْقَى فِيَّ قُوتَهُ وَدَفَعَ عَنِّي أَذَاهُ. اَلْحَمْدُ لِلّٰهِ الَّذِي أَخْرَجَ عَنِّي مَا يُؤْذِينِي وَأَمْسَكَ فِيَّ مَا يَنْفَعُنِي.

وَلَا يَحْمِلُ ذِكْرَ اللهِ وَرَسُولِهِ كَخَاتَمٍ أَوْ دِرْهَمٍ. وَلَا يَسْتَقْبِلُ الْقِبْلَةَ وَلَا يَسْتَدْبِرُهَا، فَمَنْ تَرَكَ ذٰلِكَ كُتِبَتْ لَهُ حَسَنَةٌ وَمُحِيَتْ عَنْهُ سَيِّئَةٌ. وَلَا يَسْتَقْبِلُ بَيْتَ الْمَقْدِسِ وَلَا الشَّمْسَ وَالْقَمَرَ وَالرِّيحَ وَلَا يَسْتَدْبِرُهَا. وَيَبْعُدُ فِي الصَّحْرَاءِ بِحَيْثُ لَا يَرَاهُ أَحَدٌ.

وَكَانَ أَحَبُّ مَا اسْتَتَرَ بِهِ النَّبِيُّ ﷺ لِحَاجَتِهِ هَدَفاً أَوْ نَخْلَةً.

فَإِنْ لَمْ يَجِدْ إِلَّا كَثِيباً مِنْ رَمْلٍ يَجْمَعُهُ وَيَسْتَدْبِرُهُ فَلْيَفْعَلْ.

When he ﷺ approached a discreet location, he would take a stick and dig a small hole in the ground until he stirred up the earth, then urinated [therein]. And he ﷺ would wear his shoes and cover his head, and he would not raise his garment [to uncover himself] until he came close to the ground. He ﷺ ordered us to lean on the left foot [when defecating] and to raise the right heel off the ground. And he ﷺ prohibited one from urinating in stagnant water, into an animal's burrow, at a watering place, in the middle of the road, in [places of] shade, into running water, under a fruit-bearing tree, at the edge of a running river,[8] into the air,[9] at the top of a mountain, in a [public or private] bath, or while standing, under a waterspout or into a drain. [He ﷺ prohibited] one from touching one's private parts with the right hand while urinating, or [using the right hand] while wiping oneself after defecating.[10] One should not talk while defecating, nor should one say, 'I pissed,' but rather, 'I urinated'.

وَكَانَ ﷺ إِذَا دَنَا بِحَزَازٍ مِنَ الْأَرْضِ أَخَذَ عُوداً فَنَكَتَ بِهِ الْأَرْضَ حَتَّى يُثِيرَ التُّرَابَ ثُمَّ يَبُولُ. وَكَانَ ﷺ يَلْبَسُ حِذَاءَهُ وَيُغَطِّي رَأْسَهُ، وَلَا يَرْفَعُ ثَوبَهُ حَتَّى يَدْنُوَ مِنَ الْأَرْضِ. وَأَمَرَ ﷺ أَن يَتَوَكَّأَ عَلَى الْيُسْرَى وَيَنْصِبُ الْيُمْنَى. وَنَهَى أَنْ يُبَالَ فِي الْمَاءِ الرَّاكِدِ وَالْجُحْرِ وَالْمَوْرُودِ وَقَارِعَةِ الطَّرِيقِ وَالظِّلِّ وَالْمَاءِ الْجَارِيِّ وَتَحْتَ شَجَرَةٍ مُثْمِرَةٍ وَعَلَى حَافَةِ نَهْرٍ جَارٍ وَفِي الْهَوَاءِ وَعَلَى رَأْسِ جَبَلٍ وَفِي الْمُسْتَحَمِ وَقَائِماً وَتَحْتَ الْمَأْزَبِ وَفِي الْبَالُوعَةِ. وَأَنْ لَا يُمْسِكَ ذَكَرَهُ بِيَمِينِهِ وَهُوَ يَبُولُ وَأَنْ لَا يَسْتَنْجِيَ بِيَمِينِهِ. وَأَنْ لَا يَتَحَدَّثَ وَهُوَ عَلَى الْخَلَاءِ، وَأَنْ لَا يَقُولَ: «أَهْرَقْتُ الْمَاءَ»، وَلْكِنْ لِيَقُلْ «بُلْتُ».

DAILY PRACTICES FOR THE LESSER ABLUTION

A prohibition has been handed down against using water warmed by the sun for [the purpose of] ritual purification (*ṭahūr*) and against using any leftover water that has been used by a woman for *ṭahūr*, or from using a copper vessel.[11]

It is *Sunna* to say at the beginning of one's lesser ablution (*wuḍū'*), *In the name of God; praise be to God.* [Also considered *Sunna* are]: using a tooth-cleaning stick; washing both palms [of the hands]; cupping one's hands and taking three copious handfuls of water and using it [for washing the nose and mouth] unless one is fasting;[12] sniffing up water [to clean] the nose, taking this water with the right hand, and doing this three times; running [water] between one's fingers and toes, proceeding with the right [hand or foot] before the left; washing one's forearms and lower legs;[13] performing these [steps of ablution] one after another without interruption;[14] and wiping one's entire head, ears and neck. One should not seek help from anyone, nor should one shake [the water] from one's hands,[15] or splash one's face with water. One should neither speak while performing the ablution nor waste water.

One should sit facing the *qibla* and in such a way as to not be splashed [by others]. One should extend one's hand towards the water and begin by [washing] the top of the face. If one is pouring the water for oneself, then one must proceed with the head and fingers; if another person pours it for one, then [one must begin with] the elbows and ankles. One should wash the feet with the left hand. One should place a vessel [for ablution] that has a wide mouth on one's right and a vessel with a small mouth on one's left.[16] [If someone else is pouring, then] the one pouring should be on one's left. One should drink from the remaining ablution water [in

وَظَائِفُ الْوُضُوءِ

وَرَدَ النَّهْيُ عَنِ الطَّهُورِ بِالْمَاءِ الْمُشَمَّسِ وَبِفَضْلِ طَهُورِ الْمَرْأَةِ، وَمِنَ الْإِنَاءِ النُّحَاسِ.

وَيُسَنُّ أَنْ يَقُولَ أَوَّلَ وُضُوئِهِ: بِسْمِ اللهِ وَالْحَمْدُ لِلَّهِ. وَالسِّوَاكُ وَغَسْلُ كَفَّيْهِ وَالْجَمْعُ بَيْنَهُمَا بِثَلَاثِ غُرَفٍ وَالْمُبَالَغَةُ فِيهِمَا إِلَّا لِلصَّائِمِ، وَالْاِسْتِنْثَارُ وَأَخْذُ مَائِهَا بِالْيُمْنَى وَالتَّثْلِيثُ وَالتَّخْلِيلُ وَتَقْدِيمُ الْيُمْنَى عَلَى الْيُسْرَى وَتَحْجِيلُهُ وَالْمُوَالَاةُ وَمَسْحُ جَمِيعِ رَأْسِهِ وَأُذُنَيْهِ وَرَقَبَتِهِ. وَلَا يَسْتَعِينُ وَلَا يَنْفُضُ يَدَيْهِ وَلَا يَلْطِمُ وَجْهَهُ بِالْمَاءِ. وَلَا يَتَكَلَّمُ أَثْنَاءَهُ وَلَا يَسْرِفُ فِي الْمَاءِ.

وَيَجْلِسُ مُسْتَقْبِلَ الْقِبْلَةِ وَبِحَيْثُ لَا يَنَالُهُ رَشَاشٌ. وَيَمُدُّ يَدَهُ عَلَى الْوَضُوءِ وَيَبْدَأُ بِأَعْلَى وَجْهِهِ. وَمُقَدَّمِ الرَّأْسِ وَبِالْأَصَابِعِ إِنْ صَبَّ عَلَى نَفْسِهِ، وَإِلَّا بِالْمِرْفَقِ وَبِالْكَعْبِ إِنْ صَبَّ عَلَيْهِ غَيْرُهُ. وَيَغْسِلُ الرِّجْلَ بِالْيَسَارِ. وَيَجْعَلُ الْإِنَاءَ الْوَاسِعَ عَنْ يَمِينِهِ وَالضِّيقَ عَنْ يَسَارِهِ وَيَقِفُ الصَّابُّ عَنْ يَسَارِهِ. وَيَشْرَبُ مِنْ فَضْلِ وَضُوئِهِ وَيَرُشُّ بَيْنَ إِزَارِهِ.

the vessel][17] and sprinkle water between one's loincloth (*izār*) [and one's private parts]. Immediately afterwards, and before speaking, one should say, while facing the *qibla* and looking towards the heavens, *I bear witness that there is no god but God alone; He has no partner. And I bear witness that Muḥammad is His servant and His messenger.* [Recite this] three times.

O God, make me one of the repentant and the purified. Glory be to You, O God, and praise be to You. I bear witness that there is no god but You. I seek Your forgiveness and turn to You in repentance. O God, forgive me my sins, bestow favours upon me in my abode, grant me blessings in my provision, make me content with what You have provided for me and tempt me not with what You have hidden from me.[C] One then prays for the Prophet ﷺ and recites *Sūrat al-Qadr* three times.[18]

Whenever the Prophet ﷺ performed the lesser ablution, he would take a handful of water and place it under his chin and lower jaw, run his fingers through his beard [with it] and rub the sides of his face a little. He ﷺ would run his fingers through his beard from below it, and place a [wet] finger in his mouth and in his earholes. When he ﷺ washed his face, his palms would reach his ears. He ﷺ would put his [left-hand] little finger in between his toes, and wash his heels and elbows. If there was any water leftover, he ﷺ would pour it over the parts of his body that touch the ground when prostrating (*sujūd*).

وَيقُولُ بَعْدَهُ عَلَى الْفَوْرِ قَبْلَ أَنْ يَتَكَلَّمَ مُسْتَقْبِلَ الْقِبْلَةِ نَاظِراً إِلَى السَّمَاءِ:
أَشْهَدُ أَنْ لَا إِلٰهَ إِلَّا اللهُ وَحْدَهُ، لَا شَرِيكَ لَهُ وَأَشْهَدُ أَنَّ مُحَمَّداً عَبْدُهُ
وَرَسُولُهُ (ثَلَاثاً).

اَللّٰهُمَّ اجْعَلْنِي مِنَ التَّوَّابِينَ وَاجْعَلْنِي مِنَ الْمُتَطَهِّرِينَ. سُبْحَانَكَ اللّٰهُمَّ
وَبِحَمْدِكَ أَشْهَدُ أَنْ لَا إِلٰهَ إِلَّا أَنْتَ أَسْتَغْفِرُكَ وَأَتُوبُ إِلَيْكَ. اَللّٰهُمَّ اغْفِرْ
لِي ذَنْبِي وَوَسِّعْ لِي فِي دَارِي وَبَارِكْ لِي فِي رِزْقِي وَقَنِّعْنِي بِمَا رَزَقْتَنِي وَلَا
تَفْتِنِّي بِمَا زَوَيْتَ عَنِّي. وَيُصَلِّي عَلَى النَّبِيِّ ﷺ وَيَقْرَأُ سُورَةَ الْقَدْرِ ثَلَاثاً.

وَكَانَ ﷺ إِذَا تَوَضَّأَ، أَخَذَ كَفّاً مِنْ مَاءٍ فَأَدْخَلَهُ تَحْتَ حَنَكِهِ فَخَلَّلَ بِهِ
لِحْيَتَهُ وَعَرَكَ عَارِضَيْهِ بَعْضَ الْعَرْكِ. وَشَبَّكَ لِحْيَتَهُ بِأَصَابِعِهِ مِنْ تَحْتِهَا وَأَدْخَلَ
إِصْبَعَهُ فِي فِيهِ وَفِي جُحْرِ أُذُنَيْهِ. وَكَانَ ﷺ يَبْلُغُ بِرَاحَتَيْهِ إِذَا غَسَلَ وَجْهَهُ
وَمَا أَقْبَلَ مِنْ أُذُنَيْهِ، وَكَانَ ﷺ يَدْلُكُ أَصَابِعَ رِجْلَيْهِ بِخِنْصَرِهِ وَيَدْلُكُ عَقِبَيْهِ
وَذِرَاعَيْهِ. وَكَانَ ﷺ إِذَا فَضَلَ مَاءٌ أَبْقَاهُ حَتَّى يَسِيلَ عَلَى مَوْضِعِ سُجُودِهِ.

He ﷺ would perform the greater ablution (*ghusl*) with a *ṣāʿ* [of water] and perform the lesser ablution (*wuḍūʾ*) with a *mudd*.[19] He ﷺ would perform the lesser ablution from a vessel when by a river, and when finished, he would empty any leftover water into the river. He ﷺ would have a cloth with which to dry off after the ablution. Once, he ﷺ performed the ablution and wiped his face with the edge of his garment. According to one narration, he ﷺ turned a coat that he was wearing inside out and wiped himself with it. The mother of ʿAbbās used to help him ﷺ perform the ablution; she would be standing and he sitting.

The *Sunna* for whoever has performed the ablution is to pray two units of prayer (*rakʿa*) after the ablution; meaning, at any time.[20]

وَكَانَ ﷺ يَغْتَسِلُ بِالصَّاعِ وَيَتَوَضَّأُ بِالْـمُدِّ. وَتَوَضَّأَ مِنْ إِنَاءٍ عَلَى نَهْرٍ فَلَمَّا فَرَغَ، أَفْرَغَ فَضْلَتَهُ فِي النَّهْرِ. وَكَانَتْ لَهُ خِرْقَةٌ يَتَنَشَّفُ بِهَا بَعْدَ الْوُضُوءِ. وَتَوَضَّأَ مَرَّةً فَمَسَحَ وَجْهَهُ بِطَرَفِ ثَوْبِهِ. وَفِي رِوَايَةٍ فَقَلَّبَ جُبَّةً كَانَتْ عَلَيْهِ فَمَسَحَ بِهَا. وَكَانَتْ أُمُّ عَبَّاسٍ تُوَضِّئُهُ، وَهِيَ قَائِمَةٌ وَهُوَ قَاعِدٌ.

وَالسُّنَّةُ لِمَنْ تَوَضَّأَ أَنْ يُصَلِّيَ بَعْدَ الْوُضُوءِ رَكْعَتَيْنِ أَيْ فِي أَيِّ وَقْتٍ كَانَ.

DAILY PRACTICES FOR THE GREATER ABLUTION

The *Sunna* for whoever has had sexual intercourse is to take a purificatory bath (*ghusl*) but only after having urinated, and not to bathe in an open space or upon a roof that does not conceal one. So if one performs the purificatory bath, one should take cover behind a wall, a camel[21] or a garment. If you do not find anything at all [for privacy], then draw a line [on the ground] in [the shape of] a circle, recite the name of God (Exalted is He) and bathe therein. One should neither bathe during the middle of the day, nor when it is dark. One should not pour the water [to begin the bath] without [some kind of] covering; and if [while washing] one has to see someone, one must do so after concealing one's private parts.

When removing one's garment, one should say, *In the name of God*, and when entering the public bath, one should beseech God [to send one to] Paradise (*Janna*) and seek refuge in Him from Hellfire (*Nār*). When one exits, one should seek forgiveness from God and thank God (Exalted is He) for this blessing [of the bath]. Before entering [the public bath], one should pay the admission fee. Entering the bath at sunset, or between the two evening prayers,[22] is disliked. One should enter with the left foot and exit with the right. One should begin [the purificatory bath] by washing off anything unclean, then washing the private parts and the surrounding area. Next, one should perform the lesser ablution (*wuḍūʾ*), then take care of the sides of the body, [after that], pour water on one's head, then on one's right side and then on one's left side. Proceed [by washing] the top of the body and rubbing [each body part]; do this three times. After [the purificatory bath], perform two *rakʿas*. The purificatory bath is *Sunna* after each act of sexual intercourse; if [the purificatory bath is not possible], then perform the lesser ablution (*wuḍūʾ*), or failing that, wash the private parts.

وَظَائِفُ الْغُسْلِ

اَلسُّنَّةُ لِمَنْ جَامَعَ أَنْ لَا يَغْتَسِلَ حَتَّى يَبُولَ وَلَا يَغْتَسِلُ بِأَرْضٍ فَلَاةٍ وَلَا فَوْقَ سَطْحٍ لَا يُوَارِيهِ. فَإِنِ اغْتَسَلَ اِسْتَتَرَ بِحَائِطٍ أَوْ بَعِيرٍ أَوْ ثَوْبٍ. فَإِنْ لَمْ يَجِدْ، خَطَّ خَطّاً كَالدَّائِرَةِ ثُمَّ يُسَمِّي اللّٰهَ تَعَالَى وَيَغْتَسِلُ فِيهَا. وَلَا يَغْتَسِلُ نِصْفَ النَّهَارِ وَلَا عِنْدَ الْعَتَمَةِ. لَا يَدْخُلُ الْمَاءَ إِلَّا بِمِئْزَرٍ فَإِنْ أَرَادَ أَنْ يُلْقِيَهُ فَبَعْدَ أَنْ يُوَارِيَ عَوْرَتَهُ.

وَإِذَا خَلَعَ ثَوْبَهُ قَالَ: «بِسْمِ اللّٰهِ» وَإِذَا دَخَلَ الْحَمَّامَ سَأَلَ اللّٰهَ الْجَنَّةَ وَتَعَوَّذَ بِهِ مِنَ النَّارِ. وَإِذَا خَرَجَ اِسْتَغْفَرَ وَشَكَرَ اللّٰهَ تَعَالَى عَلَى هٰذِهِ النِّعْمَةِ. وَيُعْطِي الْأُجْرَةَ قَبْلَ الدُّخُولِ. وَيُكْرَهُ دُخُولُهُ عِنْدَ الْغُرُوبِ وَبَيْنَ الْعِشَاءَيْنِ. وَيُقَدِّمُ الْيُسْرَى فِي دُخُولِهِ وَالْيُمْنَى فِي خُرُوجِهِ. وَيَبْدَأُ بِغَسْلِ الْقَذِرِ ثُمَّ غَسْلِ الْفَرْجِ وَمَا حَوْلَهُ. ثُمَّ يَتَوَضَّأُ ثُمَّ يَتَعَهَّدُ مُعَاطَفَهُ ثُمَّ يُفِيضُ عَلَى رَأْسِهِ ثُمَّ شِقِّهِ الْأَيْمَنِ ثُمَّ الْأَيْسَرِ. وَيُقَدِّمُ أَعْلَى بَدَنِهِ وَيَدْلُكُ وَيُثَلِّثُ. وَيُصَلِّي بَعْدَهُ رَكْعَتَيْنِ. وَيُسَنُّ لِكُلِّ وَطْءٍ غُسْلٌ، وَإِلَّا فَوُضُوءٌ، وَإِلَّا فَغَسْلُ الذَّكَرِ.

DAILY PRACTICES FOR THE RITUAL PRAYER

The most beloved of works to God (Exalted is He) is the ritual prayer (*ṣalāt*) [performed] at the beginning of its [appointed] time. The beginning of the appointed time is the pleasure of God (*riḍwān Allāh*), its middle is the mercy of God (*raḥmat Allāh*) and its end is the pardon of God (*ʿafw Allāh*).

When one hears the call to prayer (*ādhān*), one should say, *Welcome to those who call to righteousness and welcome to the prayer.* Then listen carefully to it; one should not speak. One should repeat what the muezzin is saying [and when he says, *Hasten to the prayer* (ḥayya ʿalā al-ṣalāt),] you should say, *There is no power and no might save in God* (lā ḥawl wa-lā quwwa illā bi'Llāh), and [when he says, *Hasten to success* (ḥayya ʿalā al-falāḥ),] say, *O God, make us eternally successful.*

After the two declarations of faith (*shahādatayn*),[23] one should add: *I am pleased with God as my Lord, with Muḥammad ﷺ as my messenger, with Islam as my religion, with the Qurʾān as my imam and with the Kaʿba as my direction [of prayer]. O God, record this declaration of mine in the Heavenly Register* (ʿIlliyyīn)*, and I make Your archangels, Your prophets who were sent and Your righteous servants [all] witnesses to it.* Conclude by saying, *Amen* (āmīn). *And make it a covenant for me with You [and] grant me my share in full for it on the Day of Resurrection. Truly, You do not break Your promise.*

At the call to prayer for the sunset prayer (*ṣalāt al-maghrib*), one should say, *O God, this is the approach of Your night, the end of Your day and the sound of Your summons, so forgive me.*

It is *Sunna* after every call to prayer (*ādhān*) and call to commence the prayer (*iqāma*), for the muezzin, the person making the call to commence the prayer and all who hear them to send prayers and

وَظَائِفُ الصَّلَاةِ

أَحَبُّ الْأَعْمَالِ إِلَى اللهِ اَلصَّلَاةُ لِأَوَّلِ وَقْتِهَا. وَأَوَّلُ الْوَقْتِ رِضْوَانُ اللهِ وَأَوْسَطُهَا رَحْمَةُ اللهِ وَآخِرُهَا عَفْوُ اللهِ.

فَإِذَا سَمِعَ الْآذَانَ قَالَ: مَرْحَباً بِالْقَائِلِينَ عَدْلاً وَبِالصَّلَاةِ مَرْحَباً وَأَهْلاً. ثُمَّ أَنْصِتْ لَهُ وَلَمْ يَتَكَلَّمْ. وَيَقُولُ مِثْلَ مَا يَقُولُ الْمُؤَذِّنُ وَزَادَ فِي كُلِّ جُمْلَةٍ: لَا حَوْلَ وَلَا قُوَّةَ إِلَّا بِاللهِ. وَفِي الثَّانِيَةِ: اَللّٰهُمَّ اجْعَلْنَا مُفْلِحِينَ.

وَزَادَ فِي الشَّهَادَتَيْنِ: رَضِيتُ بِاللهِ رَبّاً وَبِمُحَمَّدٍ رَسُولاً وَبِالْإِسْلَامِ دِيناً وَبِالْقُرْآنِ إِمَاماً وَبِالْكَعْبَةِ قِبْلَةً. اَللّٰهُمَّ اكْتُبْ شَهَادَتِي هٰذِهِ فِي عِلِّيِينَ، وَأُشْهِدُ عَلَيْهَا مَلَائِكَتَكَ الْمُقَرَّبِينَ وَأَنْبِيَاءَكَ الْمُرْسَلِينَ وَعِبَادَكَ الصَّالِحِينَ. وَاخْتِمْ عَلَيْهَا بِآمِينَ. وَاجْعَلْهَا لِي عِنْدَكَ عَهْداً تُوَفِّينِيهِ يَوْمَ الْقِيَامَةِ، إِنَّكَ لَا تُخْلِفُ الْمِيعَادَ.

وَيَقُولُ عِنْدَ أَذَانِ الْمَغْرِبِ: اَللّٰهُمَّ هٰذَا إِقْبَالُ لَيْلِكَ وَإِدْبَارُ نَهَارِكَ وَأَصْوَاتُ دُعَاتِكَ فَاغْفِرْ لِي.

وَيُسَنُّ لِكُلِّ مِنَ الْمُؤَذِّنِ وَالْمُقِيمِ وَسَامِعِهَا أَنْ يُصَلِّيَ وَيُسَلِّمَ عَلَى النَّبِيِّ ﷺ عَقْبَ الْآذَانِ وَالْاِقَامَةِ، ثَمَّ يَقُولُ: اَللّٰهُمَّ رَبَّ هٰذِهِ الدَّعْوَةِ التَّامَّةِ وَالصَّلَاةِ

invoke peace upon the Prophet ﷺ. Then one should say: *O God, Lord of this perfect call, Lord of the established prayer, bestow [upon] our Master Muḥammad the virtuous means, and grant him the praiseworthy station that You have promised Him. O God, Lord of this perfect call, Lord of the established prayer, bless Muḥammad, be pleased with me with such a pleasure that entails no anger afterwards. O God, Lord of this perfect call, the call of truth, the speech of God-fearingness* (taqwā), *make us live and die by it, resurrect us through it and make us amongst the best of its people in our life and our death.* One should ask God (Exalted is He) for forgiveness, well-being in this world and the Hereafter, and then ask for that which one desires.

Then one should wear two garments for the prayer, because truly God has more right to our adornment [than others].

The Prophet ﷺ would pray upon a mat, a tanned hide, a rug or on the thin bedding that he would sleep on.[24]

When leaving for the mosque one should say, *In the name of God. I believe in God, I trust in God. There is no power and no might save in God.*

O God, truly I ask You by the truth of those who are travelling towards You and I ask you by the truth of this way of mine towards You. I have not come out in pride, ostentation, or to gain a good reputation [for piety]. I have only come out seeking Your pleasure and guarding against Your wrath. I ask You to spare me from Hellfire, admit me to Paradise and forgive me of my sins. Truly, sins are only forgiven by You.

O God, make light be in my heart and in my tongue. Make light be in my hearing and in my sight. Make light be behind me and in front of me. Make light be above me and beneath me. O God, make me light.[D]

الْقَائِمَةِ آتِ سَيِّدَنَا مُحَمَّداً اَلْوَسِيلَةَ وَالْفَضِيلَةَ، وَابْعَثْهُ مَقَاماً مَحْمُوداً اَلَّذِي وَعَدْتَهُ. اَللّٰهُمَّ رَبَّ هٰذِهِ الدَّعْوَةِ التَّامَّةِ وَالصَّلَاةِ الْقَائِمَةِ، صَلِّ عَلَى مُحَمَّدٍ وَارْضَ عَنِّي رِضاً لَا سَخَطَ بَعْدَهُ. اَللّٰهُمَّ رَبَّ هٰذِهِ الدَّعْوَةِ التَّامَّةِ، دَعْوَةِ الْحَقِّ وَكَلِمَةِ التَقْوَى، أَحْيِنَا عَلَيْهَا وَأَمِتْنَا عَلَيْهَا وَابْعَثْنَا عَلَيْهَا وَاجْعَلْنَا مِنْ خِيَارِ أَهْلِهَا مَحْيَانَا وَمَمَاتَنَا. وَيَسْأَلُ اللهَ تَعَالَى الْعَفْوَ فِي الدُّنْيَا وَالْآخِرَةِ وَيَدْعُو بِمَا أَحَبَّ.

ثُمَّ يَلْبَسُ ثَوْبَيْنِ لِلصَّلَاةِ فَإِنَّ اللهَ تَعَالَى أَحَقُّ مَنْ يُتَزَيَّنُ لَهُ.

وَكَانَ ﷺ يُصَلِّي عَلَى الْحَصِيرِ وَالْفَرْوَةِ الْمَدْبُوغَةِ وَالْبِسَاطِ وَالْفِرَاشِ الَّذِي يَنَامُ عَلَيْهِ.

فَإِذَا خَرَجَ إِلَى الْمَسْجِدِ قَالَ: بِسْمِ اللهِ. آمَنْتُ بِاللهِ تَوَكَّلْتُ عَلَى اللهِ لَا حَوْلَ وَلَا قُوَّةَ إِلَّا بِاللهِ.

اَللّٰهُمَّ إِنِّى أَسْأَلُكَ بِحَقِّ السَّائِلِينَ عَلَيْكَ وَبِحَقِّ مَمْشَايَ هٰذَا إِلَيْكَ فَإِنِّي لَمْ أَخْرُجْ بَطَراً وَلَا مِرَاءً وَلَا رِيَاءً وَلَا سُمْعَةً، خَرَجْتُ اتِّقَاءَ سَخَطِكَ وَابْتِغَاءَ وَجْهِكَ. أَسْأَلُكَ أَنْ تَفُكَّ رَقَبَتِي مِنَ النَّارِ وَتُدْخِلَنِيَ الْجَنَّةَ وَتَغْفِرَ لِي ذُنُوبِي إِنَّه لَا يَغْفِرُ الذُّنُوبَ إِلَّا أَنْتَ.

اَللّٰهُمَّ اجْعَلْ فِي قَلْبِي نُوراً وَفِي لِسَانِي نُوراً وَاجْعَلْ فِي سَمْعِي نُوراً وَفِي بَصَرِي نُوراً. وَاجْعَلْ مِنْ خَلْفِي نُوراً وَمِنْ أَمَامِي نُوراً. وَاجْعَلْ مِنْ تَحْتِي نُوراً وَمِنْ فَوْقِي نُوراً. اَللّٰهُمَّ اجْعَلْنِي نُوراً.

One should walk with measured steps, peacefully and with dignity. When entering the mosque, one should enter with the right foot and say: *I seek refuge in God Almighty—by His noble Face and His eternal authority—from Satan the accursed. In the name of God. Praise be to God and peace be upon the Messenger of God. O God, bless Muḥammad and the family of Muḥammad. O God, forgive me my sins, open the doors of Your mercy for me and make the door of Your provisions easy for us.*

One should say the same when one exits the mosque, [replacing *open the doors of Your mercy for me* with] *open the doors of Your bounty for me*, and adding, *O God, truly I seek refuge in You from Iblīs and his army*, or, *O God, preserve me from Satan.*

On the day of *Jumʿa* (*yawm al-Jumʿa*), one should add upon entering [the mosque], *O God, make me the most focused of those who focus their attention upon You, make me the closest of those who come close to You and the most virtuous of those who implore You and desire You.*

When one reaches the prayer row (*ṣaff*) one should say, *O God, grant me the best of what you give to your righteous servants*, and pray two *rakʿa*s in salutation to the mosque (*taḥiyyat al-masjid*).[25]

One should sit intent upon [observing] spiritual seclusion (*iʿtikāf*).[26] One should not interlock one's fingers as long as one remains in the mosque, or when going to the mosque, and one should not spit while inside it. If one suddenly has to [spit], then one should spit in one's clothes and then fold that part up [to conceal it]. If one finds lice, one should bundle it up in one's clothes and not discard it in the mosque.[27]

وَيَمْشِي مُتَقَارِباً خُطَاهُ بِسَكِينَةٍ وَوَقَارٍ. فَإِذَا دَخَلَ الْمَسْجِدَ قَدَّمَ رِجْلَهُ الْيُمْنَى وَقَالَ: أَعُوذُ بِاللهِ الْعَظِيمِ وَبِوَجْهِهِ الْكَرِيمِ وَسُلْطَانِهِ الْقَدِيمِ مِنَ الشَّيْطَانِ الرَّجِيمِ. بِسْمِ اللهِ وَالْحَمْدُ لِلهِ وَالسَّلَامُ عَلَى رَسُولِ اللهِ. اَللّٰهُمَّ صَلِّ عَلَى مُحَمَّدٍ وَعَلَى آلِ مُحَمَّدٍ. اَللّٰهُمَّ اغْفِرْ لِي ذُنُوبِي وَافْتَحْ لِي أَبْوَابَ رَحْمَتِكَ وَسَهِّلْ لَنَا أَبْوَابَ رِزْقِكَ.

وَيَقُولُ مِثْلَ ذٰلِكَ إِذَا خَرَجَ مِنَ الْمَسْجِدِ وَلٰكِنْ يَقُولُ: وَافْتَحْ لِي أَبْوَابَ فَضْلِكَ، وَيَزِيدُ: اَللّٰهُمَّ إِنِّي أَعُوذُ بِكَ مِنْ إِبْلِيسَ وَجُنُودِهِ، أَوْ: اَللّٰهُمَّ اعْصِمْنِي مِنَ الشَّيْطَانِ.

وَيَزِيدُ يَوْمَ الْجُمُعَةِ فِي الدُّخُولِ: اَللّٰهُمَّ اجْعَلْنِي مِنْ أَوْجَهِ مَنْ تَوَجَّهَ إِلَيْكَ وَأَقْرَبِ مَنْ تَقَرَّبَ إِلَيْكَ وَأَفْضَلِ مَنْ سَأَلَكَ وَرَغِبَ إِلَيْكَ.

فَإِذَا انْتَهَى إِلَى الصَّفِّ قَالَ: اَللّٰهُمَّ ائْتِنِي أَفْضَلَ مَا تُؤْتِي عِبَادَكَ الصَّالِحِينَ، وَيُصَلِّي رَكْعَتَيْنِ تَحِيَّةَ الْمَسْجِدِ.

وَيَجْلِسُ وَيَنْوِي الْاِعْتِكَافَ. وَلَا يُشَبِّكُ يَدَيْهِ مَا دَامَ فِي الْمَسْجِدِ وَلَا فِي ذِهَابِهِ إِلَيْهِ وَيَجْتَنِبُ الْبُصَاقَ فِيهِ. فَإِذَا بَدَرَهُ، بَصَقَ فِي ثَوْبِهِ وَرَدَّ بَعْضَهُ عَلَى بَعْضٍ. وَإِنْ وَجَدَ قُمْلَةً صَرَّهَا فِي ثَوْبِهِ وَلَا يَطْرَحُهَا فِي الْمَسْجِدِ.

One should not sing poetry in the mosque[28] or [announce] a lost object. To anyone who announces [having lost something] in the mosque, it is said, 'May you not find it and may God not return it to you.'

One should not sell or purchase anything therein, and to anyone who does that, it is said, 'May God grant you no profit on your transaction.'

One should not swear by God or take an oath about affairs of the world.

One should not argue, raise the voice or openly bear arms, swords, bows or arrows.

One should not pass through [the mosque] with raw meat, remove pebbles from it or designate an exclusive spot for oneself in which to pray.

When the call to commence the prayer (*iqāma*) is called, one should answer [and repeat everything said during the *iqāma*], and instead of the expression, [*The prayer has begun* (qad qāmat al-ṣalāt)], one should say, *May God establish it and preserve it* (aqāmahā Allāh wa-adāmahā), and supplicate [to God] for what one wants. Just before the *iqāma*, one should pronounce the *tasbīh* (*subḥan Allāh*) and say the *tahlīl* (*lā ilāh illā Allāh*), the *taḥmīd* (*al-ḥamd li-Llāh*), the *takbīr* (*Allāh Akbar*) and the *istighfār* (*astaghfiru Allāh*) in sets of ten. The people of the mosque should not compete with one another to lead the prayer[29] and the followers should not stand until the muezzin has completed the *iqāma*.

When [the muezzin] makes the opening *takbīr* [*takbīr al-taḥrīm*], one should say: *God is utterly the Greatest, abundant praise be to God. Glory be to God morning and evening. I have turned my face to He Who originated the heavens and the earth, and I have turned away from everything*

وَلَا يَنْشُدُ فِي الْمَسْجِدِ شِعْراً وَلَا ضَالَّةً. وَيُقَالُ لِمَنْ أَنْشَدَهَا فِيهِ: لَا وَجَدْتَهَا وَلَا رَدَّهَا اللهُ عَلَيْكَ.

وَلَا يَبِيعُ فِيهِ وَلَا يُبْتَاعُ، وَيُقَالُ لِمَنْ فَعَلَ ذٰلِكَ: لَا رَبِحَ اللهُ تِجَارَتَكَ.

وَلَا يَحْلِفُ بِاللهِ وَلَا يَسْتَحْلِفُ لِحَدِيثِ الدُّنْيَا.

وَلَا يُخَاصِمُ وَلَا يَرْفَعُ فِيهِ الْأَصْوَاتَ، وَلَا يُشْهَرُ فِيهِ سِلَاحٌ، سَيْفٌ أَوْ قَوْسٌ أَوْ نَبْلٌ.

وَلَا يَمُرُّ فِيهِ بِلَحْمٍ نِيْءٍ وَلَا يَخْرُجُ مِنْهُ حُصَاةً وَلَا يَتَّخِذُ مِنْهُ مَكَاناً مَعْلُوماً لَا يُصَلِّي إِلَّا فِيهِ.

فَإِذَا أُقِيمَتِ الصَّلَاةُ، أَجَابَ وَقَالَ بَدَلَ لَفْظِ الْإِقَامَةِ: أَقَامَهَا اللهُ وَأَدَامَهَا، وَيَدْعُو بِمَا شَاءَ. وَقُبَيْلَ الْإِقَامَةِ يُسَبِّحُ وَيُهَلِّلُ وَيُحَمِّدُ وَيُكَبِّرُ وَيَسْتَغْفِرُ عَشْراً عَشْراً. وَلَا يَتَدَافَعُ أَهْلُ الْمَسْجِدِ الْإِمَامَةَ، وَلَا يَقُومُ الْمَأْمُومُونَ حَتَّى يَفْرُغَ الْمُؤَذِّنُ مِنَ الْإِقَامَةِ.

فَإِذَا أَحْرَمَ، قَالَ: اللهُ أَكْبَرُ كَبِيراً وَالْحَمْدُ لِلهِ كَثِيراً وَسُبْحَانَ اللهِ بُكْرَةً وَأَصِيلاً. وَجَّهْتُ وَجْهِيَ لِلَّذِي فَطَرَ السَّمَاوَاتِ وَالْأَرْضَ حَنِيفاً وَمَا أَنَا مِنَ

else but You (ḥanīf^an);[30] *and I am not one of the polytheists. Truly, my prayer, my rites, my life and my death belong to God, Lord of the worlds. He has no partner. With that I have been commanded and I am the first of those who submit.*

O God, You are the King; there is no god but You. You are my Lord and I am Your servant. I have wronged myself and I have confessed my sins, so forgive me for them. No one forgives sins except You. I am here and at Your service. All good is in Your Hands and evil does not reach You. O God, distance me from my mistakes just as you have made the east and the west distant from one another. O God, purify me of my mistakes just as a white garment is purified of dirt. O God, cleanse me of my sins [as if cleansed] with snow, water and ice. O God, truly I seek refuge in You that You may prevent me from seeing Your Face on the Day of Resurrection. O God, grant me life as a Muslim and grant me death as a Muslim. Glory be to You, O God, and praise be to You. Blessed be Your Name and exalted be Your Majesty. There is no god besides You. Abundant, pure and blessed praise be to God, commensurate with what befits Your noble Face; our Lord, Great and Glorious is He.

[In each *ṣalāt*] one should pronounce the expression of seeking refuge in God (*taʿawwudh*), and then recite the *Fātiḥa*[31] and a *sūra* for the first two *rakʿa*s only. In the morning prayer (*ṣubḥ* [also known as the dawn prayer, *fajr*]) and the midday prayer (*ẓuhr*), [the *sūra*s that are recited] should be from [the part of the Qurʾān referred to as the] *ṭiwāl mufaṣṣal*;[32] in the afternoon (*ʿaṣr*) and evening (*ʿishāʾ*) prayers, [the *sūra*s that are recited] should be from its middle parts; and in the sunset prayer (*maghrib*), [the *sūra*s that are recited] should be from [the part consisting of] short *sūra*s.

In the second [*rakʿa*] of the *maghrib* prayer, one should recite, '*Our Lord, do not misguide our hearts…*'[33]

الْمُشْرِكِينَ. إِنَّ صَلَاتِي وَنُسُكِي وَمَحْيَايَ وَمَمَاتِي لِلّهِ رَبِّ الْعَالَمِينَ. لَا شَرِيكَ لَهُ. وَبِذٰلِكَ أُمِرْتُ وَأَنَا أَوَّلُ الْمُسْلِمِينَ.

اَللّٰهُمَّ أَنْتَ الْمَلِكُ، لَا إِلٰهَ إِلَّا أَنْتَ. أَنْتَ رَبِّي وَأَنَا عَبْدُكَ. ظَلَمْتُ نَفْسِي وَاعْتَرَفْتُ بِذَنْبِي فَاغْفِرْ لِي ذُنُوبِي. فَإِنَّهُ لَا يَغْفِرُ الذُّنُوبَ إِلَّا أَنْتَ. لَبَّيْكَ وَسَعْدَيْكَ وَالْخَيْرُ كُلُّهُ فِي يَدَيْكَ وَالشَّرُّ لَيْسَ إِلَيْكَ. اَللّٰهُمَّ بَاعِدْ بَيْنِي وَبَيْنَ خَطَايَايَ كَمَا بَاعَدْتَ بَيْنَ الْمَشْرِقِ وَالْمَغْرِبِ. اَللّٰهُمَّ نَقِّنِي مِنْ خَطَايَايَ كَمَا يُنَقَّى الثَّوْبُ الْأَبْيَضُ مِنَ الدَّنَسِ. اَللّٰهُمَّ اغْسِلْنِي مِنْ خَطَايَايَ بِالثَّلْجِ وَالْمَاءِ وَالْبَرَدِ. اَللّٰهُمَّ إِنِّي أَعُوذُ بِكَ أَنْ تَصُدَّ عَنِّي وَجْهَكَ يَوْمَ الْقِيَامَةِ. اَللّٰهُمَّ أَحْيِنِي مُسْلِماً وَأَمِتْنِي مُسْلِماً. سُبْحَانَكَ اللّٰهُمَّ وَبِحَمْدِكَ وَتَبَارَكَ اسْمُكَ وَتَعَالَى جَدُّكَ وَلَا إِلٰهَ غَيْرُكَ. اَلْحَمْدُ لِلّهِ حَمْداً كَثِيراً طَيِّباً مُبَارَكاً فِيهِ كَمَا يَنْبَغِي لِكَرِيمِ وَجْهِكَ رَبَّنَا عَزَّ وَجَلَّ.

وَيَتَعَوَّذُ وَيَقْرَأُ سُورَةَ الْفَاتِحَةِ وَسُورَةً فِي الْأُولَيَيْنِ خَاصَّةً. وَتَكُونُ فِي الصُّبْحِ وَالظُّهْرِ مِنْ طِوَالِ الْمُفَصَّلِ، وَفِي الْعَصْرِ وَالْعِشَاءِ مِنْ أَوْسَاطِهِ، وَفِي الْمَغْرِبِ مِنْ قِصَارِهِ.

وَيَقْرَأُ فِي ثَانِيَةِ الْمَغْرِبِ: ﴿رَبَّنَا لَا تُزِغْ قُلُوبَنَا﴾

In the *maghrib* prayer on the eve of the day of *Jumʿa*, the *sūras al-Kāfirūn*[34] and *al-Ikhlāṣ*[35] [should be recited].

In the *ʿishāʾ* prayer on the eve of the day of *Jumʿa*, [one should recite] *Sūrat al-Munāfiqūn.*[36]

In the *ṣubḥ* [or, *fajr*] prayer on the day of *Jumʿa*, [one should recite] *Sūrat* [*al-Sajda*, which begins,] '*Alif lām mīm. This is the revelation...*'[37] and [one should recite *Sūrat al-Insān*, which begins,] '*Has there [not] come...*'[38] One should not read fewer than twenty verses of the Qurʾān in the *ṣubḥ* [or, *fajr*] prayer, or fewer than ten verses in the *ʿishāʾ* prayer.[39]

It has been transmitted that the Messenger of God ﷺ would count the verses during the prayer. He would place his right hand over his left and press them upon his chest,[40] and he would be silent and at ease after reciting, asking God (Exalted is He) for His bounty.[41]

When bowing one should say, *Glory be to God the Almighty and praise be to Him*. [This should be said] three times, at a minimum, or five, seven, nine or eleven times, which would be the most complete. *Glory be to You; Yours is the dominion, the kingdom and the majesty. Glory be to You; there is no god but You. Glory be to You, O God, our Lord, and praise be to You. O God, forgive me; You are the Ever-Relenting, the Most Merciful. Most Glorious, Most Holy, Lord of the angels and the spirit. O God, to You I bow, in You I believe and to You I surrender. I humble my hearing and my sight, my flesh and my bones to You, and whatever firmness I have in my feet belongs to You, Lord of the worlds.*[E]

وَفِي الْمَغْرِبِ لَيْلَةَ الْجُمُعَةِ بِسُورَةِ الْكَافِرِينَ وَالْإِخْلَاصِ.

وَفِي الْعِشَاءِ لَيْلَتَهَا بِسُورَةِ الْمُنَافِقِينَ.

وَفِي الصُّبْحِ يَوْمَهَا ﴿الٓمٓ تنزِيلُ﴾، وَ﴿هَلْ أَتَى﴾. وَلَا يَقْرَأُ فِي الصُّبْحِ بِدُونِ عِشْرِينَ آيَةً، وَلَا فِي الْعِشَاءِ بِدُونِ عَشْرِ آيَاتٍ.

وَوَرَدَ أَنَّهُ ﷺ كَانَ يَعُدُّ الآيَ فِي الصَّلَاةِ وَكَانَ يَضَعُ يَدَهُ الْيُمْنَى عَلَى الْيُسْرَى ثُمَّ يَشُدُّ بِهِمَا عَلَى صَدْرِهِ وَكَانَ يَسْكُتُ بَعْدَ القِرَاءَةِ سَكْتَةً هِينَةً يَسْأَلُ اللّٰهَ تَعَالَى مِنْ فَضْلِهِ.

فَإِذَا رَكَعَ، قَالَ: سُبْحَانَ رَبِّيَ الْعَظِيمِ وَبِحَمْدِهِ (ثَلَاثاً) وَهُوَ الْأَقَلُّ، أَوْ خَمْساً أَوْ سَبْعاً أَوْ تِسْعاً أَوْ إِحْدَى عَشَرَ، وَهُوَ الْأَكْمَلُ. سُبْحَانَكَ ذِي الْمُلْكِ وَالْمَلَكُوتِ وَالْعَظَمَةِ. سُبْحَانَكَ لَا إِلٰهَ إِلَّا أَنْتَ. سُبْحَانَكَ اللّٰهُمَّ رَبَّنَا وَبِحَمْدِكَ. اَللّٰهُمَّ اغْفِرْ لِي أَنْتَ التَّوَّابُ الرَّحِيمُ، سُبُّوحٌ قُدُّوسٌ رَبُّ الْمَلَائِكَةِ وَالرُّوحِ. اَللّٰهُمَّ لَكَ رَكَعْتُ وَبِكَ آمَنْتُ وَلَكَ أَسْلَمْتُ. خَشَعَ لَكَ سَمْعِي وَبَصَرِي وَلَحْمِي وَعَظْمِي وَمَا اسْتَقَلَّتْ بِهِ قَدَمَايَ لِلّٰهِ رَبِّ الْعَالَمِينَ.

When the Prophet ﷺ bowed [during the prayer] he would place his hands on his knees and would keep his back so straight that if water were to be poured on it, the water would remain [and not run off]. When he ﷺ bowed, he would spread his fingers apart and when he prostrated, he would keep them together. When he ﷺ raised his head [after bowing] he would say, *God has heard the one who has praised Him.*

When standing up [after bowing] one should say: *Our Lord, abundant, pure and blessed praise be to You, enough to fill the heavens and the earth, to fill what is between them and to fill what You wish from anything after. You are befitting of praise and splendour, more deserving than what Your servant has said, and all of us are servants to You. O God, there is no one who can withhold what You bestow and no one who can bestow what You withhold, and before You [on the Day of Judgement] the wealth of the wealthy will be of no benefit.*

When prostrating one should say, *Glory be to my Lord, the Most Exalted and praise be to Him*, [once] at a minimum, or seven times, which would be most complete. *Glory be to You, O God, and praise be to You. O God, forgive me. Most Glorious, Most Holy, Lord of the angels and the spirit. O God, to You I have prostrated, in You I believe and to You I surrender. My face has prostrated to He Who created it, shaped it and Who shaped its ears and eyes. Blessed be God, the Best of creators. O God, forgive me for all of my sin, the small of it and the large of it, the first of it and the last of it, what is public of it and what is private of it. O God, I seek refuge in Your pleasure from Your wrath and in Your protection from Your punishment. I seek refuge with You from You. We do not praise You [in any way other than] how You have praised Yourself. Lord, grant my soul its God-fearingness and purify it; You are the most excellent of those who purify it. You are its Patron and its Protector. My body and soul prostrate to You; my heart believes in You. O Lord, these are my hands, and [these] are sins I have committed against myself. O Almighty One, Who is sought in all great matters, forgive [my] great sins.*

وَكَانَ ﷺ إِذَا رَكَعَ، أَبَانَ يَدَيْهِ عَلَى رُكْبَتَيْهِ وَسَوَّى ظَهْرَهُ حَتَّى لَوْ صُبَّ عَلَيْهِ الْمَاءُ، لَاسْتَقَرَّ. وَكَانَ ﷺ إِذَا رَكَعَ، فَرَّجَ بَيْنَ أَصَابِعِهِ وَإِذَا سَجَدَ، ضَمَّ أَصَابِعَهُ. فَإِذَا رَفَعَ رَأْسَهُ مِنَ الرُّكُوعِ، قَالَ: سَمِعَ اللهُ لِمَنْ حَمِدَهُ.

فإِذَا انْتَصَبَ، قَالَ: رَبَّنَا لَكَ الْحَمْدُ حَمْداً كَثِيراً طَيِّباً مُبَارَكاً فِيهِ مِلْءَ السَّمَاوَاتِ وَالْأَرْضِ وَمِلْءَ مَا بَيْنَهُمَا وَمِلْءَ مَا شِئْتَ مِنْ شَيْءٍ بَعْدُ. أَهْلُ الثَّنَاءِ وَالْمَجْدِ أَحَقُّ مَا قَالَ الْعَبْدُ وَكُلُّنَا لَكَ عَبْدٌ اَللّٰهُمَّ لَا مَانِعَ لِمَا أَعْطَيْتَ وَلَا مُعْطِيَ لِمَا مَنَعْتَ، وَلَا يَنْفَعُ ذَا الْجَدِّ مِنْكَ الْجَدُّ.

فَإِذَا سَجَدَ، قَالَ: سُبْحَانَ رَبِّيَ الْأَعْلَى وَبِحَمْدِهِ ثَلَاثاً، وَهُوَ الْأَقَلُّ أَوْ سَبْعاً وَهُوَ الْأَكْمَلُ. سُبْحَانَكَ اللّٰهُمَّ وَبِحَمْدِكَ اَللّٰهُمَّ اغْفِرْ لِي. سُبُّوحٌ قُدُّوسٌ، رَبُّ الْمَلَائِكَةِ وَالرُّوحِ. اَللّٰهُمَّ لَكَ سَجَدْتُ وَبِكَ آمَنْتُ وَلَكَ أَسْلَمْتُ. سَجَدَ وَجْهِي لِلَّذِي خَلَقَهُ وَصَوَّرَهُ وَشَقَّ سَمْعَهُ وَبَصَرَهُ تَبَارَكَ اللهُ أَحْسَنُ الْخَالِقِينَ. اَللّٰهُمَّ اغْفِرْ لِي ذَنْبِي كُلَّهُ، دِقَّهُ وَجِلَّهُ، وَأَوَّلَهُ وَآخِرَهُ وَعَلَانِيَتَهُ وَسِرَّهُ. اَللّٰهُمَّ أَعُوذُ بِرِضَاكَ مِنْ سَخَطِكَ وَبِمُعَافَاتِكَ مِنْ عُقُوبَتِكَ وَأَعُوذُ بِكَ مِنْكَ. لَا نُحْصِي ثَنَاءً عَلَيْكَ أَنْتَ كَمَا أَثْنَيْتَ عَلَى نَفْسِكَ. رَبِّ أَعْطِ نَفْسِي تَقْوَاهَا وَزَكِّهَا أَنْتَ خَيْرُ مَنْ زَكَّاهَا. أَنْتَ وَلِيُّهَا وَمَوْلَاهَا. سَجَدَ لَكَ سَوَادِي وَخَيَالِي وَآمَنَ بِكَ فُؤَادِي. يَا رَبِّ هٰذِهِ يَدَايَ وَمَا جَنَيْتُ عَلَى نَفْسِي. يَا عَظِيماً يُرْجَى لِكُلِّ عَظِيمٍ فَاغْفِرِ الذَّنْبَ الْعَظِيمَ.

Then one says, *O Lord, forgive me my sins*, three times. *O God, aid me in remembering You, in thanking You and beautifully worshipping You.*

When the Prophet ﷺ prostrated, he would aim his fingers and toes towards the *qibla* and place his nose and forehead on the ground. He ﷺ would hold his hands away from his sides and place his palms in line with his shoulders. When he ﷺ prostrated, he would put his knees down before his hands. He ﷺ said, 'When one of you prostrates, put your palms on the ground.' They complained to him about the difficulty of prostration when they sit up. He said. 'Seek help with the knees.' Ibn ʿAjlān (may God be pleased with him) said, 'One does that by resting one's elbows on the knees when the prostration lasts a long time in supplication.'

When sitting between the two prostrations one should say, *Lord forgive me and have mercy upon me, compel me, guide me, grant me well-being, provide for me and elevate me. 'Indeed, I am in need of whatever good You send down to me.'*[42]

If the Prophet ﷺ was in an odd-numbered *rakʿa* in his prayer, he would sit up until he was completely straight.

Samura (may God be pleased with him) said, 'He ﷺ used to order us to remain motionless while sitting on the ground when we lifted our heads from prostration and to not be agitated [by sitting] on our heels.'

He ﷺ would raise his hands when starting the prayer, before bowing, when rising from bowing and when standing up after two *rakʿas*.[43] He ﷺ prohibited a person from putting one foot in front of the other to stand up during the prayer.

وَيَقُولُ: يَا رَبِّ اغْفِرْ لِي ذَنْبِي (ثَلَاثاً). اَللّٰهُمَّ أَعِنِّي عَلَى ذِكْرِكَ وَشُكْرِكَ وَحُسْنِ عِبَادَتِكَ.

وَكَانَ ﷺ إِذَا سَجَدَ اسْتَقْبَلَ بِأَصَابِعِهِ وَبِأَطْرَافِ رِجْلَيْهِ الْقِبْلَةَ وَأَمْكَنَ أَنْفَهُ وَجَبْهَتَهُ مِنَ الْأَرْضِ. وَنَحَّى يَدَيْهِ عَنْ جَنْبَيْهِ وَوَضَعَ كَفَّيْهِ حَذْوَ مَنْكِبَيْهِ. وَكَانَ ﷺ إِذَا سَجَدَ، وَضَعَ رُكْبَتَيْهِ قَبْلَ يَدَيْهِ، وَقَالَ ﷺ: «إِذَا سَجَدَ أَحَدُكُمْ فَلْيُبَاشِرْ بِكَفَّيْهِ الْأَرْضَ.» وَشَكَوْا إِلَيْهِ مَشَقَّةَ السُّجُودِ إِذَا نَهَضُوا، فَقَالَ: «اسْتَعِينُوا بِالرُّكَبِ» قَالَ ابْنُ عَجْلَانَ: «وَذٰلِكَ أَنْ يَضَعَ مِرْفَقَيْهِ عَلَى رُكْبَتَيْهِ إِذَا طَالَ السُّجُودُ وَدَعَا.»

فَإِذَا جَلَسَ بَيْنَ السَّجْدَتَيْنِ قَالَ: رَبِّ اغْفِرْ لِي وَارْحَمْنِي وَأَجْبِرْنِي وَاهْدِنِي وَعَافِنِي وَارْزُقْنِي وَارْفَعْنِي. ﴿إِنِّي لِمَا أَنْزَلْتَ إِلَيَّ مِنْ خَيْرٍ فَقِيرٌ﴾.

وَكَانَ ﷺ إِذَا كَانَ فِي وِتْرٍ مِنْ صَلَاتِهِ يَنْهَضُ حَتَّى يَسْتَوِيَ قَاعِداً.

قَالَ سَمُرَةُ: «كَانَ ﷺ يَأْمُرُنَا إِذَا رَفَعْنَا رُؤُوسَنَا مِنَ السُّجُودِ أَنْ نَطْمَئِنَّ عَلَى الْأَرْضِ جُلُوساً وَلَا نَسْتَوْفِزَ عَلَى أَطْرَافِ الْأَقْدَامِ.»

وَكَانَ ﷺ يَرْفَعُ يَدَيْهِ إِذَا دَخَلَ الصَّلَاةَ وَإِذَا رَكَعَ وَإِذَا قَامَ مِنَ الرَّكْعَتَيْنِ. وَنَهَى ﷺ أَنْ يُقَدِّمَ الرَّجُلُ فِي الصَّلَاةِ إِحْدَى رِجْلَيْهِ إِذَا نَهَضَ.

When one sits to recite the *shahāda* (*tashahhud*),[44] one should say: *In the name of God—the best of names—and by God.*[45] *Blessed greetings and pure prayers be to God. Peace be upon you, O Prophet, and the mercy of God and His blessings. Peace be upon us and upon the righteous servants of God. I bear witness that there is no god but God and I bear witness that Muḥammad is His Messenger. O God, send prayers upon Muḥammad.* At the final [*tashahhud*], add: *And upon the family of Muḥammad, just as you have sent prayers upon Abraham. And bless Muḥammad and the family of Muḥammad, just as you have blessed Abraham and the family of Abraham in all the worlds. Truly, You are the Most Praiseworthy and Majestic. O God, I seek refuge in You from the torment of the grave; I seek refuge in You from the temptation of the Antichrist* (al-Masīḥ al-Dajjāl); *and I seek refuge in You from the trials of life and the trials of death.*

O God, I seek refuge in You from sins and penalties. O God, indeed I have done myself a great wrong, and no one forgives sins except You, so forgive me with forgiveness from You and have mercy on me. Truly, You are the All-Forgiving and the Most Merciful. O God, forgive me for what I have sent ahead and what I may yet commit; for what I have performed secretly and for what I have performed publicly; for what I have squandered and for what You know more about than I. You are the Expediter and You are the Delayer; there is no god but You. O God, truly I ask You [to admit me to] Paradise, and I seek refuge in You from Hellfire. O God, I ask You for all that is good, both what is immediate and what is to come, for that which I know and of which I know not. O God, I ask You for all that is good that righteous servants have asked You for.

O Lord, grant us [that which is] good in this world and [that which is] good in the Hereafter, and save us from the punishment of Hellfire. Our Lord, truly we believe, so forgive us our sins, grant us pardon for our misdeeds and grant us death amongst the [ranks of the] righteous. Our Lord, grant us what You promised us through Your messengers and do not disgrace

فإذَا جَلَسَ لِلتَّشَهُّدِ قَالَ: بِسْمِ اللهِ خَيْرِ الأَسْمَاءِ، وَبِاللهِ اَلتَّحِيَّاتُ الْمُبَارَكَاتُ، الصَّلَوَاتُ الطَّيِّبَاتُ لِلهِ. اَلسَّلَامُ عَلَيْكَ أَيُّهَا النَّبِيُّ وَرَحْمَةُ اللهِ وَبَرَكَاتُهُ. اَلسَّلَامُ عَلَيْنَا وَعَلَى عِبَادِ اللهِ الصَّالِحِينَ. أَشْهَدُ أَنْ لَا إِلٰهَ إِلَّا اللهُ وَأَشْهَدُ أَنَّ مُحَمَّداً رَسُولُ اللهِ. اَللّٰهُمَّ صَلِّ عَلَى مُحَمَّدٍ. وَيَزِيدُ فِي الْأَخِيرِ: وَعَلَى آلِ مُحَمَّدٍ كَمَا صَلَّيْتَ عَلَى إِبْرَاهِيمَ وَبَارِكْ عَلَى مُحَمَّدٍ وَعَلَى آلِ مُحَمَّدٍ كَمَا بَارَكْتَ عَلَى إِبْرَاهِيمَ وَعَلَى آلِ إِبْرَاهِيمَ فِي الْعَالَمِينَ إِنَّكَ حَمِيدٌ مَجِيدٌ. اَللّٰهُمَّ إِنِّي أَعُوذُ بِكَ مِنْ عَذَابِ الْقَبْرِ وَأَعُوذُ بِكَ مِنْ فِتْنَةِ الْمَسِيحِ الدَّجَّالِ وَأَعُوذُ بِكَ مِنْ فِتْنَةِ الـمَحْيَا وَمِنْ فِتْنَةِ الْمَمَاتِ.

اَللّٰهُمَّ إِنِّى أَعُوذُ بِكَ مِنَ الْمَأْثَمِ وَالْمَغْرَمِ. اَللّٰهُمَّ إِنِّي ظَلَمْتُ نَفْسِي ظُلْماً كَثِيراً وَلَا يَغْفِرُ الذُّنُوبَ إِلَّا أَنْتَ فَاغْفِرْ لِي مَغْفِرَةً مِنْ عِنْدِكَ وَارْحَمْنِي إِنَّكَ أَنْتَ الْغَفُورُ الرَّحِيمُ. اَللّٰهُمَّ اغْفِرْ لِي مَا قَدَّمْتُ وَمَا أَخَّرْتُ وَمَا أَسْرَرْتُ وَمَا أَعْلَنْتُ وَمَا أَسْرَفْتُ وَمَا أَنْتَ أَعْلَمُ بِهِ مِنِّي أَنْتَ الْمُقَدِّمُ وَأَنْتَ الْمُؤَخِّرُ، لَا إِلٰهَ إِلَّا أَنْتَ. اَللّٰهُمَّ إِنِّي أَسْأَلُكَ الْجَنَّةَ وَأَعُوذُ بِكَ مِنَ النَّارِ. اَللّٰهُمَّ إِنِّي أَسْأَلُكَ مِنَ الْخَيْرِ كُلِّهُ، عَاجِلِهِ وآجِلِهِ، مَا عَلِمْتُ مِنْهُ وَمَا لَمْ أَعْلَمْ. اَللّٰهُمَّ إِنِّي أَسْأَلُكَ مِنْ خَيْرِ مَا سَأَلَكَ بِهِ عِبَادُكَ الصَّالِحُونَ.

رَبَّنَا آتِنَا فِي الدُّنْيَا حَسَنَةً وَفِي الْآخِرَةِ حَسَنَةً وَقِنَا عَذَابَ النَّارِ. رَبَّنَا إِنَّنَا آمَنَّا فَاغْفِرْ لَنَا ذُنُوبَنَا وَكَفِّرْ عَنَّا سَيِّئَاتِنَا وَتَوَفَّنَا مَعَ الْأَبْرَارِ. رَبَّنَا وَآتِنَا مَا وَعَدْتَنَا عَلَى رُسُلِكَ وَلَا تُخْزِنَا يَوْمَ الْقِيَامَةِ، إِنَّكَ لَا تُخْلِفُ الْمِيعَادَ. اَللّٰهُمَّ إِنِّي

us on the Day of Resurrection; truly, You do not fail in [Your] promise. O God, I seek refuge in You from the evil of which I know and of which I know not. O Changer of hearts (Muqallib al-Qulūb), *firmly establish my heart upon Your religion.* One should then supplicate for what one wishes and ask for one's needs, especially during the morning prayer (*ṣubḥ* [*fajr*]).

Whenever he ﷺ would sit for the *tashahhud,* he would place his hands on his thighs. When raising his ﷺ finger [to pronounce the *shahāda*], he would join his thumb and middle finger and point with his index finger, not moving it at all. He ﷺ would wipe the sweat on his forehead during the prayer. He would notice [what was] to his left and to his right, but he would not turn his neck.

During the prayer, he ﷺ prohibited: turning one's head or lifting one's gaze to the heavens; tying one's hair back; gathering one's clothes; rushing; wiping pebbles away or wiping one's forehead of the traces of dirt before finishing [the prayer]; flatulence; cracking the knuckles or interlocking the fingers; leaving one's garment dangling;[46] covering the nose or mouth; closing one's eyes; stretching; yawning or sneezing; and [unnecessarily] snorting phlegm during the prayer is from Satan. If one of you yawns, then resist it as much as possible.

Mujāhid (may God be pleased with him) said, 'Let one refrain from reciting [the Qur'ān] when someone behind one sneezes.' He said, [say]: '*Abundant, pure and blessed praise be to God until You are pleased, our Lord, and after You are pleased, from the affairs of this world and the Hereafter.* This [prayer] only stops at the Throne.'

The Prophet ﷺ prohibited anyone who was praying from greeting others, or vice versa. Once, a man complained to him about [Satanic] whisperings during the prayer, for he did not know [if

أَعُوذُ بِكَ مِنْ شَرِّ مَا عَلِمْتُ وَمِنْ شَرِّ مَا لَمْ أَعْلَمْ. يَا مُقَلِّبَ الْقُلُوبِ ثَبِّتْ قَلْبِي عَلَى دِينِكَ. وَيَدْعُو بِمَا أَحَبَّ وَيَسْأَلُ حَاجَتَهُ وَخُصُوصاً فِي الصُّبْحِ.

وَكَانَ ﷺ إِذَا قَعَدَ فِي التَّشَهُّدِ وَضَعَ يَدَيْهِ عَلَى رُكْبَتَيْهِ. وَعَقَدَ الْيُمْنَى ثَلَاثاً وَخَمْسِينَ وَأَشَارَ بِالسَّبَّابَةِ وَحَنَاهَا وَلَمْ يُحَرِّكْهَا بِشَيْءٍ. وَكَانَ ﷺ يَمْسَحُ الْعِرْقَ عَنْ وَجْهِهِ فِي الصَّلَاةِ وَكَانَ يُلْحِظُ فِي الصَّلَاةِ يَمِيناً وَشِمَالاً، وَلَا يَلْوِي عُنُقَهُ.

وَنَهَى ﷺ فِي الصَّلَاةِ عَنِ الْإِلْتِفَاتِ وَرَفْعِ الْبَصَرِ إِلَى السَّمَاءِ وَعَنْ عَقْصِ الشَّعْرِ وَكَفِّ الثَّوْبِ وَالْاِخْتِصَارِ وَمَسْحِ الْحَصَى وَمَسْحِ الْجَبْهَةِ مِنْ أَثَرِ التُّرَابِ قَبْلَ الْفَرَاغِ وَالنَّفْخِ وَتَفْقِيعِ الْأَصَابِعِ وَتَشْبِيكِهَا وَالسَّدْلِ وَتَغْطِيَةِ الْأَنْفِ وَالْفَمِ وَتَغْمِيضِ الْعَيْنَيْنِ وَالتَّمَطِّي. وَالتَّثَاؤُبُ وَالْعُطَاسُ وَالْمُخَاطُ فِي الصَّلَاةِ مِنَ الشَّيْطَانِ فَإِذَا تَثَاءَبَ أَحَدُكُمْ فَلْيَكْظِمْ مَا اسْتَطَاعَ.

قَالَ مُجَاهِدٌ: «وَلْيُمْسِكْ عَنِ الْقِرَاءَةِ» وَعَطَسَ رَجُلٌ خَلْفَهُ فَقَالَ: اَلْحَمْدُ لِلّٰهِ حَمْداً كَثِيراً طَيِّباً مُبَارَكاً فِيهِ حَتَّى يَرْضَى رَبُّنَا وَبَعْدَ مَا يَرْضَى مِنْ أَمْرِ الدُّنْيَا والآخِرَةِ. فَقَالَ «مَا تَنَاهَتْ دُونَ الْعَرْشِ.»

وَنَهَى ﷺ أَنْ يُسَلِّمَ الْمُصَلِّي عَلَى أَحَدٍ أَوْ يُسَلَّمَ عَلَيْهِ. وَشَكَى إِلَيْهِ رَجُلٌ اَلْوَسْوَسَةَ فِي الصَّلَاةِ فَمَا يَدْرِي أَشَفَعَ أَمْ وَتَرَ، فَقَالَ ﷺ: «إِذَا وَجَدْتَ

he had prayed] an even number [of *rakʿas*], or an odd number. He ﷺ replied, 'Whenever this happens to you, raise your right index finger and poke your left thigh [with it] and say, *In the name of God*, for verily, that stills Satan.'[47]

He ﷺ said, 'If one of you breaks your ablution during the prayer, then one should put one's hand over one's nose and leave.'[48]

When one says the concluding prayer for peace (*taslīm*), one should say, *May peace and the mercy of God be upon you* (al-salām ʿalaykum wa-raḥmat Allāh), two times, [once to the] right and [once to the] left. For each one [of these *salāms*], one should turn [far enough] so that one's cheek may be seen [when viewed from behind]. One may shorten the *salām*, but not lengthen it, and then one should wipe one's forehead with the right hand.[49] One should seek God's forgiveness three times by saying: *I seek forgiveness from God; there is no god but He, the Living, the Self-Subsisting. I turn to Him in repentance.* One should wipe one's head with one's right hand and say, *In the name of God. There is no god but He, the Most Compassionate, the Most Merciful. O God, remove worries, sorrow and sadness from me.*

Then one should say, *O God, You are [the Source of] peace and peace is from You. Blessed be You; O Lord of Majesty and Generosity.* Then one recites the *Fātiḥa* and the *Āyat al-Kursī* (the 'Throne Verse'),[50] and '*God bears witness that there is no god but He…*,'[51] and '*O God, King of All Sovereignty…*,' up until His Words, '*…without reckoning;*'[52] [recite] *Sūrat al-Ikhlāṣ* ten times;[53] the *muʿawwadhatayn* (the last two chapters of the Qurʾān);[54] pronounce the *tasbīḥ*, the *taḥmīd* and the *takbīr* in sets of ten—which would be the most complete and perhaps the best form. Or [one may repeat them] thirty-three times each, and upon completing the one hundredth, say: *There is no god but God alone; He has no partner. To Him is the dominion, to Him is all praise and He has power over all things. O God, there is no*

ذٰلِكَ، فَارْفَعْ أَصْبَعَكَ السَّبَّابَةَ الْيُمْنَى فَاطْعَنْ فِي فَخِذِكَ الْيُسْرَى وَقُلْ: بِسْمِ اللهِ، فَإِنَّهَا تُسْكِنُ الشَّيْطَانَ.»

وَقَالَ ﷺ: «إِذَا أَحْدَثَ أَحَدُكُمْ وَهُوَ فِي الصَّلَاةِ فَلْيَضَعْ يَدَهُ عَلَى أَنْفِهِ وَلْيَنْصَرِفْ.»

فَإِذَا سَلَّمَ، قَالَ: اَلسَّلَامُ عَلَيْكُمْ وَرَحْمَةُ اللهِ، مَرَّتَيْنِ يَمِيناً وَشِمَالاً يَلْتَفِتُ فِي كُلِّ وَاحِدَةٍ حَتَّى يُرَى خَدُّهُ. وَيَحْذِفُ السَّلَامَ وَلَا يَمُطُّهُ، ثُمَّ يَمْسَحُ جَبْهَتَهُ بِيَدِهِ الْيُمْنَى وَيَسْتَغْفِرُ ثَلَاثاً وَيَقُولُ: أَسْتَغْفِرُ اللهَ الَّذِي لَا إِلٰهَ إِلَّا هُوَ الْحَيُّ الْقَيُّومُ وَأَتُوبُ إِلَيْهِ. وَيَمْسَحُ بِيَمِينِهِ عَلَى رَأْسِهِ وَيَقُولُ: بِسْمِ اللهِ الَّذِي لَا إِلٰهَ إِلَّا هُوَ الرَّحْمٰنُ الرَّحِيمُ. اَللّٰهُمَّ أَذْهِبْ عَنِّي الْهَمَّ وَالْغَمَّ وَالْحُزْنَ.

ثُمَّ يَقُولُ: اَللّٰهُمَّ أَنْتَ السَّلَامُ وَمِنْكَ السَّلَامُ تَبَارَكْتَ يَا ذَا الْجَلَالِ وَالْإِكْرَامِ. ثُمَّ يَقْرَأُ الْفَاتِحَةَ وَآيَةَ الْكُرْسِيِّ وَ﴿شَهِدَ اللهُ أَنَّهُ لَا إِلٰهَ إِلَّا هُوَ﴾ وَ﴿قُلِ اللّٰهُمَّ مَالِكَ الْمُلْكِ﴾ إِلَى قَوْلِهِ: ﴿بِغَيْرِ حِسَابٍ﴾. وَسُورَةَ الْإِخْلَاصِ عَشْرَ مَرَّاتٍ وَالْمُعَوِّذَتَيْنِ وَيُسَبِّحُ وَيُحَمِّدُ وَيُكَبِّرُ عَشْراً عَشْراً، وَهُوَ الْأَكْمَلُ وَلَعَلَّهُ الْأَوْلَى أَوْ ثَلَاثاً وَثَلَاثِينَ وَيَقُولُ تَمَامَ الْمِائَةِ: لَا إِلٰهَ إِلَّا اللهُ وَحْدَهُ، لَا شَرِيكَ لَهُ، لَهُ الْمُلْكُ وَلَهُ الْحَمْدُ وَهُوَ عَلَى كُلِّ شَيْءٍ

power and no might save in God, the Most High, the Almighty. There is no god but God and we do not worship anything besides Him. To Him is the blessing, to Him is the bounty and to Him is all beautiful praise. There is no god but God. [We are] sincere before Him in our religion, even if the disbelievers abhor [it].

One should say three times, *Glory be to God, the Almighty, and praise be to Him. There is no power and no might save in God, the Most High, the Almighty.* [And then continue by saying,] *O God, there is no one who can withhold what You bestow and no one who can bestow what You withhold, and before You [on the Day of Judgement] the wealth of the wealthy will be of no benefit.*

Then one supplicates: *O God, truly I seek refuge in You from cowardice, I seek refuge in You from being returned to the worst stage of life,*[55] *I seek refuge in You from the trials of the world and I seek refuge in You from the torment of the grave. O God, I seek refuge in You from disbelief, from poverty and from the torment of the grave. O God, aid me in remembering You, in thanking You and in beautifully worshipping You.*

O God, I seek refuge in You from the punishment of Hellfire, from the trials of life and death, and from the evil temptation of the Antichrist. O God, Our Lord and the Lord of everything, I am a witness that You Alone are the Lord; You have no partner. O God, Our Lord and the Lord of everything, I bear witness that Muḥammad ﷺ is Your servant and Your messenger. O God, Our Lord and the Lord of everything, I am a witness that all of the servants are brothers. O God, Our Lord and the Lord of everything, make my family and I sincere before You at every hour of the day and night. Lord of Majesty and Generosity, listen and respond!

قَدِيرٌ. اَللّٰهُمَّ لَا حَوْلَ وَلَا قُوَّةَ إِلَّا بِاللهِ الْعَلِيِّ الْعَظِيمِ. لَا إِلٰهَ إِلَّا اللهُ وَلَا نَعْبُدُ إِلَّا إِيَّاهُ لَهُ النِّعْمَةُ وَلَهُ الْفَضْلُ وَلَهُ الثَّنَاءُ الْحَسَنُ. لَا إِلٰهَ إِلَّا اللهُ مُخْلِصِينَ لَهُ الدِّينَ وَلَوْ كَرِهَ الكَافِرُونَ.

وَيَقُولُ: سُبْحَانَ اللهِ الْعَظِيمِ وَبِحَمْدِهِ. وَلَا حَوْلَ وَلَا قُوَّةَ إِلَّا بِاللهِ الْعَلِيِّ الْعَظِيمِ (ثَلَاثاً). اَللّٰهُمَّ لَا مَانِعَ لِمَا أَعْطَيْتَ وَلَا مُعْطِيَ لِمَا مَنَعْتَ، وَلَا يَنْفَعُ ذَا الْجَدِّ مِنْكَ الْجَدُّ.

ثُمَّ يَدْعُو: اَللّٰهُمَّ إِنِّي أَعُوذُ بِكَ مِنَ الْجُبْنِ وَأَعُوذُ بِكَ مِنْ أَنْ أُرَدَّ إِلَى أَرْذَلِ الْعُمْرِ وَأَعُوذُ بِكَ مِنْ فِتْنَةِ الدُّنْيَا وَأَعُوذُ بِكَ مِنْ عَذَابِ الْقَبْرِ. اَللّٰهُمَّ إِنِّي أَعُوذُ بِكَ مِنَ الْكُفْرِ وَالْفَقْرِ وَعَذَابِ الْقَبْرِ. اَللّٰهُمَّ أَعِنِّي عَلَى ذِكْرِكَ وَشُكْرِكَ وَحُسْنِ عِبَادَتِكَ.

اَللّٰهُمَّ إِنِّي أَعُوذُ بِكَ مِنْ عَذَابِ النَّارِ وَمِنْ فِتْنَةِ الْمَحْيَا وَالْمَمَاتِ وَمِنْ شَرِّ فِتْنَةِ الْمَسِيحِ الدَّجَّالِ. اَللّٰهُمَّ رَبَّنَا وَرَبَّ كُلِّ شَيْءٍ، أَنَا شَهِيدٌ أَنَّكَ أَنْتَ الرَّبُّ وَحْدَكَ لَا شَرِيكَ لَكَ. اَللّٰهُمَّ رَبَّنَا وَرَبَّ كُلِّ شَيْءٍ، أَنَا أَشْهَدُ أَنَّ مُحَمَّداً عَبْدُكَ وَرَسُولُكَ. اَللّٰهُمَّ رَبَّنَا وَرَبَّ كُلِّ شَيْءٍ، أَنَا شَهِيدٌ أَنَّ الْعِبَادَ كُلَّهُمْ إِخْوَةٌ. اَللّٰهُمَّ رَبَّنَا وَرَبَّ كُلِّ شَيْءٍ، اِجْعَلْنِي مُخْلِصاً لَكَ وَأَهْلِي فِي كُلِّ سَاعَةٍ مِنْ لَيْلٍ أَوْ نَهَارٍ يَا ذَا الْجَلَالِ وَالْإِكْرَامِ اسْمَعْ وَاسْتَجِبْ.

God is most Great, God is most Great; the Light of the heavens and the earth. God is most Great, God is most Great. God [Alone] is sufficient for me and how excellent a Trustee. God is most Great, God is most Great. O God, rectify my religion that You have made as [a form of] protection for me. Rectify my worldly life, in which You have made my livelihood. O God, I seek refuge in Your pleasure from Your wrath. I seek refuge in Your pardon from Your revenge. I seek refuge in You, from You. O God, there is no one who can withhold what You bestow and no one who can bestow what You withhold, and before You [on the Day of Judgement] the wealth of the wealthy will be of no benefit. Save me from Hellfire, admit me to Paradise and wed me to a houri (ḥūr ʿayn).[56] *O God, I ask you for all good things of which I know and of which I know not. O God, I seek refuge in You from all evil of which I know and of which I know not.*

O God, I seek refuge in You from every action that embarrasses me and I seek refuge in You from every friend who disgraces me. I seek refuge in You from every action that distracts me. I seek refuge in You from every poverty that makes me forget and I seek refuge in You from every affluence that makes me transgress. O God, forgive me for all of my sins and mistakes. Rescue me, save me and guide me to wholesome actions and character traits, for no one but You can guide one to wholesome actions or divert one from bad actions.

O God, make the best of my days be the day that I meet You. O God, grant Muḥammad ﷺ the means (wasīla),[57] *instil his love in the chosen people, make his rank high in all the worlds and his abode amongst those brought near [to You].*

One should say three times: *Glory be to Your Lord, Lord of Honour, [He is above] what they ascribe to Him. Peace be upon the messengers. Praise be to God, Lord of the worlds.* The morning prayer (*ṣubḥ* [*fajr*]) and the sunset prayer (*maghrib*) are distinguished by one's saying the following [words] ten or one hundred times as a litany (*wird*)

اَللهُ أَكْبَرُ اللهُ أَكْبَرُ، نُورُ السَّموَاتِ وَالأَرْضِ اَللهُ أَكْبَرُ اللهُ أَكْبَرُ، حَسْبِيَ اللهُ وَنِعْمَ الْوَكِيْلُ اَللهُ أَكْبَرُ اللهُ أَكْبَرُ. اَللّٰهُمَّ اَصْلِحْ لِي دِيْنِيَ الَّذِي جَعَلْتَهُ عِصْمَةً لِي وَأَصْلِحْ دُنْيَايَ الَّتِي جَعَلْتَ فِيهَا مَعَاشِي. اَللّٰهُمَّ إِنِّي أَعُوذُ بِرِضَاكَ مِنْ سَخَطِكَ وَأَعُوذُ بِعَفْوِكَ مِنْ نِقْمَتِكَ وَأَعُوذُ بِكَ مِنْكَ. لَا مَانِعَ لِمَا اَعْطَيْتَ وَلَا مُعْطِيَ لِمَا مَنَعْتَ، وَلَا يَنْفَعُ ذَا الْجَدِّ مِنْكَ الْجَدُّ. أَجِرْنِي مِنَ النَّارِ وَأَدْخِلْنِيَ الْجَنَّةَ وَزَوِّجْنِي مِنَ الْحُورِ الْعِيْنِ. اَللّٰهُمَّ إِنِّي أَسْأَلُكَ مِنَ الْخَيْرِ كُلِّهِ، مَا عَلِمْتُ مِنْهُ وَمَا لَمْ أَعْلَمْ. اَللّٰهُمَّ إِنِّي اَعُوذُ مِنَ الشَّرِ كُلِّهُ، مَا عَلِمْتُ مِنْهُ وَمَا لَمْ أَعْلَمْ.

اَللّٰهُمَّ إِنِّي أَعُوذُ بِكَ مِنْ كُلِّ عَمَلٍ يُخْزِينِي وَأَعُوذُ بِكَ مِنْ كُلِّ صَاحِبٍ يُرْدِينِي وَأَعُوذُ بِكَ مِنْ كُلِّ عَمَلٍ يُلْهِينِي وَأَعُوذُ بِكَ مِنْ كُلِّ فَقْرٍ يُنْسِينِي وَأَعُوذُ بِكَ مِنْ كُلِّ غِنًى يُطْغِينِي. اَللّٰهُمَّ اغْفِرْ لِي ذُنُوبِي وَخَطَايَايَ كُلَّهَا أَغِثْنِي وَأَجِرْنِي وَاهْدِنِي لِصَالِحِ الأَعْمَالِ وَالأَخْلَاقِ، فَإِنَّهُ لَا يَهْدِي لِصَالِحِهَا وَلَا يَصْرِفُ عَنْ سَيِّئَاتِهَا إِلَّا أَنْتَ.

اَللّٰهُمَّ اجْعَلْ خَيْرَ أَيَّامِي يَوْمَ لِقَائِكَ. اَللّٰهُمَّ أَعْطِ مُحَمَّداً اَلْوَسِيلَةَ وَاجْعَلْ فِي الْمُصْطَفَيْنَ مَحَبَّتَهُ وَفِي الْعَالَمِينَ دَرَجَتَهُ وَفِي الْمُقَرَّبِينَ دَارَهُ.

وَيَقُولُ: سُبْحَانَ رَبِّكَ رَبِّ الْعِزَّةِ عَمَّا يَصِفُونَ. وَسَلَامٌ عَلَى الْمُرْسَلِينَ. وَالْحَمْدُ لِلهِ رَبِّ الْعَالَمِينَ (ثَلَاثًا). وَيَخْتَصُّ الصُّبْحَ وَالْمَغْرِبَ بِأَنْ يَقُولَ بَعْدَهُمَا قَبْلَ أَنْ يُثْنِيَ رِجْلَيْهِ وَقَبْلَ أَنْ يَتَكَلَّمَ: لَا إِلٰهَ إِلَّا اللهُ وَحْدَهُ لَا شَرِيْكَ لَهُ،

after the two [preceding phrases], before stretching out one's feet or speaking: *There is no god but God alone; He has no partner. To Him is the dominion and to Him is all praise. He gives life and He gives death. In His Hand is all that is good and He has power over all things.*

[One should say,] *O God, save me from Hellfire*, seven times. The morning prayer (*ṣubḥ* [*fajr*]) is distinguished by one's saying afterwards (while one's legs are still in the *tashahhud* position), *Glory be to God and praise be to Him. I seek forgiveness from God. Truly, He is Ever-Relenting.* [This should be repeated] seventy times. One should recite *Sūrat al-Ikhlāṣ*[58] twelve or one hundred times before one speaks. And one should say three times: *O God, truly I ask you for beneficial knowledge, pure provisions and accepted actions. O God, through You do I try, through You do I strive and through You do I fight. O God, guide me with special guidance from You, pour Your bounty upon me, envelop me with Your mercy and send down Your blessings upon me.*

[Repeat] three times: *O God, rectify for me my worldly life, in which You made my livelihood. O God, rectify my religion that You have made as [a form of] protection for me.* [And repeat] three times: *O God, rectify my Hereafter, which you have made my place of return.* [And repeat] three times: *O God, I seek refuge in Your pardon from Your punishment.*

It is incumbent upon anyone praying the morning prayer (*ṣubḥ* [*fajr*]) to not stand up from their place [immediately]. Instead, one should remain seated and remember God until the sun rises, then pray two *rakʿas*. Sleeping after the morning prayer is disliked.

لَهُ ٱلْمُلْكُ وَلَهُ الْحَمْدُ يُحْيِي وَيُمِيتُ بِيَدِهِ الْخَيْرُ وَهُوَ عَلَى كُلِّ شَيْءٍ قَدِيرٌ (عَشْراً أَوْ مِائَةً وِرْداً).

اَللّٰهُمَّ أَجِرْنِي مِنَ النَّارِ (سَبْعاً). وَيَخْتَصُّ الصُّبْحَ بِأَنْ يَقُولَ بَعْدَهَا وَهُوَ ثَانٍ رِجْلَيْهِ: سُبْحَانَ اللهِ وَبِحَمْدِهِ أَسْتَغْفِرُ اللهَ إِنَّهُ كَانَ تَوَّاباً (سَبْعِيْنَ). وَبِأَنْ يَقْرَأَ سُورَةَ الْإِخْلَاصِ اِثْنَتَيْ عَشْرَةَ مَرَّةً أَوْ مِائَةً قَبْلَ أَنْ يَتَكَلَّمَ. وَبِأَنْ يَقُولَ: اَللّٰهُمَّ إِنِّي أَسْأَلُكَ عِلْماً نَافِعاً وَرِزْقاً طَيِّباً وَعَمَلاً مُتَقَبَّلاً. اَللّٰهُمَّ بِكَ أُحَاوِلُ وَبِكَ أُصَاوِلُ وَبِكَ أُقَاتِلُ. اَللّٰهُمَّ اهْدِنِي مِنْ عِنْدِكَ وَأَفِضْ عَلَيَّ مِنْ فَضْلِكَ وَأَسْبِغْ عَلَيَّ رَحْمَتَكَ وَأَنْزِلْ عَلَيَّ مِنْ بَرَكَاتِكَ (ثَلاثاً).

اَللّٰهُمَّ أَصْلِحْ لِي دُنْيَايَ الَّتِي جَعَلْتَ فِيهَا مَعَاشِي اَللّٰهُمَّ أَصْلِحْ لِي دِيْنِيَ الَّذِي جَعَلْتَهُ لِي عِصْمَةً (ثَلَاثاً). اَللّٰهُمَّ أَصْلِحْ آخِرَتِيَ الَّتِي جَعَلْتَ إِلَيْهَا مَرْجِعِي (ثَلَاثاً). اَللّٰهُمَّ إِنِّي أَعُوذُ بِعَفْوِكَ مِنْ عُقُوبَتِكَ (ثَلَاثاً).

وَيَنْبَغِي لِمَنْ صَلَّى الصُّبْحَ أَنْ لَا يَقُومَ مِنْ مَجْلِسِهِ بَلْ يَثْبُتُ فِيهِ يَذْكُرُ اللهَ حَتَّى تَطْلُعَ الشَّمْسُ، وَيُصَلِّي رَكْعَتَيْنِ. وَيُكْرَهُ النَّوْمُ بَعْدَ صَلَاةِ الصُّبْحِ.

SUPEREROGATORY PRAYERS

The two *rak'as* of the dawn prayer (*fajr*): One should recite *Sūrat al-Kāfirūn*[59] [during the first *rak'a*] and *Sūrat al-Ikhlāṣ*[60] [during the second]. Or [recite], '*Say: We have believed in God and what has been revealed to us...*'[61] [and continue reciting] to the end of the verse; and, '*Say: O People of the Book, come to a common word...*'[62] [and continue reciting] to the end of the verse; and, '*The Messenger has believed...*'[63] [and continue reciting] to the end of the *sūra*; and, '*Say: We have believed in God and in what was revealed to us...*'[64] [and continue reciting] to the end of the *sūra*; and, '*Our Lord, we have believed in what You revealed...*'[65] [and continue reciting] to the end of the verse; and, '*Indeed, We have sent you with the truth as a bringer of good tidings and as a warner...*'[66] [and continue reciting] to the end of the verse. All of these are mentioned.

It is *Sunna* to lighten [shorten] them and to lie down after them[67] on one's right side[68] and say three times, *O God, Lord of Gabriel, Michael, Isrāfīl and Muḥammad ﷺ; I seek refuge in You from Hellfire.*

O God, we bear witness that You are not a god that we have concocted and are not a Lord Whose remembrance we can reject. You have no partners decreeing [anything] with You and we have no god before You that we supplicate, or humble ourselves towards. No one has helped You in creating us [which would warrant us to] associate him with You. There is no god but You, so forgive me.

If it is the day of *Jum'a*, one should add, *I seek forgiveness from God Almighty; there is no god but He, the Living, the Self-Subsisting, and I turn to Him.* [One should repeat this] three times.

نَوَافِلُ الصَّلَاةِ

رَكْعَتَا الْفَجْرِ: يَقْرَأُ فِيهِمَا الْكَافِرُونَ وَالْإِخْلَاصَ أَوْ ﴿قُولُوا: آمَنَّا بِاللهِ وَمَا أُنْزِلَ إِلَيْنَا﴾ اَلْآيَةُ، وَ﴿قُلْ يَا أَهْلَ الْكِتَابِ تَعَالَوْا إِلَى كَلِمَةٍ﴾ اَلْآيَة، وَ﴿آمَنَ الرَسُولُ﴾ إِلَى آخِرِ السُّورَةِ، وَ﴿قُلْ آمَنَّا بِاللهِ وَمَا أُنْزِلَ عَلَيْنَا﴾ اَلْآيَةُ، وَ﴿رَبَّنَا آمَنَّا بِمَا أَنْزَلْتَ﴾ اَلْآيَةُ، وَ﴿إِنَّا أَرْسَلْنَاكَ بِالْحَقِّ بَشِيراً وَنَذِيراً﴾ اَلْآيَةُ. كُلٌّ وَارِدٌ.

وَالسُّنَّةُ تَخْفِيفُهَا. وَالْاِضْطِجَاعُ بَعْدَهَا عَلَى الشِّقِّ الْأَيْمَنِ، وَيَقُولُ بَعْدَهَا: اَللّٰهُمَّ رَبَّ جِبْرِيلَ وَمِيكَائِيلَ وَإِسْرَافِيلَ وَمُحَمَّدٍ ﷺ، أَعُوذُ بِكَ مِنَ النَّارِ (ثَلَاثاً).

اَللّٰهُمَّ إِنَّا نَشْهَدُ أَنَّكَ لَسْتَ بِإِلٰهٍ اِسْتَحْدَثْنَاهُ وَلَا رَبٍّ نَنْبُذُ ذِكْرَهُ وَلَا عَلَيْكَ شُرَكَاءُ يَقْضُونَ مَعَكَ وَلَا لَنَا قَبْلَكَ إِلٰهٌ نَدْعُوهُ وَنَتَضَرَّعُ إِلَيْهِ وَلَا أَعَانَكَ عَلَى خَلْقِنَا أَحَدٌ فَنُشْرِكَهُ فِيكَ. لَا إِلٰهَ إِلَّا أَنْتَ فَاغْفِرْ لِي.

فَإِنْ كَانَ يَوْمُ الْجُمُعَةِ زَادَ: أَسْتَغْفِرُ اللهَ الْعَظِيمَ الَّذِي لَا إِلٰهَ إِلَّا هُوَ الْحَيُّ الْقَيُّومُ وَأَتُوبُ إِلَيْهِ (ثَلَاثاً).

The two *rakʿas* of the sunrise prayer (*ishrāq*): The Prophet ﷺ used to pray two *rakʿas* when the sun had risen above the horizon by the height of one or two spears.[69]

The forenoon prayer (*ṣalāt al-ḍuhā*): [It is performed] if a quarter of the morning has passed. Its minimum is two *rakʿas,* then [the next increment] is four, then six, then eight *rakʿas*.[70] One should say the *salām* after every two *rakʿas*; then [perform as many prayers] as you wish to occupy your time with, just as with the night vigil (*qiyām al-layl*). ʿAbd Allāh b. Ghālib (may God be pleased with him) used to pray the forenoon prayer by [reciting] the *Fātiḥa*,[71] *Sūrat al-Kāfirūn*,[72] *Sūrat al-Ikhlāṣ*,[73] the *Āyat al-Kursī* (the 'Throne Verse')[74] and *Sūrat al-Ikhlāṣ* in sets of ten. *Sūrat al-Kāfirūn* and *Sūrat al-Ikhlāṣ* [are recited] during the first *rakʿa*, and the *muʿawwadhatayn* (the last two chapters of the Qurʾān)[75] during the second *rakʿa*. After them, one should say, *O God, through You do I try, through You do I strive and through You do I fight*. And one should say one hundred times, *Lord forgive me and turn unto me; truly, You are the Ever-Relenting, the All-Forgiving*.

The declination prayer (*ṣalāt al-zawāl*): [The prayer consists of] four *rakʿas* after [the beginning of] the sun's declination (*zawāl*) [from its zenith and it is performed] before the midday prayer (*ẓuhr*) with no separation between them. During [the declination prayer], the recitation is lengthened [and] one should recite two *sūras* from the [the part of the Qurʾān referred to as the] *ṭiwāl* or from the [part referred to as the] *awsaṭ*.[76] ʿUmar b. al-Khattab (may God be pleased with him) recited *Sūrat Qāf*[77] during [this prayer].

The fixed supererogatory midday prayer (*rātibat al-ẓuhr*):[78] [The prayer consists of] four *rakʿas* before [the midday prayer (*ẓuhr*)] and four after it; the *Sunna* that is emphasised (*muʾakkad*) is [praying] two *rakʿas*. On the day of *Jumʿa*, the *Sunna* that is emphasised is [praying] four *rakʿas* beforehand and afterwards, with no interruption [between them]. The *Sunna* that is not non-emphasised (*ghayr muʾakkad*) is [praying] six *rakʿas*.

رَكْعَتَا الْإِشْرَاقِ: كَانَ النَّبِيُّ ﷺ إِذَا زَالَتِ الشَّمْسُ مِنْ مَطْلِعِهَا قَدْرَ رُمْحٍ أَوْ رُمْحَيْنِ صَلَّى رَكْعَتَيْنِ.

صَلَاةُ الضُّحَى: إِذَا مَضَى رُبْعُ النَّهَارِ. وَأَقَلُّهَا رَكْعَتَانِ ثُمَّ أَرْبَعٌ ثُمَّ سِتٌّ ثُمَّ ثَمَانٍ. يُسَلِّمُ فِي كُلِّ رَكْعَتَيْنِ ثُمَّ مَا شِئْتَ أَنْ تَسْتَغْرِقَ الْوَقْتَ كَقِيَامِ اللَّيْلِ. وَكَانَ عَبْدُ اللهِ بْنُ غَالِبٍ يُصَلِّي الضُّحَى بِالْفَاتِحَةِ وَسُورَةِ الْكَافِرُونَ وَالْإِخْلَاصِ وَآيَةِ الْكُرْسِيِّ وَسُورَةِ الْإِخْلَاصِ عَشْراً عَشْراً، وَسُورَةُ الْكَافِرُونَ وَالْإِخْلَاصِ فِي الْأُولَى، وَالْمُعَوِّذَتَيْنِ فِي الثَّانِيَةِ. وَيَقُولُ بَعْدَهَا: اللَّهُمَّ بِكَ أُحَاوِلُ وَبِكَ أُصَاوِلُ وَبِكَ أُقَاتِلُ. وَيَقُولُ: رَبِّ اغْفِرْ لِي وَتُبْ عَلَيَّ، إِنَّكَ أَنْتَ التَّوَّابُ الْغَفُورُ مِائَةً.

صَلَاةُ الزَّوَالِ: أَرْبَعُ رَكْعَاتٍ بَعْدَ زَوَالِ الشَّمْسِ قَبْلَ الظُّهْرِ، لَا يَفْصِلُ بَيْنَهُنَّ. يُطَوِّلُ فِيهَا الْقِرَاءَةَ، يَقْرَأُ فِيهَا سُورَتَيْنِ مِنَ الطِّوَالِ أَوْ مِنَ الْأَوْسَاطِ. وَقَرَأَ فِيهَا عُمَرُ بْنُ الْخَطَّابِ بِسُورَةِ قٓ.

رَاتِبَةُ الظُّهْرِ: أَرْبَعٌ قَبْلَهَا وَأَرْبَع بَعْدَهَا وَالْمُؤَكَّدُ فِيهَا رَكْعَتَانِ. وَالْمُؤَكَّدُ فِي الْجُمُعَةِ أَرْبَعٌ قَبْلُ وَبَعْدُ مِنْ غَيْرِ فَصْلٍ. وَغَيْرُ الْمُؤَكَّدِ فِيهَا سِتُّ رَكَعَاتٍ.

The prayer between the midday (*ẓuhr*) and afternoon (*ʿaṣr*) prayers: They used to occupy themselves between the midday (*ẓuhr*) and afternoon (*ʿaṣr*) prayers in a similar manner to the night vigil (*ṣalāt al-layl*). During this period of time, Ibn ʿUmar (may God be pleased with him) would pray twelve *rakaʿas*.

The fixed supererogatory afternoon prayer (*rātibat al-ʿaṣr*) is four *rakʿas*. [There should be] a separation between them by saying the *taslīm* or by [praying] two *rakʿas*.

The fixed supererogatory sunset prayer (*rātibat al-maghrib*) is two short *rakʿas* before it,[79] and two after it.[80] The *Sunna* is to perform the latter before speaking. One should *recite Sūrat al-Kāfirūn* and *Sūrat al-Ikhlāṣ* in them,[81] and afterwards say, *O Changer of hearts, firmly establish my heart upon Your religion*.

The prayer between the sunset (*maghrib*) and evening (*ʿishāʾ*) prayers is called the prayer of the penitent (*ṣalāt al-awwābīn*). [It consists of] six *rakʿas* with no speaking in between them, or ten or twenty *rakʿas*.

The fixed supererogatory evening prayer (*rāṭibat al-ʿishāʾ*): [The prayer consists of] two *rakʿas* before it, and two after it; or four with no interruption. During it, one should recite *Sūrat al-Sajda*,[82] *Sūrat Tabārak*,[83] *Sūrat al-Kāfirūn*[84] and *Sūrat al-Ikhlāṣ*.[85]

The odd-numbered prayer (*ṣalāt al-witr*): Its minimum is one *rakʿa*; then [the next increment] is three, then five, then seven, then nine, then eleven *rakʿas*, which is the maximum. In what is more than three [*rakʿas*], it is best to separate them;[86] and in the three [*rakʿas*] to join them together.[87] One should recite *Sūrat Sabbiḥ*[88] during the first *rakʿa*, *Sūrat al-Kāfirūn*[89] during the second and *Sūrat al-Ikhlāṣ*[90] and the *muʿawwadhatayn*[91] during the third. Or one should recite, '*Competition in [worldly] increase diverts you*' [*Sūrat al-Takāthur*],[92] *Sūrat al-Qadr*[93] and *Sūrat al-Zilzāl*[94] during the first *rakʿa*; during the second *Sūrat al-ʿAṣr*,[95] *Sūrat al-Naṣr*[96] and *Sūrat al-Kawthar*;[97] and during the third *Sūrat al-Kāfirūn*,[98] *Sūrat Tabbat*[99] and *Sūrat al-Ikhlāṣ*.[100]

صَلَاةُ مَا بَيْنَ الظُّهْرِ وَالعَصْرِ: كَانَ يُحْيُوْنَ مَا بَيْنَ الظُّهْرِ وَالْعَصْرِ وَيُشْبِهُونَ ذٰلِكَ بِصَلَاةِ اللَّيْلِ. وَكَانَ اِبْنُ عُمَرَ يُصَلِّي فِي ذٰلِكَ الْوَقْتِ اِثْنَتَيْ عَشْرَةَ رَكْعَةً.

رَاتِبَةُ الْعَصْرِ: أَرْبَعُ رَكْعَاتٍ فِيهَا، يَفْصُلُ بَيْنَهُنَّ بِتَسْلِيمٍ أَوْ رَكْعَتَانِ.

رَاتِبَةُ الْمَغْرِبِ: قَبْلَهَا رَكْعَتَانِ خَفِيفَتَانِ وَبَعْدَهَا رَكْعَتَانِ. وَالسُّنَّةُ اَلْمُبَادَرَةُ بِهِمَا قَبْلَ أَنْ يَتَكَلَّمَ. وَيَقْرَأُ فِيهَا اَلْكَافِرُونَ وَالْإِخْلَاصَ وَيَقُولُ بَعْدَهَا: يَا مُقَلِّبَ الْقُلُوبِ، ثَبِّتْ قُلُوبَنَا عَلَى دِينِكَ.

صَلَاةُ مَا بَيْنَ الْمَغْرِبِ وَالْعِشَاءِ: تُسَمَّى صَلَاةُ الْأَوَّابِينَ. سِتُّ رَكْعَاتٍ لَا يَتَكَلَّمُ فِيمَا بَيْنَهُنَّ أَوْ عَشْرَ رَكْعَاتٍ أَوْ عِشْرُونَ رَكْعَةً.

رَاتِبَةُ الْعِشَاءِ: قَبْلَهَا رَكْعَتَانِ وَبَعْدَهَا رَكْعَتَانِ أَوْ أَرْبَعٌ بِلَا فَاصِلٍ. يَقْرَأُ فِيهَا اَلسَّجْدَةَ وَتَبَارَكَ وَالْكَافِرُونَ وَالْإِخْلَاصَ.

صَلَاةُ الْوِتْرِ: أَقَلُّهُ رَكْعَةً ثُمَّ ثَلَاثٌ ثُمَّ خَمْسٌ ثُمَّ سَبْعٌ ثُمَّ تِسْعٌ ثُمَّ أَحَدَ عَشَرَ، وَهُوَ أَكْثَرُهُ. وَالْأَفْضَلُ فِي غَيْرِ الثَّلَاثِ اَلْفَصْلُ، وَفِي الثَّلَاثِ اَلْوَصْلُ. وَيَقْرَأُ فِي الْأُولَى سَبِّحِ وَالثَّانِيَةِ اَلْكَافِرُونَ وَالثَّالِثَةِ اَلْإِخْلَاصَ وَالْمُعَوِّذَتَيْنِ. أَوْ يَقْرَأُ فِي الْأُولَى ﴿أَلْهَاكُمُ التَّكَاثُرُ﴾ وَالْقَدْرَ وَالزَّلْزَلَةَ، وَالثَّانِيَةِ اَلْعَصْرَ وَالنَّصْرَ وَالْكَوْثَرَ، وَالثَّالِثَةِ اَلْكَافِرُونَ وَتَبَّتْ وَالْإِخْلَاصَ.

During the second half of Ramaḍān one should recite the 'standing' prayer (*du'ā' al-qunūt*) after bowing during the last *rak'a* [of *witr*].[101]

[The *du'ā' al-qunūt*] is: *In the name of God, the Most Compassionate, Most Merciful.*[102] *O God, truly we seek Your help, we seek Your guidance and we seek Your forgiveness. We praise You with all that is good. We thank You and we do not disbelieve in You. We humble ourselves before You and we renounce those who reject You. O God, it is You that we worship, to You that we pray and prostrate and to You that we strive. We are quick to obey You, we hope for Your mercy and fear Your punishment. Indeed, Your severe punishment shall overtake the disbelievers. O God, guide me along with those whom You have guided, pardon me along with those whom You have pardoned, be an ally to me along with those for whom You are an ally and bless for me that which You have bestowed. Protect me from the evil that You have decreed, for truly [it is] You [Who] decrees and none can issue a decree against You. Truly, those to whom You show allegiance are never abased and those You take as an enemy are never honoured. Blessed be You, our Lord, and may You be exalted. May God's blessings and peace be upon the Prophet Muḥammad and his family.*

One should say three times, *Glory be to the King, the Most Holy*; raising one's voice the third time. *Lord of the angels and the spirit. O God, I seek refuge in Your pleasure from Your wrath, I seek refuge in Your pardon from Your punishment and I seek refuge in You, from You. I do not praise You [in any other way than] how You have praised Yourself.* It is *Sunna* to use the *miswāk* afterwards.

Prayer of glorification (*ṣalāt at-tasbīḥ*): [The prayer consists of] four *rak'as* with no interruption. During it one should recite '*Competition in [worldly] increase diverts you*' [*Sūrat al-Takāthur*],[103] *Sūrat al-'Aṣr*,[104] *Sūrat al-Kāfirūn*[105] and *Sūrat al-Ikhlāṣ*.[106] One should say twenty-five times: *Glory be to God, praise be to God, there is no god but God and God is most Great. There is no power and no might*

وَيَقْنُتُ فِي الْأَخِيرَةِ بَعْدَ الرُّكُوعِ فِي النِّصْفِ الْأَخِيرِ مِنْ رَمَضَانَ.

وَهُوَ: بِسْمِ اللهِ الرَّحْمٰنِ الرَّحِيمِ. اَللّٰهُمَّ إِنَّا نَسْتَعِينُكَ وَنَسْتَهْدِيكَ وَنَسْتَغْفِرُكَ وَنُثْنِي عَلَيْكَ الْخَيْرَ كُلَّهُ. نَشْكُرُكَ وَلَا نَكْفُرُكَ وَنَخْلَعُ وَنَتْرُكُ مَنْ يَفْجُرُكَ. اَللّٰهُمَّ إِيَّاكَ نَعْبُدُ وَلَكَ نُصَلِّي وَنَسْجُدُ وَإِلَيْكَ نَسْعَى وَنَحْفِدُ نَرْجُو رَحْمَتَكَ وَنَخْشَى عَذَابَكَ إِنَّ عَذَابَكَ الْجِدَّ بِالْكُفَّارِ مُلْحِقٌ. اللّٰهُمَّ اهْدِنِي فِيمَنْ هَدَيْتَ وَعَافِنِي فِيمَنْ عَافَيْتَ وَتَوَلَّنِي فِيمَنْ تَوَلَّيْتَ وَبَارِكْ لِي فِيمَا أَعْطَيْتَ. وَقِنِي شَرَّ مَا قَضَيْتَ فَإِنَّكَ تَقْضِي وَلَا يُقْضَى عَلَيْكَ. وَإِنَّهُ لَا يَذِلُّ مَنْ وَالَيْتَ تَبَارَكْتَ رَبَّنَا وَتَعَالَيْتَ. وَصَلَّى اللهُ عَلَى النَّبِيِّ مُحَمَّدٍ وَآلِهِ وَسَلَّمَ.

وَيَقُولُ: سُبْحَانَ الْمَلِكِ الْقُدُّوسِ (ثَلَاثاً). وَيَرْفَعُ صَوْتَهُ فِي الثَّالِثَةِ. رَبُّ الْمَلَائِكَةِ وَالرُّوحِ. اللّٰهُمَّ إِنِّي أَعُوذُ بِرِضَاكَ عَنْ سَخَطِكَ وَأَعُوذُ بِمُعَافَاتِكَ مِنْ عُقُوبَتِكَ وَأَعُوذُ بِكَ مِنْكَ. لَا أُحْصِي ثَنَاءً عَلَيْكَ أَنْتَ كَمَا أَثْنَيْتَ عَلَى نَفْسِكَ. وَالسِّوَاكُ بَعْدَهُ سُنَّةٌ.

صَلَاةُ التَّسْبِيحِ: أَرْبَعُ رَكْعَاتٍ بِلَا فَصْلٍ. يَقْرَأُ فِيهَا ﴿أَلْهَاكُمُ﴾ وَالْعَصْرَ وَالْكَافِرُونَ وَالْإِخْلَاصَ. وَيَقُولُ: سُبْحَانَ اللهِ وَالْحَمْدُ لِلّٰهِ وَلَا إِلٰهَ إِلَّا اللهُ وَاللهُ أَكْبَرُ، وَلَا حَوْلَ وَلَا قُوَّةَ إِلَّا بِاللهِ (خَمْساً وَعِشْرِينَ مَرَّةً). فِي كُلِّ قِيَامٍ

save in God. [During the prayer,] at each instance of standing (*qiyām*), bowing (*rukūʿ*), drawing oneself up [after bowing] (*iʿtidāl*), prostration (*sujūd*), sitting (*julūs*) between the two prostrations, sitting in rest and [kneeling to say the] *tashahhud*, [one should recite this] ten times. One then says before the final *salāms*: *O God, I ask You for the Divine Success* (tawfīq) *of the people of guidance, the deeds of the people of certainty, the sincerity of the people of repentance, the resolve of the people of patience, the seriousness of the people of dread, the enthusiasm of the people of zeal [for God], the devotion of the people of scrupulousness and the gnosis of the people of knowledge so that I fear You. O God, I ask you for fear that protects me from disobeying You so that I perform deeds in obedience to You that make me deserving of Your pleasure, so that I am sincere to You in repentance out of fear of You, so that I make my intention purely for You and attain Your place of safety and so that I place my trust in You in all affairs. O God, make good my belief in You. Glory be to You, Creator of Light.* This prayer is performed every day, or every day of *Jumʿa*, every month or every year.[107]

The prayer of repentance (*ṣalāt al-tawba*): [The prayer consists of] two *rakʿas* and after them one says: *O God, I turn to You in repentance from such-and-such sins. Truly, You will not see the same from me again.*

The prayer of need (*ṣalāt al-ḥāja*): [The prayer consists of] two *rakʿas*, and when one bows, one should praise God and invoke blessings upon the Prophet ﷺ, then say: *There is no god but God, the Indulgent, the Generous. Glory be to God, Lord of the almighty Throne. Praise be to God, Lord of the worlds. I ask You for that which causes Your mercy, for that which determines Your forgiveness, for the spoils of every righteous [deed] and for safety from every sin. Do not leave any one of my sins without forgiving it, or any worry without removing it, or any need amongst the needs of this world and the Hereafter that is pleasing to You without decreeing it [to be bestowed], O Most Merciful of the merciful. O God, I beseech You and turn towards You by means of Your Prophet*

عَشْراً، وَفِي كُلِّ رُكُوعٍ وَاعْتِدَالٍ وَسُجُودٍ وَجُلُوسٍ بَيْنَ السَّجْدَتَيْنِ وَجُلُوسِ الْاِسْتِرَاحَةِ وَالتَّشَهُّدِ. وَيَقُولُ فِيهِ قَبْلَ السَّلَامِ: اَللّٰهُمَّ إِنِّي أَسْأَلُكَ تَوْفِيقَ أَهْلِ الْهُدَى وَأَعْمَالَ أَهْلِ الْيَقِينِ وَمُنَاصَحَةَ أَهْلِ التَّوْبَةِ وَعَزْمَ أَهْلِ الصَّبْرِ وَجِدَّ أَهْلِ الْخَشْيَةِ وَطَلَبَ أَهْلِ الرَّغْبَةِ وَتَعَبُّدَ أَهْلِ الْوَرَعِ وَعِرْفَانَ أَهْلِ الْعِلْمِ حَتَّى أَخَافَكَ. اللّٰهُمَّ إِنِّي أَسْأَلُكَ مَخَافَةً تَحْجِزُنِي عَنْ مَعْصِيَتِكَ حَتَّى أَعْمَلَ بِطَاعَتِكَ عَمَلاً أَسْتَحِقُّ بِهِ رِضَاكَ وَحَتَّى أُنَاصِحَكَ بِالتَّوْبَةِ خَوْفاً مِنْكَ وَحَتَّى أَخْلِصَ النِّيَّةَ بِمَأْمَنِكَ وَحَتَّى أَتَوَكَّلَ عَلَيْكَ فِي الْأُمُورِ كُلِّهَا. اَللّٰهُمَّ حَسِّنْ ظَنِّي بِكَ سُبْحَانَكَ خَالِقَ النُّورِ. تُصَلَّى هٰذِهِ الصَّلَاةُ كُلَّ يَوْمٍ أَوْ كُلَّ جُمُعَةٍ أَوْ كُلَّ شَهْرٍ أَوْ كُلَّ سَنَةٍ.

صَلَاةُ التَّوْبَةِ: رَكْعَتَانِ وَيَقُولُ بَعْدَهُمَا: اَللّٰهُمَّ إِنِّي أَتُوبُ إِلَيْكَ مِنْ ذَنْبِ كَذَا. إِنَّ هٰذَا آخِرُ الْعَهْدِ بِكَ.

صَلَاةُ الْحَاجَةِ: رَكْعَتَانِ فَإِذَا رَكَعَ أَثْنَى عَلَى اللهِ وَصَلَّى عَلَى النَّبِيِّ ﷺ، ثُمَّ يَقُولُ: لَا إِلٰهَ إِلَّا اللهُ الْحَلِيمُ الْكَرِيمُ سُبْحَانَ اللهِ رَبِّ الْعَرْشِ الْعَظِيمِ. اَلْحَمْدُ لِلّٰهِ رَبِّ الْعَالَمِينَ. أَسْأَلُكَ مُوجِبَاتِ رَحْمَتِكَ وَعَزَائِمَ مَغْفِرَتِكَ وَالْغَنِيمَةَ مِنْ كُلِّ بِرٍّ وَالسَّلَامَةَ مِنْ كُلِّ إِثْمٍ لَا تَدَعْ لِي ذَنْباً إِلَّا غَفَرْتَهُ وَلَا هَمّاً إِلَّا فَرَّجْتَهُ وَلَا حَاجَةً مِنْ حَوَائِجِ الدُّنْيَا وَالْآخِرَةِ هِيَ لَكَ رِضاً إِلَّا قَضَيْتَهَا يَا أَرْحَمَ الرَّاحِمِينَ.

Muḥammad, the prophet of mercy. O Muḥammad, truly I turn towards my Lord by means of you in my need of this to be decreed for me.[108] *O God, allow him to intercede on my behalf.*

Prayer for retrieving something lost (*ṣalāt radd al-ḍālla*): [The prayer consists of] two *rakʿas*; when one has finished, one should say: *O God, Returner of the lost, Guider of the misguided. Return my lost item to me through Your power and Your authority; for indeed, it is from Your bounty and Your gifts.*

Prayer for guidance (*ṣalāt al-istikhāra*): [The prayer consists of] two *rakʿas*; after them one should say: *O God, I seek guidance from You through Your Knowledge and I seek strength through Your Power. I ask of Your almighty bounty, for You have the power and I do not; You know and I know not; and You are the Knower of the unseen. O God, if You know that this matter is good for me in my religion, my livelihood and its consequences, both what is immediate and what is to come, then decree it for me, make it easy for me and then bless it for me. And if You know that this matter is bad for me in my religion, my livelihood and its consequences, both what is immediate and what is to come, then turn it away from me and turn me away from it, and decree for me whatever is good, then make me content with it.*[F] Then one names the need.

In a *ḥadīth* [it was reported that], 'If you are worrying about something, then seek the guidance of Your Lord about it seven times. Then look at what happens, for truly there is good in it.' When the Messenger of God ﷺ would want something, he would say, *O God, choose for me and make my choice for me.*

Other supererogatory prayers (*min al-nawāfil*): [One may pray] two *rakʿas* upon entering the home and upon leaving it; if hard times, intense problems or lack of provisions befall one; if one's child, brother or relative dies; or if something makes one sad. There are narrations concerning [the supererogatory prayers for] all of these.

اللّٰهُمَّ إِنِّي أَسْأَلُكَ وَأَتَوَجَّهُ إِلَيْكَ بِنَبِيِّكَ مُحَمَّدٍ نَبِيِّ الرَّحْمَةِ. يَا مُحَمَّدُ، إِنِّي أَتَوَجَّهُ بِكَ إِلَى رَبِّي فِي حَاجَتِي هٰذِهِ لِتَقْضِيَ لِي. اَللّٰهُمَّ شَفِّعْهُ فِيَّ.

صَلَاةُ رَدِّ الضَّالَّةِ: رَكْعَتَانِ فَإِذَا فَرَغَ، قَالَ: اَللّٰهُمَّ رَادَّ الضَّالَّةِ هَادِيَ الضَّلَالَةِ رَدِّ عَلَيَّ ضَالَّتِي بِقُوَّتِكَ وَسُلْطَانِكَ فَإِنَّهَا مِنْ فَضْلِكَ وَعَطَايَاكَ.

صَلَاةُ الْاِسْتِخَارَةِ: رَكْعَتَانِ تَقُولُ بَعْدَهُمَا: اَللّٰهُمَّ إِنِّي أَسْتَخِيرُكَ بِعِلْمِكَ وَأَسْتَقْدِرُكَ بِقُدْرَتِكَ وَأَسْأَلُكَ مِنْ فَضْلِكَ الْعَظِيمِ فَإِنَّكَ تَقْدِرُ وَلَا أَقْدِرُ وَتَعْلَمُ وَلَا أَعْلَمُ وَأَنْتَ عَلَّامُ الْغُيُوبِ. اَللّٰهُمَّ إِنْ كُنْتَ تَعْلَمُ أَنَّ هٰذَا الْأَمْرَ خَيْرٌ لِي فِي دِينِي وَمَعَاشِي وَعَاقِبَةِ أَمْرِي، وَعَاجِلِ أَمْرِي وَآجِلِهِ، فَاقْدُرْهُ لِي وَيَسِّرْهُ لِي ثُمَّ بَارِكْ لِي فِيهِ. وَإِنْ كُنْتَ تَعْلَمُ أَنَّ هٰذَا الْأَمْرَ شَرٌّ لِي فِي دِينِي وَمَعَاشِي، وَعَاقِبَةِ أَمْرِي، وَعَاجِلِ أَمْرِي وَآجِلِهِ، فَاصْرِفْهُ عَنِّي وَاصْرِفْنِي عَنْهُ وَاقْدُرْ لِيَ الْخَيْرَ حَيْثُ كَانَ، ثُمَّ اَرْضِنِي بِهِ. ثُمَّ يُسَمِّي حَاجَتَهُ.

وَفِي الْحَدِيثِ: «إِذَا هَمَمْتَ بِأَمْرٍ فَاسْتَخِرْ رَبَّكَ فِيهِ سَبْعَ مَرَّاتٍ ثُمَّ انْظُرْ إِلَى الَّذِي يَسْبِقُ فَإِنَّ الْخَيْرَ فِيهِ.» وَكَانَ ﷺ إِذَا أَرَادَ الْأَمْرَ قَالَ: اَللّٰهُمَّ خِرْ لِي وَاخْتَرْ لِي.

وَمِنَ النَّوَافِلِ: رَكْعَتَانِ عِنْدَ دُخُولِ الْمَنْزِلِ وَعِنْدَ الْخُرُوجِ مِنْهُ وَإِذَا نَزَلَ بِهِ ضِيقٌ أَوْ شِدَّةٌ أَوْ خَصَاصَةٌ فِي الرِّزْقِ أَوْ مَاتَ لَهُ وَلَدٌ أَوْ أَخٌ أَوْ قَرِيبٌ أَوْ أَحْزَنَهُ أَمْرٌ. وَرَدَتِ الْآثَارُ بِكُلِّ ذٰلِكَ.

SUPPLICATIONS FOR THE MORNING AND THE EVENING

O God, You created me and I am Your servant. I adhere to Your covenant and Your promise as much as I am able. I acknowledge Your blessings upon me and I acknowledge my sins, so forgive me; truly no one forgives sins save You. I seek refuge in You from the evil I have performed.

O God, through You I have reached the morning (or, *evening*), *through You we are given life, through You we die and to You is the return*. In the evening, [instead of, *to You is the return*, one should say], *and to You is the final destination*.

We have reached the morning, and the entire kingdom has reached the morning, belonging to You. We have reached the evening, and the entire kingdom has reached the evening, belonging to God. Praise be to God. There is no god but God alone; He has no partner. To Him is the kingdom, to Him is all praise and He has power over all things. Lord, I ask You for the good of this day and for the good of what is after it. I seek refuge in You from the evil of this day and from the evil of what is after it (or, *the night*). *Lord, I seek refuge in You from laziness and from the evil of arrogance. I seek refuge in You from punishment in Hellfire and from the torment of the grave.*

You should say three times, *I seek refuge in the perfect words of God from the evil of what He has created. In the name of God, with [the protection provided by] His name, nothing upon the earth or in the heavens can cause harm; He is the All-Hearing, the All-Knowing*. [And say] three times, *I am pleased with God as a Lord, with Islam as a religion and with Muḥammad ﷺ as a Prophet*. [And say] four times, *O God, I have reached the morning and I have reached the evening. I ask you to bear witness, and those who carry Your Throne and Your angels to bear witness,*

أَذْكَارُ الصَّبَاحِ وَالْمَسَاءِ

اَللّٰهُمَّ أَنْتَ خَلَقْتَنِي وَأَنَا عَبْدُكَ وَأَنَا عَلَى عَهْدِكَ وَوَعْدِكَ مَا اسْتَطَعْتُ. أَبُوءُ بِنِعْمَتِكَ عَلَيَّ وَأَبُوءُ بِذَنْبِي فَاغْفِرْ لِي فَإِنَّهُ لَا يَغْفِرُ الذُّنُوبَ إِلَّا أَنْتَ. أَعُوذُ بِكَ مِنْ شَرِّ مَا صَنَعْتُ.

اَللّٰهُمَّ بِكَ أَصْبَحْنَا (أَوْ أَمْسَيْنَا) وَبِكَ نَحْيَا وَبِكَ نَمُوتُ وَإِلَيْكَ النُّشُورُ. وَفِي الْمَسَاءِ: وَإِلَيْكَ الْمَصِيرُ.

أَصْبَحْنَا وَأَصْبَحَ الْمُلْكُ لَكَ. وَأَمْسَيْنَا وَأَمْسَى الْمُلْكُ لِلّٰهِ. وَالْحَمْدُ لِلّٰهِ وَلَا إِلٰهَ إِلَّا اللّٰهُ وَحْدَهُ لَا شَرِيكَ لَهُ، لَهُ الْمُلْكُ وَلَهُ الْحَمْدُ وَهُوَ عَلَى كُلِّ شَيْءٍ قَدِيرٌ. رَبِّ أَسْأَلُكَ خَيْرَ هٰذَا الْيَوْمِ وَخَيْرَ مَا بَعْدَهُ. وَأَعُوذُ بِكَ مِنْ شَرِّ هٰذَا الْيَوْمِ وَشَرِّ مَا بَعْدَهُ (أَوِ اللَّيْلَةِ). رَبِّ أَعُوذُ بِكَ مِنَ الْكَسَلِ وَشَرِّ الْكِبَرِ وَأَعُوذُ بِكَ مِنْ عَذَابٍ فِي النَّارِ وَعَذَابٍ فِي الْقَبْرِ.

وَتَقُولُ: أَعُوذُ بِكَلِمَاتِ اللّٰهِ التَّامَّاتِ كُلِّهَا مِنْ شَرِّ مَا خَلَقَ. بِسْمِ اللّٰهِ الَّذِي لَا يَضُرُّ مَعَ اسْمِهِ شَيْءٌ فِي الْأَرْضِ وَلَا فِي السَّمَاءِ وَهُوَ السَّمِيعُ الْعَلِيمُ (ثَلَاثاً). رَضِيتُ بِاللّٰهِ رَبّاً وَبِالْإِسْلَامِ دِيناً وَبِمُحَمَّدٍ ﷺ نَبِيّاً (ثَلَاثاً). اَللّٰهُمَّ إِنِّي أَصْبَحْتُ وَأَمْسَيْتُ أُشْهِدُكَ وَأُشْهِدُ حَمَلَةَ عَرْشِكَ وَمَلَائِكَتَكَ

and Your entire creation [to bear witness] that You are God—there is no god but You alone, You have no partner—and that Muḥammad is Your servant and Your messenger.

O God, truly I ask you for pardon, and well-being in religion, this world and the Hereafter.

O God, truly I ask You for well-being in my religion, in my worldly life, for myself, my family and my wealth. O God, cover my faults and calm my fears. O God, protect me from in front of me and from behind me, on my right and on my left and from above me. I seek refuge in Your greatness lest I be seized unexpectedly from below.

O God, whatever blessing has [reached] me, or anyone from amongst Your creation, in the morning or the evening is from You alone; You have no partner. So praise be to You and thanks be to You. And you should say three times, *O God, grant me well-being in my body. O God, grant me well-being in my hearing. O God, grant me well-being in my sight. O God, I seek refuge in You from disbelief and poverty. O God, truly I seek refuge in You from the torment of the grave. There is no god but You.*

Glory be to God and praise be to Him. There is no power and no might save in God, the Most High, the Almighty. I know that God is powerful over all things and that God has encompassed all things [with His] knowledge. I seek refuge in God, Who prevents the heavens from falling to the earth—except by His permission—and from the evil of each creature that my Lord takes by its forelock [by rewarding the good-doers and punishing the wrongdoers].[109] *Truly, my Lord is on a straight path.*

O God, truly I seek refuge in You from worry and sadness. I seek refuge in You from inability and laziness. I seek refuge in You from cowardice and miserliness. I seek refuge in You from overwhelming debt and from being

وَجَمِيعَ خَلْقِكَ أَنَّكَ أَنْتَ اللهُ، لَا إِلٰهَ إِلَّا أَنْتَ وَحْدَكَ لَا شَرِيكَ لَكَ، وَأَنَّ مُحَمَّداً عَبْدُكَ وَرَسُولُكَ (أَرْبَعاً).

اَللّٰهُمَّ إِنِّي أَسْأَلُكَ الْعَفْوَ وَالْعَافِيَةَ فِي الدِّينِ وَالدُّنْيَا وَالْآخِرَةِ.

اَللّٰهُمَّ إِنِّي أَسْأَلُكَ الْعَافِيَةَ فِي دِينِي وَدُنْيَايَ وَنَفْسِي وَأَهْلِي وَمَالِي. اَللّٰهُمَّ اسْتُرْ عَوْرَاتِي وَآمِنْ رَوْعَاتِي. اَللّٰهُمَّ احْفَظْنِي مِنْ بَيْنِ يَدَيَّ وَمِنْ خَلْفِي وَعَنْ يَمِينِي وَعَنْ شِمَالِي وَمِنْ فَوْقِي وَأَعُوذُ بِعَظَمَتِكَ أَنْ أُغْتَالَ مِنْ تَحْتِي.

اَللّٰهُمَّ مَا أَصْبَحَ وَمَا أَمْسَى بِي مِنْ نِعْمَةٍ أَوْ بِأَحَدٍ مِنْ خَلْقِكَ فَمِنْكَ وَحْدَكَ، لَا شَرِيكَ لَكَ فَلَكَ الْحَمْدُ وَلَكَ الشُّكْرُ. وَتَقُولُ: اَللّٰهُمَّ عَافِنِي فِي بَدَنِي. اَللّٰهُمَّ عَافِنِي فِي سَمْعِي. اَللّٰهُمَّ عَافِنِي فِي بَصَرِي. اَللّٰهُمَّ إِنِّي أَعُوذُ بِكَ مِنَ الْكُفْرِ وَالْفَقْرِ. اَللّٰهُمَّ إِنِّي أَعُوذُ بِكَ مِنْ عَذَابِ الْقَبْرِ لَا إِلٰهَ إِلَّا أَنْتَ (ثَلَاثاً).

سُبْحَانَ اللهِ وَبِحَمْدِهِ وَلَا حَوْلَ وَلَا قُوَّةَ إِلَّا بِاللهِ الْعَلِيِّ الْعَظِيمِ. أَعْلَمُ أَنَّ اللهَ عَلَى كُلِّ شَيْءٍ قَدِيرٌ وَأَنَّ اللهَ قَدْ أَحَاطَ بِكُلِّ شَيْءٍ عِلْماً. أَعُوذُ بِاللهِ الَّذِي يُمْسِكُ السَّمَاءَ أَنْ تَقَعَ عَلَى الْأَرْضِ إِلَّا بِإِذْنِهِ مِنْ شَرِّ كُلِّ دَابَّةٍ رَبِّي آخِذٌ بِنَاصِيَتِهَا إِنَّ رَبِّي عَلَى صِرَاطٍ مُسْتَقِيمٍ.

اَللّٰهُمَّ إِنِّي أَعُوذُ بِكَ مِنَ الْهَمِّ وَالْحُزْنِ. وَأَعُوذُ بِكَ مِنَ الْعَجْزِ وَالْكَسْلِ. وَأَعُوذُ بِكَ مِنَ الْجُبْنِ وَالْبُخْلِ. وَأَعُوذ بِكَ مِنْ غَلَبَةِ الدَّيْنِ وَقَهْرِ الرِّجَالِ.

subjugated by men. We have begun our morning (or, *we have begun our evening*) *in accordance with the natural constitution* (fiṭra) *of Islam, with the sincere word, with the religion* (dīn) *of our Prophet Muḥammad* ﷺ *and the religion* (milla) *of our father Abraham* ﷺ, *the* ḥanīf,[110] *the Muslim, who was not one of the polytheists.*

We have reached the morning, and the entire kingdom has reached the morning, belonging to God (or, *we have reached the evening, and the entire kingdom has reached the evening, for God*). *Praise be to God, all grandeur and greatness be to God. [All of] creation, [every] affair, the night, the day and what resides in them belongs to God (Exalted is He) alone; He has no partner. Power, might, authority, the heavens, the earth and every single thing belongs to God, Lord of the worlds. O God, make the first part of this day* (or, *night*) *[full of] virtue, its middle part successful and its end prosperous. I ask You for the good of this world and the good of the Hereafter, O Most Merciful of the merciful. O God, I ask You for the good of this day, for its victory, its light, its blessings and its guidance. And I seek refuge in You from its evil, from the evil that is in it and from the evil of what will come after it.*

And you should say three times, *O God, praise be to You. There is no god but You, my Lord, and I am Your servant. I believe in You, sincere to You in my religion. Truly, I have reached the morning and reached the evening adhering to Your covenant and Your promise as much as I am able. I turn towards You in repentance [for] the evil of my actions and I seek Your forgiveness for my sins that none can forgive save You.*

Praise be to God; I do not associate anything with Him. I bear witness that there is no god but God. Praise be to God Who has takes the day away, Who brings forth the night and follows it again with the day [all] in well-being.

أَصْبَحْنَا (أَوْ أَمْسَيْنَا) عَلَى فِطْرَةِ الْإِسْلَامِ وَكَلِمَةِ الْإِخْلَاصِ وَدِينِ نَبِيِّنَا مُحَمَّدٍ ﷺ وَمِلَّةِ أَبِينَا إِبْرَاهِيمَ حَنِيفاً مُسْلِماً وَمَا كَانَ مِنَ الْمُشْرِكِينَ.

أَصْبَحْنَا وَأَصْبَحَ الْمُلْكُ لِلّٰهِ (أَوْ أَمْسَيْنَا وَأَمْسَى الْمُلْكُ لِلّٰهِ) وَالْحَمْدُ لِلّٰهِ وَالْكِبْرِيَاءُ وَالْعَظَمَةُ لِلّٰهِ. وَالْخَلْقُ وَالْأَمْرُ وَاللَّيْلُ وَالنَّهَارُ وَمَا سَكَنَ فِيهِمَا لِلّٰهِ تَعَالَى وَحْدَهُ لَا شَرِيكَ لَهُ. وَالْحَوْلُ وَالْقُوَّةُ وَالسُّلْطَانُ وَالسَّمَاوَاتُ وَالْأَرْضُ وَكُلُّ شَيْءٍ لِلّٰهِ رَبِّ الْعَالَمِينَ. اَللّٰهُمَّ اجْعَلْ أَوَّلَ هٰذَا النَّهَارِ (أَوْ أَوَّلَ اللَّيْلَةِ) صَلَاحاً وَأَوْسَطَهُ نَجَاحاً وَآخِرَهُ فَلَاحاً. أَسْأَلُكَ خَيْرَ الدُّنْيَا وَخَيْرَ الْآخِرَةِ يَا أَرْحَمَ الرَّاحِمِينَ. اللّٰهُمَّ إِنِّي أَسْأَلُكَ خَيْرَ هٰذَا الْيَوْمِ وَنَصْرَهُ وَنُورَهُ وَبَرَكَتَهُ وَهُدَاهُ وَأَعُوذُ بِكَ مِنْ شَرِّهِ وَشَرِّ مَا فِيهِ وَشَرِّ مَا بَعْدَهُ.

وَتَقُولُ: اللّٰهُمَّ لَكَ الْحَمْدُ لَا إِلٰهَ إِلَّا أَنْتَ رَبِّي، وَأَنَا عَبْدُكَ. آمَنْتُ بِكَ مُخْلِصاً لَكَ دِينِي. إِنِّي أَصْبَحْتُ وَأَمْسَيْتُ عَلَى عَهْدِكَ وَوَعْدِكَ مَا اسْتَطَعْتُ. أَتُوبُ إِلَيْكَ مِنْ شَرِّ عَمَلِي وَأَسْتَغْفِرُكَ لِذُنُوبِيَ الَّتِي لَا يَغْفِرُهَا إِلَّا أَنْتَ (ثَلَاثاً).

اَلْحَمْدُ لِلّٰهِ الَّذِي لَا أُشْرِكُ بِهِ شَيْئاً. وَأَشْهَدُ أَنْ لَا إِلٰهَ إِلَّا اللّٰهُ. اَلْحَمْدُ لِلّٰهِ الَّذِي ذَهَبَ بِالنَّهَارِ وَجَاءَ بِاللَّيْلِ وَجَاءَ بِالنَّهَارِ فِي عَافِيَةٍ.

O God, here is Your creation, so whatever misdeed I have done [as part of] it, overlook it, and whatever good [thing] I have done [as part of] it, accept it and multiply it many times over. O God, truly You are aware of all of my states and truly You are capable of making them successful. O God, in this day (or, *night*) *make successful [my request for] every need I have. Do not increase me in my worldly life with that which does not benefit me in my Hereafter. O God, truly I ask You for unexpected goodness and I seek refuge in You from unexpected evil, O Living, O Self-Subsisting. With You I seek aid. So rectify for me all of my affairs and do not leave me to myself for [even] the blink of an eye. [I invoke] the name of God upon myself, upon my family, for my safety and for my wealth. Glory be to the King, the Most Holy.*[G]

One should say three times, *O God, because of You I have reached the morning with blessing, well-being and concealment.*[111] *So complete Your [bestowal of] blessing, well-being and concealment upon me in this world and the Hereafter.* [And one should say] seven times, *God [alone] is sufficient for me; there is no god but He. I have put my trust in Him and He is the Lord of the almighty Throne.*

O God, Originator of the heavens and the earth, Knower of the unseen and the seen, Lord of each thing and its Proprietor, I bear witness that there is no god but You. I seek refuge in You from the evil of my soul, from the evil of Satan and his associating [other with You], lest I commit a misdeed against myself or bring it upon a Muslim.

One should say: *Glory be to God (*subḥān Allāh*); may it be to the measure of what He has created. Glory be to God; may it fill [all] that He has created. Glory be to God; may it fill the heavens and the earth. Glory be to God; may it be to the measure of what is in the heavens and the earth. Glory be to God; may it be commensurate with what He has enumerated in His Book. Glory be to God; may it be commensurate with the quantity of everything. Glory be to God; may it fill everything.*

اَللّٰهُمَّ هٰذَا خَلْقٌ قَدْ جَاءَ، فَمَا عَمِلْتُ فِيهِ مِنْ سَيِّئَةٍ فَتَجَاوَزْ عَنْهَا وَمَا عَمِلْتُ فِيهِ مِنْ حَسَنَةٍ فَتَقَبَّلْهَا وَضَاعِفْهَا أَضْعَافاً مُضَاعَفَةً. اَللّٰهُمَّ إِنَّكَ بِجَمِيعِ أَحْوَالِي عَالِمٌ، وَإِنَّكَ عَلَى جَمِيعِ نَجْحِهَا قَادِرٌ اَللّٰهُمَّ أَنْجِحِ الْيَوْمَ (أَوِ اللَّيْلَةَ) كُلَّ حَاجَةٍ لِي وَلَا تَزِدْنِي فِي دُنْيَايَ بِمَا لَا يَنْفَعُنِي مِنْ آخِرَتِي. اَللّٰهُمَّ إِنِّي أَسْأَلُكَ مِنْ فُجَاءَةِ الْخَيْرِ وَأَعُوذُ بِكَ مِنْ فُجَاءَةِ الشَّرِّ. يَا حَيُّ يَا قَيُّومُ بِكَ أَسْتَغِيثُ فَأَصْلِحْ لِي شَأْنِي كُلَّهُ وَلَا تَكِلْنِي إِلَى نَفْسِي طَرْفَةَ عَيْنٍ. بِسْمِ اللهِ عَلَى نَفْسِي وَأَهْلِي وَأَمْنِي وَمَالِي. سُبْحَانَ الْمَلِكِ الْقُدُّوسِ.

وَيَقُولُ: اَللّٰهُمَّ إِنِّي أَصْبَحْتُ مِنْكَ فِي نِعْمَةٍ وَعَافِيَةٍ وَسِتْرٍ فَأَتْمِمْ نِعْمَتَكَ عَلَيَّ وَعَافِيَتَكَ وَسِتْرَكَ فِي الدُّنْيَا وَالْآخِرَةِ (ثَلاثاً). حَسْبِيَ اللّٰهُ لَا إِلٰهَ إِلَّا هُوَ. عَلَيْهِ تَوَكَّلْتُ وَهُوَ رَبُّ الْعَرْشِ الْعَظِيمِ (سَبْعاً).

اَللّٰهُمَّ فَاطِرَ السَّمَاوَاتِ وَالْأَرْضِ، عَالِمَ الْغَيْبِ وَالشَّهَادَةِ، رَبَّ كُلِّ شَيْءٍ وَمَلِيكَهُ، أَشْهَدُ أَنْ لَا إِلٰهَ إِلَّا أَنْتَ. أَعُوذُ بِكَ مِنْ شَرِّ نَفْسِي وَمِنْ شَرِّ الشَّيْطَانِ وَشِرْكِهِ وَأَنْ أَقْتَرِفَ عَلَى نَفْسِي سُوءاً أَوْ أَجُرَّهُ إِلَى مُسْلِمٍ.

وَيَقُولُ: سُبْحَانَ اللهِ عَدَدَ مَا خَلَقَ. وَسُبْحَانَ اللهِ مِلْءَ مَا خَلَقَ. وَسُبْحَانَ اللهِ مِلْءَ السَّمَاوَاتِ وَالْأَرْضِ. وَسُبْحَانَ اللهِ عَدَدَ مَا فِي السَّمَاوَاتِ وَالْأَرْضِ. وَسُبْحَانَ اللهِ عَدَدَ مَا أَحْصَى كِتَابُهُ. وَسُبْحَانَ اللهِ عَدَدَ كُلِّ شَيْءٍ. وَسُبْحَانَ اللهِ مِلْءَ كُلِّ شَيْءٍ.

One should say: *Praise be to God* (al-ḥamd li-Llāh) *equal to that [mentioned above]; God is most Great* (Allāh Akbar) *equal to that [mentioned above]. Praise be to God Who has made the night wane by His Power and, with His Greatness, has brought the day as a new creation. Welcome to you the guardian angels* (ḥāfiẓīn) *on the right and greetings to you writers of deeds* (kātibīn) *on the left.*[112] *Write in the name of God, Most Compassionate and Merciful that I bear witness there is no god but God and I bear witness that Muḥammad is His servant and His messenger; I bear witness that the Hour is coming—there is no doubt about it—and that God will resurrect those in the graves. [It is] in accordance with this that I live, that I die and shall be resurrected, if God so wills. O God, call Muḥammad's attention to the greeting from us.*

One should say three times, *In the name of God. It is what God has willed; there is no blessing save [that which is] from God. It is what God has willed; there is no power and no might save in God.* [And one should say] seven times, *No one but God brings good. In the name of God, no one but God diverts evil. O God, You have created me, You guide me, You feed me, You give me to drink, You cause me to die and You cause me to live.*

O God, truly I seek refuge in You from the evil of my soul and from the evil of every creature that You take by its forelock. Truly, my Lord is on a straight path.

And one should say three times, *I seek refuge in God, the All-Hearing, the All-Knowing, from Satan the accursed.* One should recite, '*He is God; there is no god besides Him…*' to the end of *Sūrat al-Ḥashr.*[113] [Then] one should recite, '*Glory be to God when you reach the evening and when you reach the morning,*' to His Words, '*And thus will you be brought out*' three times.[114] [And recite,] '*So did you reckon that We created you in vain?*' to the end of the *sūra.*[115] One should

وَيَقُولُ: اَلْحَمْدُ لِلّٰهِ مِثْلَ ذٰلِكَ وَاللّٰهُ أَكْبَرُ مِثْلَ ذٰلِكَ. اَلْحَمْدُ لِلّٰهِ الَّذِي ذَهَبَ بِاللَّيْلِ بِقُدْرَتِهِ وَجَاءَ بِالنَّهَارِ بِعَظَمَتِهِ خَلْقاً جَدِيداً. مَرْحَباً بِكُمْ وَأَهْلاً مِنْ حَافِظِينَ عَنْ يَمِينِهِ، وَحَيَّاكُمُ اللّٰهُ الْكَاتِبِينَ عَنْ يَسَارِهِ. أُكْتُبُوا بِسْمِ اللّٰهِ الرَّحْمٰنِ الرَّحِيمِ. أَشْهَدُ أَنْ لَا إِلٰهَ إِلَّا اللّٰهُ وَأَشْهَدُ أَنَّ مُحَمَّداً عَبْدُهُ وَرَسُولُهُ وَأَشْهَدُ أَنَّ السَّاعَةَ آتِيَةٌ لَا رَيْبَ فِيهَا، وَأَنَّ اللّٰهَ يَبْعَثُ مَنْ فِي الْقُبُورِ. عَلَى ذٰلِكَ أَحْيَا وَعَلَى ذٰلِكَ أَمُوتُ وَعَلَى ذٰلِكَ أُبْعَثُ إِنْ شَاءَ اللّٰهُ. اَللّٰهُمَّ أَذْكِرْ مُحَمَّداً مِنَّا بِالسَّلَامِ.

وَيَقُولُ: بِسْمِ اللّٰهِ. مَا شَاءَ اللّٰهُ، مَا كَانَ مِنْ نِعْمَةٍ فَمِنَ اللّٰهِ. مَا شَاءَ اللّٰهُ لَا قُوَّةَ إِلَّا بِاللّٰهِ (ثَلَاثاً). لَا يَسُوقُ الْخَيْرَ إِلَّا اللّٰهُ. بِسْمِ اللّٰهِ لَا يَصْرِفُ السُّوءَ إِلَّا اللّٰهُ. اَللّٰهُمَّ أَنْتَ خَلَقْتَنِي وَأَنْتَ تَهْدِينِي وَأَنْتَ تُطْعِمُنِي وَأَنْتَ تَسْقِينِي وَأَنْتَ تُمِيتُنِي وَأَنْتَ تُحْيِينِي (سَبْعاً).

اَللّٰهُمَّ إِنِّي أَعُوذُ بِكَ مِنْ شَرِّ نَفْسِي وَمِنْ شَرِّ كُلِّ دَابَّةٍ أَنْتَ آخِذٌ بِنَاصِيَتِهَا. إِنَّ رَبِّي عَلَى صِرَاطٍ مُّسْتَقِيمٍ.

وَيَقُولُ: أَعُوذُ بِاللّٰهِ السَّمِيعِ الْعَلِيمِ مِنَ الشَّيْطَانِ الرَّجِيمِ (ثَلَاثاً). وَيَقْرَأُ: ﴿هُوَ اللّٰهُ الَّذِي لَا إِلٰهَ إِلَّا هُوَ﴾ إِلَى آخِرِ سُورَةِ الْحَشْرِ. وَيَقْرَأُ: ﴿فَسُبْحَانَ اللّٰهِ حِينَ تُمْسُونَ وَحِينَ تُصْبِحُونَ﴾ إِلَى قَوْلِهِ: ﴿وَكَذٰلِكَ تُخْرَجُونَ﴾ ثَلَاثَ مَرَّاتٍ. ﴿أَفَحَسِبْتُمْ أَنَّمَا خَلَقْنَاكُمْ عَبَثاً﴾ إِلَى آخِرِهَا. وَيَقْرَأُ مِنْ أَوَّلِ غَافِرٍ إِلَى

recite from the beginning of *Sūrat Ghāfir* as far as, '*to Him is the destination,*'[116] the Throne Verse (*Āyat al-Kursī*)[117] and four verses from the beginning of *Sūrat al-Baqara.*[118] [Then] the Throne Verse, the two verses after it and three [verses] from the end of *Sūrat al-Baqara*. [Then] the end of *Sūrat al-Isrā'*,[119] *Sūrat al-Ikhlāṣ*[120] and the *mu'awwadhatayn*[121] three times.

One should say, *Glory be to God and praise be to Him*, one hundred or one thousand times. [Then,] *There is no god but God alone; He has no partner. To Him is the Kingdom and to Him is all praise. He gives life and He gives death. He is the Living; He does not die. All that is good is in His Hand and He has power over all things*, ten or one hundred times. And [say], *Glory be to God and praise be to God*, one hundred times; *There is no god but God*, one hundred times; and, *God is most Great*, one hundred times. One should invoke God's blessing and peace upon the Prophet ﷺ ten times.

[Supplications] one should designate for the morning: *I am here, O God, I am here and at Your service. All good is in Your Hand and is from You, through You and to You. O God, whatever I have said, or have ever vowed or have ever taken an oath for, I submit it to Your Will and disposal. What You will, is, and what You have not willed, is not. There is no power and no might save in You. Truly, You have power over all things. O God, whatever salutations I send, then they are for those whom You have also blessed; and whoever I have cursed then it is upon those whom You have also cursed. You are my Patron in this world and the Hereafter. Give me death as a Muslim and let me follow the righteous.*

O God, truly I ask You for contentment with Your Decree, for ease of life after death, for the pleasure of looking upon Your Face, for longing to meet You, [to arrive at all this] without suffering harm or causing harm and without the temptation to go astray. I seek refuge in You, O God, lest I oppress [anyone] or am [myself] oppressed, lest I show enmity or enmity is shown to me and lest I accrue all-encompassing mistakes or sins that are not forgiven.

﴿إِلَيْهِ الْمَصِيرُ﴾. وَآيَةَ الْكُرْسِيِّ وَأَرْبَعَ آيَاتٍ مِنْ أَوَّلِ الْبَقَرَةِ. وَآيَةَ الْكُرْسِيِّ وَآيَتَيْنِ بَعْدَهَا وَثَلَاثاً مِنْ آخِرِهَا وَآخِرَ الْإِسْرَاءِ وَالْإِخْلَاصَ وَالْمُعَوِّذَتَيْنِ ثَلَاثَ مَرَّاتٍ.

وَيَقُولُ: سُبْحَانَ اللهِ وَبِحَمْدِهِ، مِائَةً أَوْ أَلْفاً. وَلَا إِلٰهَ إِلَّا اللهُ وَحْدَهُ، لَا شَرِيكَ لَهُ، لَهُ الْمُلْكُ وَلَهُ الْحَمْدُ يُحْيِي وَيُمِيتُ وَهُوَ حَيٌّ لَا يَمُوتُ بِيَدِهِ الْخَيْرُ وَهُوَ عَلَى كُلِّ شَيْءٍ قَدِيرٌ (عَشْراً أَوْ مِائَةً). وَسُبْحَانَ اللهِ وَالْحَمْدُ لِلّٰهِ (مِائَةً). وَلَا إِلٰهَ إِلَّا اللهُ (مِائَةً). وَاللهُ أَكْبَرُ (مِائَةً). وَيُصَلِّي عَلَى النَّبِيِّ ﷺ عَشْراً.

وَيَخُصُّ الصَّبَاحَ: لَبَّيْكَ اللّٰهُمَّ لَبَّيْكَ وَسَعْدَيْكَ وَالْخَيْرُ فِي يَدَيْكَ وَمِنْكَ وَبِكَ وَإِلَيْكَ. اَللّٰهُمَّ مَا قُلْتُ مِنْ قَولٍ أَوْ نَذَرْتُ مِنْ نَذْرٍ أَوْ حَلَفْتُ مِنْ حَلْفٍ فَمَشِيئَتُكَ بَيْنَ يَدَيْهِ. مَا شِئْتَ كَانَ، وَمَا لَمْ تَشَأْ لَمْ يَكُنْ. لَا حَوْلَ وَلَا قُوَّةَ إِلَّا بِكَ. إِنَّكَ عَلَى كُلِّ شَيْءٍ قَدِيرٌ. اَللّٰهُمَّ وَمَا صَلَّيْتُ مِنْ صَلَاةٍ فَعَلَى مَنْ صَلَّيْتَ وَما لَعَنْتُ مِنْ لَعْنَةٍ، فَعَلَى مَنْ لَعَنْتَ. أَنْتَ وَلِيٌّ فِي الدُّنْيَا وَالْآخِرَةِ. تَوَفَّنِي مُسْلِماً وَأَلْحِقْنِي بِالصَّالِحِينَ.

اَللّٰهُمَّ إِنِّي أَسْأَلُكَ الرِّضَا بِالْقَضَاءِ وَبَرْدَ الْعَيْشِ بَعْدَ الْمَوْتِ وَلَذَّةَ النَّظَرِ إِلَى وَجْهِكَ وَشَوْقاً إِلَى لِقَائِكَ مِنْ غَيْرِ ضَرَّاءَ مُضِرَّةٍ وَلَا فِتْنَةٍ مُضِلَّةٍ. أَعُوذُ بِكَ اللّٰهُمَّ أَنْ أَظْلِمَ أَوْ أُظْلَمَ أَوْ أَعْتَدِيَ أَوْ يُعْتَدَى عَلَيَّ أَوْ أَرْتَكِبَ خَطِيئَةً مُحِيطَةً أَوْ ذَنْباً لَا يُغْفَرُ.

O God, Originator of the heavens and the earth, Knower of the unseen and the seen, Lord of Majesty and Generosity. Truly I bear witness to You in this worldly life and I make You a witness—sufficient is God as a witness. Indeed, I bear witness that there is no god but You alone; You have no partner. To Him is the Kingdom and to Him is all praise. Truly, You have power over all things. I bear witness that Muḥammad is Your servant and Your messenger. I bear witness that Your promise is true, that meeting You is true, that Paradise is true, that Hellfire is true and that the Hour is coming—there is no doubt about it—truly, You will resurrect those in the graves. I bear witness that, truly, if You leave me to myself, You leave me to uselessness, deficiency, sin and error. Certainly, I have confidence in Your mercy. So forgive me all of my sins; truly, no one forgives sins but You. Turn towards me, for You are the Ever-Relenting and Most Merciful.

O God, make me amongst the greatest of Your servants in share in every good that you distribute. In what is to come, grant me a light with which You guide me, a mercy that you spread out [for me], a provision that You expand, a harm that You uncover, calamities that You remove, temptations that You cast away and evil that You avert.

At the rising of the dawn you should say, *O God, truly I seek refuge in You from the torment of the grave and from the trial of the grave.*

At the rising of the sun [you should say], *Praise be to God Who has bestowed this day upon us, Who has given us twelve [*rakʿas *to pray]*[122] *in it and Who has not punished us with Hellfire. Praise be to God, Who has honoured us today [with] His well-being and has brought forth the sun from its place of rising. O God, I have reached the morning; to You I bear witness to what You have borne witness for Yourself—and to which You called Your angels as witnesses, [as well as] those carrying Your Throne and*

اَللّٰهُمَّ فَاطِرَ السَّمَاوَاتِ وَالْأَرْضِ، عَالِمَ الْغَيْبِ وَالشَّهَادَةِ، ذَا الْجَلَالِ وَالْإِكْرَامِ. فَإِنِّي أَشْهَدُ إِلَيْكَ فِي هٰذِهِ الْحَيَاةِ الدُّنْيَا وَأُشْهِدُكَ وَكَفَى بِاللّٰهِ شَهِيداً، أَنِّي أَشْهَدُ أَنْ لَا إِلٰهَ إِلَّا أَنْتَ وَحْدَكَ لَا شَرِيكَ لَكَ. لَهُ الْمُلْكُ وَلَهُ الْحَمْدُ. أَنَّكَ عَلَى كُلِّ شَيْءٍ قَدِيرٌ. وَأَشْهَدُ أَنْ مُحَمَّداً عَبْدُكَ وَرَسُولُكَ. وَأَشْهَدُ أَنَّ وَعْدَكَ حَقٌّ وَلِقَاءَكَ حَقٌّ وَالْجَنَّةَ حَقٌّ وَالنَّارَ حَقٌّ وَالسَّاعَةَ آتِيَةٌ لَا رَيْبَ فِيهَا، وَأَنَّكَ تَبْعَثُ مَنْ فِي الْقُبُورِ. وَأَشْهَدُ أَنَّكَ إِنْ تَكِلْنِي إِلَى نَفْسِي، تَكِلْنِي إِلَى ضَيْعَةٍ وَعَوْرَةٍ وَذَنْبٍ وَخَطِيئَةٍ. وَإِنِّي أَثِقُ إِلَى رَحْمَتِكَ فَاغْفِرْ لِي ذَنْبِي كُلَّهُ، إِنَّهُ لَا يَغْفِرُ الذُّنُوبَ إِلَّا أَنْتَ. وَتُبْ عَلَيَّ، إِنَّكَ أَنْتَ التَّوَّابُ الرَّحِيمُ.

اَللّٰهُمَّ اجْعَلْنِي مِنْ أَعْظَمِ عِبَادِكَ نَصِيباً، فِي كُلِّ خَيْرٍ تُقْسِمُهُ، فِي الْغَدَاةِ مِنْ نُورٍ تَهْدِنِي بِهِ، وَرَحْمَةٍ تَنْشُرُهَا، وَرِزْقٍ تُبْسِطُهُ، وَضُرٍّ تُكْشِفُهُ، وَبَلَاءٍ تَرْفَعُهُ، وَفِتْنَةٍ تُصْرِفُهَا، وَشَرٍّ تَدْفَعُهُ.

وَتَقُولُ عِنْدَ طُلُوعِ الْفَجْرِ: اَللّٰهُمَّ إِنِّي أَعُوذُ بِكَ مِنْ عَذَابِ الْقَبْرِ وَمِنْ فِتْنَةِ الْقَبْرِ.

وَعِنْدَ طُلُوعِ الشَّمْسِ: اَلْحَمْدُ لِلّٰهِ الَّذِي وَهَبَ لَنَا هٰذَا الْيَوْمَ وَأَقَالَنَا فِيهِ اثْنَتَا عَشَرَةَ وَلَمْ يُعَذِّبْنَا بِالنَّارِ. اَلْحَمْدُ لِلّٰهِ الَّذِي جَلَّلَنَا الْيَوْمَ عَافِيَتَهُ وَجَاءَ بِالشَّمْسِ مِنْ مَطْلَعِهَا. اَللّٰهُمَّ إِنِّي أَصْبَحْتُ، أُشْهِدُكَ بِمَا شَهِدْتَ بِهِ عَلَى نَفْسِكَ وَأَشْهَدْتَ بِهِ مَلَائِكَتَكَ وَحَمَلَةَ عَرْشِكَ وَجَمِيعَ خَلْقِكَ بِأَنَّكَ أَنْتَ

all of Your creation—namely, that You are God, the Eminent, the Wise. Record my bearing witness with that of Your angels and of those possessing knowledge. And [as for] anyone who has not borne witness to You in what You have borne witness to [Yourself], record my bearing witness in place of his. O God, You are [the Source of] peace, peace is from You and peace returns to You. I ask You, O Lord of Majesty and Generosity, to answer our supplications, to give us our hearts' desire, to exceed what we desire and to make us independent of those whom You have made independent of us amongst Your creation.

O God, rectify my religion, which is [a form of] protection for my affairs; rectify my worldly life, which contains my livelihood; and rectify my Hereafter, to which I am going.

At sunset [you should say], *I seek refuge in the perfect Words of God from the evil of what He has created.*

And you should say every day (at any time of the day), *There is no god but God, the King, the evident Truth*, one hundred times; *There is no power and no might save in God*, one hundred times; you should seek God's forgiveness (*istighfār*) one hundred times; and you should seek refuge from Satan ten times. [You should say,] *O God, bless us in death and in what is after death*, twenty-five times and seek forgiveness for the believing men and believing women twenty-seven times. Every day, you should recite *Sūrat al-Ikhlāṣ*[123] [either] fifty, one hundred or two hundred times.

You should say: *Glory be to God, commensurate with His creation, with what pleases Him, with the weight of His Throne and with the ink of His Words.*[124] *Praise be to God, before Whom everything is humbled due to His might. Praise be to God Who has subjugated everything to His rule. Praise be to God to Whose power everything submits.*

اللهُ الْعَزِيزُ الْحَكِيمُ. أُكْتُبْ شَهَادَتِي مَعَ مَلَائِكَتِكَ وَأُولِي الْعِلْمِ. وَمَنْ لَمْ يَشْهَدْ لَكَ بِمَا شَهِدْتَ فَاكْتُبْ شَهَادَتِي مَكَانَ شَهَادَتِهِمْ. اَللّٰهُمَّ أَنْتَ السَّلَامُ وَمِنْكَ السَّلَامُ وَإِلَيْكَ يَعُودُ السَّلَامُ. أَسْأَلُكَ يَا ذَا الْجَلَالِ وَالْإِكْرَامِ أَنْ تَسْتَجِيبَ لَنَا دَعْوَتَنَا وَأَنْ تُعْطِيَنَا رَغْبَتَنَا وَأَنْ تَزِيدَ فَوْقَ رَغْبَتِنَا وَأَنْ تُغْنِيَنَا عَمَّنْ أَغْنَيْتَهُ عَنَّا مِنْ خَلْقِكَ.

اَللّٰهُمَّ أَصْلِحْ لِي دِينِيَ الَّذِي هُوَ عِصْمَةُ أَمْرِي وَأَصْلِحْ لِي دُنْيَايَ الَّتِي فِيهَا مَعَاشِي وَأَصْلِحْ لِي آخِرَتِي الَّتِي إِلَيْهَا مُنْقَلَبِي.

وَعِنْدَ الْغُرُوبِ: أَعُوذُ بِكَلِمَاتِ اللهِ التَّامَّاتِ مِنْ شَرِّ مَا خَلَقَ.

وَتَقُولُ كُلَّ يَوْمٍ فِي أَيِّ وَقْتٍ كَانَ مِنَ النَّهَارِ: لَا إِلٰهَ إِلَّا اللهُ الْمَلِكُ الْحَقُّ الْمُبِينُ مِائَةَ مَرَّةٍ. وَلَا حَوْلَ وَلَا قُوَّةَ إِلَّا بِاللهِ مِائَةَ مَرَّةٍ، وَتَسْتَغْفِرُ مِائَةً، وَتَسْتَعِيذُ مِنَ الشَّيْطَانِ عَشْراً. اَللّٰهُمَّ بَارِكْ لَنَا فِي الْمَوْتِ وَفِيمَا بَعْدَ الْمَوْتِ (خَمْساً وَعِشْرِينَ). وَتَسْتَغْفِرُ لِلْمُؤْمِنِينَ وَالْمُؤْمِنَاتِ سَبْعاً وَعِشْرِينَ. وَتَقْرَأُ كُلَّ يَوْمٍ سُورَةَ الْإِخْلَاصِ خَمْسِينَ مَرَّةً أَوْ مِائَةً أَوْ مَائَتَيْنِ.

وَتَقُولُ: سُبْحَانَ اللهِ عَدَدَ خَلْقِهِ وَرِضَا نَفْسِهِ وَزِنَةَ عَرْشِهِ وَمِدَادَ كَلِمَاتِهِ. اَلْحَمْدُ لِلّٰهِ الَّذِي تَوَاضَعَ كُلُّ شَيْءٍ لِعِزَّتِهِ. وَالْحَمْدُ لِلّٰهِ الَّذِي خَضَعَ كُلُّ شَيْءٍ لِمُلْكِهِ. وَالْحَمْدُ لِلّٰهِ الَّذِي اِسْتَسْلَمَ كُلُّ شَيْءٍ لِقُدْرَتِهِ.

DAILY PRACTICES FOR THE DAY OF JUMʿA

[Daily practices for this day include:] engaging in sexual intercourse,[125] the purificatory bath,[126] trimming the moustache,[127] paring the nails, wearing a white garment and turban,[128] using perfume, burning incense, using a *miswāk,* applying oil [to the skin], combing the beard, waking early, going to sleep late, walking early to the [*Jumʿa*] prayer.

One should enter the mosque,[129] pray eight *rakʿas*, then sit[130] and focus completely on listening (*inṣāt*)[131] to the imam when he begins the sermon (*khuṭba*)—with the exception of responding when someone greets him and when someone who sneezes [by saying, *May God have mercy upon you* (yarḥamuka Allāh)].[132] If one should nod off [in light sleep[133]] while the imam is giving the *khuṭba*, one should move from one's seat to that of one's companion, while one's companion moves to one's own seat. While the imam is delivering the *khuṭba*, it is prohibited to sit with a cloth wrapped around one or with one's hands clasped around one's legs.[134] However, the majority of people have said that this has been abrogated (*mansūkh*).

After *Jumʿa*, one should recite *Sūrat al-Ikhlāṣ*,[135] the *muʿawwadhatayn*[136] and the *Fātiḥa*[137] seven times each before speaking. One should send abundant blessings (*ṣalawāt*) upon the Prophet ﷺ on the day of *Jumʿa* and the night of *Jumʿa*, so one should recite one hundred *ṣalawāt* or one thousand. One should say, *O God, shower blessings upon Muḥammad and upon the family of Muḥammad, the unlettered Prophet.*

وَظَائِفُ يَوْمِ الْجُمُعَةِ

اَلْجِمَاعُ، الْغُسْلُ وَقَصُّ الشَّارِبِ وَقَلْمُ الْأَظْفَارِ وَلَبْسُ أَبْيَضِ الثِّيَابِ وَالْعِمَامَةِ وَالطِّيبُ وَالْبَخُورُ وَالسِّوَاكُ وَالدُّهْنُ وَتَسْرِيحُ اللِّحْيَةِ وَالتَّبْكِيرُ وَتَأْخِيرُ النَّوْمِ وَالْغَدْوُ إِلَى الصَّلَاةِ.

وَإِذَا دَخَلَ الْمَسْجِدَ يُصَلِّي ثَمَانَ رَكَعَاتٍ ثُمَّ يَجْلِسُ وَالْإِنْصَاتُ إِذَا خَطَبَ الْإِمَامُ إِلَّا فِي السَّلَامِ، وَتَشْمِيتُ الْعَاطِسِ. وَإِذَا نَعَسَ وَالْإِمَامُ يَخْطُبُ، تَحَوَّلَ مِنْ مَجْلِسِهِ إِلَى مَجْلِسِ صَاحِبِهِ وَيَتَحَوَّلُ صَاحِبُهُ إِلَى مَجْلِسِهِ. وَنَهَى عَنِ الْحَبْوَةِ وَالْإِمَامُ يَخْطُبُ. لٰكِنْ قَالَ الْجُمْهُورُ إِنَّهُ مَنْسُوخٌ.

يَقْرَأُ بَعْدَ الْجُمُعَةِ قَبْلَ أَنْ يَتَكَلَّمَ اَلْإِخْلَاصَ وَالْمُعَوِّذَتَيْنِ وَالْفَاتِحَةَ سَبْعاً سَبْعاً. وَيُكْثِرُ مِنَ الصَّلَاةِ عَلَى النَّبِيِّ ﷺ يَوْمَ الْجُمُعَةِ وَلَيْلَةَ الْجُمُعَةِ، فَيُصَلِّي مِائَةَ مَرَّةٍ أَوْ أَلْفَ مَرَّةٍ. يَقُولُ: اللّٰهُمَّ صَلِّ عَلَى مُحَمَّدٍ وَعَلَى آلِ مُحَمَّدٍ، النَّبِيِّ الْأُمِّيِّ.

One should complete the fixed supererogatory prayer of *Jumʿa* (*rātibat al-jumʿa*), which is recited afterwards in one's home, not in the mosque.[138] After that, one should walk to visit a brother [in Islam], visit the sick, or attend a funeral or wedding. On the day of *Jumʿa,* one should recite *Sūrat al-Kahf*[139] before the imam comes out to give the *khuṭba,* [as well as] *Sūrat Āl ʿImrān,*[140] *Sūrat Hūd*[141] and *Sūrat al-Dukhān.*[142] One should give as much charity as one can afford. One should not attend a social gathering of one's people on the evening of this day; [rather,] one should busy oneself with remembrance of God (*dhikr*) and supplications (*duʿāʾ*) until the end of sunset.

On the day of *Jumʿa* and that night one should say seven times: *O God, You are my Lord. There is no god but You. You have created me and I am Your servant, the son of Your servant and the son of Your female servant. I am in Your complete control and my forelock is in Your Hand. I have reached the evening adhering to Your covenant and Your promise as much as I am able. I seek refuge in You from the evil that I have done. I acknowledge Your blessings upon me and I acknowledge my sins, so forgive me for no one forgives sins save You.*[H]

One should avidly desire to do abundant good and avoid evil on this day—because good and evil deeds are multiplied therein—and to supplicate, hoping that it coincides with the hour of acceptance (*sāʿat al-ijāba*). And the best times for this are at the rising of the sun, from [the beginning of] the sun's declination (*zawāl*) [from its zenith] until the *salāms* of the imam [at the start of the *khuṭba*],[143] from after the afternoon prayer (*ʿaṣr*) until sunset and at the end of the *iqāma* for the *Jumʿa* prayer. It is *Sunna* for whoever misses the *Jumʿa* prayer without an excuse to give a dinar (or half a dinar), a dirham (or half a dirham) or a *ṣāʿ* of wheat (or half a *ṣāʿ*).[144]

وَيُصَلِّي رَاتِبَةَ الْجُمُعَةِ الَّتِي بَعْدَهَا فِي بَيْتِهِ، لَا فِي الْمَسْجِدِ. وَيَمْشِي بَعْدَهَا لِزِيَارَةِ أَخٍ أَوْ عِيَادَةِ مَرِيضٍ أَوْ حُضُورِ جَنَازَةٍ أَوْ عَقْدِ نِكَاحٍ. وَيَقْرَأُ يَوْمَ الْجُمُعَةِ سُورَةَ الْكَهْفِ قَبْلَ أَنْ يَخْرُجَ الْإِمَامُ، وَآلَ عِمْرَانَ وهُوداً وَالدُّخَانَ. وَيَتَصَدَّقُ بِمَا تَيَسَّرَ. وَلَا يَحْضُرُ مَجْلِسَ قَوْمِهِ عَشِيَّةَ هٰذَا النَّهَارِ، وَيَشْتَغِلُ بِالذِّكْرِ وَالدُّعَاءِ إِلَى آخِرِ الْغُرُوبِ.

وَيَقُولُ سَبعَ مَرَّاتٍ يَوْمَ الْجُمُعَةِ وَلَيْلَتِهَا: اَللّٰهُمَّ أَنْتَ رَبِّي. لَا إِلٰهَ إِلَّا أَنْتَ. خَلَقْتَنِي وَأَنَا عَبْدُكَ وَابْنُ عَبْدِكَ وَابْنُ أَمَتِكَ، وَفِي قَبْضَتِكَ وَنَاصِيَتِي بِيَدِكَ أَمْسَيْتُ عَلَى عَهْدِكَ وَوَعْدِكَ مَا اسْتَطَعْتُ. أَعُوذُ بِكَ مِنْ شَرِّ مَا صَنَعْتُ. أَبُوءُ بِنِعْمَتِكَ عَلَيَّ وَأَبُوءُ بِذَنْبِي فَاغْفِرْ لِي ذُنُوبِي، إِنَّهُ لَا يَغْفِرُ الذُّنُوبَ إِلَّا أَنْتَ.

وَيَحْرِصُ فِيهِ عَلَى الْاِسْتِكْثَارِ مِنَ الْحَسَنَاتِ وَاجْتِنَابِ السَّيِّئَاتِ، فَإِنَّ الْحَسَنَةَ وَالسَّيِّئَةَ تُضَاعَفُ فِيهِ وَعَلَى الدُّعَاءِ رَجَاءً أَنْ يُصَادِفَ سَاعَةَ الْإِجَابَةِ. وَأَرْجَى الْأَوْقَاتِ لَهَا عِنْدَ طُلُوعِ الشَّمْسِ وَعِنْدَ زَوَالِهَا إِلَى أَنْ يُسَلِّمَ الْإِمَامُ وَمِنْ بَعْدِ الْعَصْرِ إِلَى الْغُرُوبِ وَعِنْدَ اِنْتِهَاءِ وَقْتِ الْإِقَامَةِ لِصَلَاةِ الْجُمُعَةِ. وَالسُّنَّةُ لِمَنْ فَاتَتْهُ الْجُمُعَةُ مِنْ غَيْرِ عُذْرٍ أَنْ يَتَصَدَّقَ بِدِينَارٍ أَوْ نِصْفِ دِينَارٍ أَوْ دِرْهَمٍ أَوْ نِصْفِ دِرْهَمٍ أَوْ صَاعِ حِنْطَةٍ أَوْ نِصْفِ صَاعِ حِنْطَةٍ.

It is desirable (*mustaḥabb*) to pass five nights[145] during the year [in remembrance of God]: the eve of *Jumʿa*, the eve of *ʿĪd al-Fiṭr*, the eve of *ʿĪd al-Aḍḥā*, the eve of the fifteenth of Shaʿbān and the first night of Rajab.

The daily practices for the eve of *Jumʿa* include visiting the sick for a period of time equivalent to that between milking a camel and then milking it again. This [visiting should be done at least] once in a lifetime and anything additional is supererogatory. It is not done every day, but every other day or every fourth [day].

The proprieties (*ādāb*) [of such a visit] include shaking hands, [gently] placing one's hand where the patient is sick, asking them how they are and cheering them up so that they recover. This should be recited in their presence: *O God, Lord of Humankind, remove the affliction. Provide a cure, You are the Curer. There is no cure except Your Cure, [which is] a cure that does not leave behind illness. In the name of God, I recite this protective prayer*[146] *on you against everything that hurts you and against the evil of every person or eye that is envious. May God cure you. In the name of God, Most Compassionate, Most Merciful. I seek protection for you with God, the One, the Utterly Independent—Who neither begets, nor is born, nor is there any equivalent to Him—from the evil of what you find. O God, Curer of this servant of Yours, Your enemy does not supplicate to You and walk [to the mosque] for You to prayer.*[147] *May God cure your illness, forgive Your sins, grant You well-being in your religion and protect you as long you live. O God, remove from him what ails him and reward him for what You have tested him with. Our Lord Who is in the heavens, blessed be Your Name. Your command is in the heavens and the earth, just as Your mercy is in the heavens. Make Your mercy be on earth; forgive us our sins and our mistakes. Truly, You are the Lord of the good people, so send down mercy upon this ailment from Your mercy and a cure from Your cures.*

وَيُسْتَحَبُّ إِحْيَاءُ خَمْسِ لَيَالٍ فِي السَّنَةِ: لَيْلَةَ الْجُمُعَةِ وَلَيْلَةَ الْفِطْرِ وَلَيْلَةَ الْأَضْحَى وَلَيْلَةَ النِّصْفِ مِنْ شَعْبَانَ وَأَوَّلَ لَيْلَةٍ مِنْ رَجَبَ.

وَمِنْ وَظَائِفِ لَيْلَةِ يَوْمِ الْجُمُعَةِ عِيَادَةُ الْمَرِيضِ قَدْرَ فُوَاقِ نَاقَةٍ. وَهِيَ مَرَّةً فِي الْعُمْرِ وَمَا زَادَ نَافِلَةٌ. وَلَا يَكُونُ كُلَّ يَوْمٍ بَلْ غِبّاً أَوْ رِبْعاً.

وَمِنْ آدَابِهَا أَنْ يُصَافِحَهُ وَيَضَعُ يَدَهُ حَيْثُ يَشْتَكِي وَيَسْأَلُهُ كَيْفَ هُوَ وَيُنَفِّسُ لَهُ فِي أَجْلِهِ. وَيُقَالُ عِنْدَهُ: اللّٰهُمَّ رَبَّ النَّاسِ أَذْهِبِ الْبَأْسَ. إِشْفِ، أَنْتَ الشَّافِي لَا شِفَاءَ إِلَّا شِفَاؤُكَ، شِفَاءً لَا يُغَادِرُ سَقَماً. بِسْمِ اللهِ أُرْقِيكَ مِنْ كُلِّ شَيْءٍ يُؤْذِيكَ مِنْ شَرِّ كُلِّ نَفْسٍ أَوْ عَيْنٍ حَاسِدٍ اَللّٰهُ يَشْفِيكَ. بِسْمِ اللهِ الرَّحْمٰنِ الرَّحِيمِ. أُعِيذُكَ بِاللهِ الْأَحَدِ الصَّمَدِ الَّذِي لَمْ يَلِدْ وَلَمْ يُولَدْ وَلَمْ يَكُنْ لَهُ كُفُواً أَحَدٌ، وَمِنْ شَرِّ مَا تَجِدُ. اَللّٰهُمَّ شَافِ عَبْدَكَ هٰذَا، لَا دَعَا لَكَ عَدُوَّكَ وَيَمْشِي لَكَ إِلَى الصَّلَاةِ. شَفَى اللهُ سَقَمَكَ وَغَفَرَ ذَنْبَكَ وَعَافَاكَ فِي دِينِكَ وَحَفِظَكَ إِلَى مُدَّةِ أَجْلِكَ. اَللّٰهُمَّ أَذْهِبْ عَنْهُ مَا يَجِدُهُ وَأَجِرْهُ مِمَّا ابْتَلَيْتَهُ. رَبَّنَا الَّذِي فِي السَّمَاءِ، تَقَدَّسَ اسْمُكَ. أَمْرُكَ فِي السَّمَاءِ وَالْأَرْضِ كَمَا رَحْمَتُكَ فِي السَّمَاءِ. اِجْعَلْ رَحْمَتَكَ فِي الْأَرْضِ وَاغْفِرْ لَنَا ذُنُوبَنَا وَخَطَايَانَا إِنَّكَ أَنْتَ رَبُّ الطَّيِّبِينَ فَأَنْزِلْ رَحْمَةً مِنْ رَحْمَتِكَ وَشِفَاءً مِنْ شِفَائِكَ عَلَى هٰذَا الْوَجَعِ.

One should say seven times, *I ask God Almighty, Lord of the almighty Throne, to grant you well-being and to cure you.*

The daily practices for the day of *Jumʿa* include visiting graves. One should say: *Peace be upon you, abode of the believers. May God show mercy to those who have gone ahead of us and to those who remain behind you. Truly, when God so wills, we will be joining you. You have lead the way for us and we are following you. I ask God for well-being, for us and for you. Peace be upon you, O people of the graves. May God forgive us and you. You have gone before us and we are at your heels. You have attained long-lasting goodness and have left behind long-lasting evil. Peace be upon you, O transient souls, worn-out bodies and disintegrated bones that have left the world believing in God. O God, grant them rest from You*[148] *and greetings from us.*

One should recite *Sūrat Yāsīn,*[149] *Āyat al-Kursī*[150] and *Sūrat al-Ikhlāṣ*[151] eleven times; [recite] the *muʿawwadhatayn*[152] and the *Fātiḥa;*[153] and supplicate for the people of the graveyards.

وَيَقُولُ سَبْعَ مَرَّاتٍ: أَسْأَلُ اللّٰهَ الْعَظِيمَ رَبَّ الْعَرْشِ الْعَظِيمِ أَنْ يُعَافِيَكَ وَيَشْفِيَكَ.

وَمِنْ وَظَائِفِ يَوْمِ الْجُمُعَةِ زِيَارَةُ الْقُبُورِ. وَيَقُولُ: اَلسَّلَامُ عَلَيْكُمْ دَارَ قَوْمٍ مُؤْمِنِينَ. وَيَرْحَمُ اللّٰهُ الْمُسْتَقْدِمِينَ مِنَّا وَمِنْكُمْ وَ الْمُسْتَأْخِرِينَ. وَإِنَّا إِنْ شَاءَ اللّٰهُ بِكُمْ لَاحِقُونَ. أَنْتُمْ لَنَا فَرَطٌ وَنَحْنُ لَكُمْ تَبَعٌ. أَسْأَلُ اللّٰهَ لَنَا وَلَكُمْ الْعَافِيَةَ. اَلسَّلَامُ عَلَيْكُمْ أَهْلَ الْقُبُورِ. يَغْفِرُ اللّٰهُ لَنَا وَلَكُمْ. أَنْتُمْ لَنَا سَلَفٌ وَنَحْنُ عَلَى الْأَثَرِ. أَصَبْتُمْ خَيْراً طَوِيلاً وَسَبَقْتُمْ شَرّاً طَوِيلاً. اَلسَّلَامُ عَلَيْكُمْ أَيَّتُهَا الْأَرْوَاحُ الْفَانِيَةُ وَالْأَبْدَانُ الْبَالِيَةُ وَالْعِظَامُ النَّخِرَةُ الَّتِي خَرَجَتْ مِنَ الدُّنْيَا وَهِيَ بِاللّٰهِ مُؤْمِنَةٌ. اَللّٰهُمَّ أَدْخِلْ عَلَيْهِمْ رَوْحاً مِنْكَ وَسَلَاماً مِنَّا.

وَيَقْرَأُ يس وَآيَةَ الْكُرْسِيِّ وَالْإِخْلَاصَ إِحْدَى عَشَرَةَ مَرَّةً وَالْمُعَوِّذَتَيْنِ وَالْفَاتِحَةَ، وَيَدْعُو لِأَهْلِ الْمَقَابِرِ.

DAILY PRACTICES DURING THE TEN DAYS OF DHŪ'L-ḤIJJA

The Messenger of God ﷺ said, 'There are no days in which a [good] deed is more beloved to God (Exalted is He), and more virtuous, than during the [first] ten days of Dhū'l-Ḥijja.'

During [these days] you should pronounce the *tahlīl*, *takbīr* and *tasbīh* abundantly. Truly, fasting [on] each of these days is equal to the fast of one year, and standing every night in prayer [during these days] is like standing in prayer during the Night of Power (*Laylat al-Qadr*).[154] Deeds [performed] during [these days] are multiplied seven hundred times.[155]

Anas (may God be pleased with him) said, 'It was said about the ten days [of Dhū'l-Ḥijja that] every day [is worth] one thousand days and that the Day of ʿArafa[156] [is worth] 10,000 days.' Bayhaqī narrated this in *The Branches of Faith* (Shuʿab al-īmān).[157]

It was also narrated from some of the wives of the Prophet ﷺ that he would fast on nine days of Dhū'l-Ḥijja.

وَظَائِفُ عَشْرِ ذِي الْحِجَّةِ

قَالَ ﷺ: «مَا مِنْ أَيَّامٍ اَلْعَمَلُ فِيهِنَّ أَحَبُّ إِلَى اللّٰهِ تَعَالَى وَأَفْضَلُ مِنْ أَيَّامِ الْعَشْرِ.»

فَأَكْثِرُوا فِيهِنَّ مِنَ التَّهْلِيلِ وَالتَّكْبِيرِ وَالتَّسْبِيحِ. وَإِنَّ صِيَامَ كُلِّ يَوْمٍ مِنْهَا يَعْدِلُ بِصِيَامِ سَنَةٍ، وَقِيَامُ كُلِّ لَيْلَةٍ بِقِيَامِ لَيْلَةِ الْقَدْرِ. وَالْعَمَلُ فِيهِنَّ يُضَاعَفُ بِسَبْعِمِائَةِ ضَعْفٍ.

وَعَنْ أَنَسٍ رَضِيَ اللّٰهُ عَنْهُ قَالَ: «كَانَ يُقَالُ فِي أَيَّامِ الْعَشْرِ بِكُلِّ يَوْمٍ أَلْفُ يَوْمٍ، وَيَوْمُ عَرَفَةَ عَشْرَةُ آلَافِ يَوْمٍ.» رَوَاهُ الْبَيْهَقِيُّ فِي شُعَبِ الْإِيمَانِ.

وَرُوِيَ أَيْضاً عَنْ بَعْضِ أَزْوَاجِ النَّبِيِّ ﷺ أَنَّهُ كَانَ يَصُومُ تِسْعَ ذِي الْحِجَّةِ.

DAILY PRACTICES FOR THE DAY OF ʿARAFA

One should say one hundred times, *There is no god but God alone; He has no partner. To Him is the Kingdom and to Him is all praise. He gives life and He gives death. In His Hand is all good and He has power over all things.*

O God, praise be to You like that which we utter—and even better than what we utter. O God, Yours is my dwelling, my life, my death, to You is my return and Yours is my legacy. O God, I seek refuge in You from the torment of the grave, from the whispering in my breast and from the dissipation of my affairs. O God, truly I ask You for the good that the wind brings. O God, truly You see my place, hear my speech, know my secret and my open dealings, and nothing from my affairs is hidden from You. I am the miserable one, the poor one, the one seeking protection, the fearful one, the anxious one, the acknowledger, the one who recognises his sins. I beg You like the begging of a poor person. I am earnest [in prayer] to You like the earnestness of a disgraced sinner. I supplicate to You like the supplication of a scared and battered person who has lowered his neck and his body for You and has put his nose upon the ground.

O God, do let me supplicate You in vain, Lord; be kind and merciful with me, O Best of those who are asked and O Best of those who provide. O God, make light be in my sight, in my hearing and in my heart. O God, expand my breast and ease my affairs. O God, truly I seek refuge in You from the whisperings in the breast, from the scattering of my affairs, from the trial of the grave, from the evil of what appears during the day, from the evil of what

وَظَائِفُ يَوْمِ عَرَفَةَ

يَقُولُ: لَا إِلٰهَ إِلَّا اللهُ وَحْدَهُ، لَا شَرِيكَ لَهُ، لَهُ الْمُلْكُ وَلَهُ الْحَمْدُ يُحْيِي وَيُمِيتُ. بِيَدِهِ الْخَيْرُ وَهُوَ عَلَى كُلِّ شَيْءٍ قَدِيرٌ (مِائَةَ مَرَّةٍ).

اَللّٰهُمَّ لَكَ الْحَمْدُ كَالَّذِي نَقُولُ وَخَيْراً مِمَّا نَقُولُ. اَللّٰهُمَّ لَكَ سُكْنَايَ وَمَحْيَايَ وَمَمَاتِي وَإِلَيْكَ مَآبِي وَلَكَ تُرَاثِي. اَللّٰهُمَّ إِنِّي أَعُوذُ بِكَ مِنْ عَذَابِ الْقَبْرِ وَوَسْوَسَةِ الصَّدْرِ وَشَتَاتِ الْأَمْرِ. اَللّٰهُمَّ إِنيِّ أَسْأَلُكَ مِنْ خَيْرِ مَا تَجِيءُ بِهِ الرِّيحُ. اَللّٰهُمَّ إِنَّكَ تَرَى مَكَانِي وَتَسْمَعُ كَلَامِي وَتَعْلَمُ سِرِّي وَعَلَانِيَتِي، لَا يَخْفَى عَلَيْكَ شَيْءٌ مِنْ أَمْرِي. أَنَا الْبَائِسُ الْفَقِيرُ الْمُسْتَجِيرُ الْوَجِلُ، اَلْمُشْفِقُ الْمُقِرُّ، اَلْمُعْتَرِفُ بِذَنْبِهِ. أَسْأَلُكَ مَسْأَلَةَ الْمِسْكِينِ وَأَبْتَهِلُ إِلَيْكَ اِبْتِهَالَ الْمُذْنِبِ الذَّلِيلِ. وَأَدْعُوكَ دُعَاءَ الْخَائِفِ الضَّرِيرِ الَّذِي خَضَعَتْ لَكَ رَقَبَتُهُ وَذَلَّ لَكَ جَسَدُهُ وَرَغِمَ أَنْفُهُ.

اَللّٰهُمَّ لَا تَجْعَلْنِي بِدُعَائِكَ رَبِّ شَقِيّاً، وَكُنْ بِي رَؤُوفاً رَحِيماً، يَا خَيْرَ الْمَسْئُولِينَ، وَيَا خَيْرَ الْمُعْطِينَ. اَللّٰهُمَّ اجْعَلْ فِي بَصَرِي نُوراً وَفِي سَمْعِي نُوراً وَفِي قَلْبِي نُوراً. اَللّٰهُمَّ اشْرَحْ لِي صَدْرِي وَيَسِّرْ لِي أَمْرِي. اَللّٰهُمَّ إِنِّي

appears during the night, from the evil that the wind blows and from the evil of the vicissitudes of time.[J] One should say this one thousand times.

Glory be to He Whose Throne is in the heavens. Glory be to He Whose domain is the earth. Glory be to He Who makes a way through the ocean. Glory be to He Whose authority is in Hellfire. Glory be to He Whose mercy is in Paradise. Glory be to He Whose decree is in the graves. Glory be to He Whose spirit is in the air. Glory be to He Who raised the heavens. Glory be to He Who laid down the earth. Glory be to He Who is the only refuge.

One should recite *Sūrat al-Ikhlāṣ*[158] one hundred times, then say, *O God, bless Muḥammad just as You blessed Abraham and the family of Abraham—truly, You are the Praised, All-Glorious—and [bless] us along with them*, one hundred times.

The Messenger of God ﷺ said, 'Whoever guards his tongue, his hearing and his sight on the Day of ʿArafa will be forgiven from one ʿArafa to [the next] ʿArafa.'

أَعُوذُ بِكَ مِنْ وَسْوَاسِ الصُّدُورِ وَشَتَاتِ الْأُمُورِ وَفِتْنَةِ الْقُبُورِ وَشَرِّ مَا يَلِجُ فِي النَّهَارِ وَشَرِّ مَا يَلِجُ فِي اللَّيْلِ وَشَرِّ مَا تَهُبُّ بِهِ الرِّيَاحُ وَمِنْ شَرِّ نَوَائِبِ الدُّهُورِ. وَيَقُولُ أَلْفَ مَرَّةٍ.

سُبْحَانَ الَّذِي فِي السَّمَاءِ عَرْشُهُ. سُبْحَانَ الَّذِي فِي الْأَرْضِ مَوْطِنُهُ. سُبْحَانَ الَّذِي فِي الْبَحْرِ سَبِيلُهُ. سُبْحَانَ الَّذِي فِي النَّارِ سُلْطَانُهُ. سُبْحَانَ الَّذِي فِي الْجَنَّةِ رَحْمَتُهُ. سُبْحَانَ الَّذِي فِي الْقُبُورِ قَضَاؤُهُ. سُبْحَانَ الَّذِي فِي الْهَوَاءِ رُوحُهُ. سُبْحَانَ الَّذِي رَفَعَ السَّمَاءَ. سُبْحَانَ الَّذِي وَضَعَ الْأَرْضَ. سُبْحَانَ الَّذِي لَا مَلْجَأَ مِنْهُ إِلَّا إِلَيْهِ.

وَيَقْرَأُ سُورَةَ الْإِخْلَاصِ مِائَةَ مَرَّةٍ، ثُمَّ يَقُولُ: اَللّٰهُمَّ صَلِّ عَلَى مُحَمَّدٍ كَمَا صَلَّيْتَ عَلَى إِبْرَاهِيمَ وَعَلَى آلِ إِبْرَاهِيمَ، إِنَّكَ حَمِيدٌ مَجِيدٌ، وَعَلَيْنَا مَعَهُمْ (مِائَةَ مَرَّةٍ).

وَقَالَ ﷺ: «مَنْ حَفِظَ لِسَانَهُ وَسَمْعَهُ وَبَصَرَهُ يَوْمَ عَرَفَةَ غُفِرَ لَهُ مِنْ عَرَفَةَ إِلَى عَرَفَةَ.»

DAILY PRACTICES FOR RECITING THE QUR'ĀN

It is recommended to recite [the Qur'ān] abundantly, for in a *ḥadīth* [it was said], 'Whoever recites one letter from the Book of God will have a good deed recorded for him, and one good deed shall be rewarded ten times over.'

The Prophet ﷺ said to ʿAbd Allāh b. ʿAmr (may God be pleased with him), 'Recite the [whole of the] Qur'ān in a month.' He responded, 'I have [the] strength [to do so].' He ﷺ said, 'Recite it in fifteen days.' He responded, 'I am stronger than that.' He ﷺ said, 'Recite it in one day of *Jumʿa*.'

Some of the scholars said, 'It is disliked to take more than forty days to complete the Qur'ān with no excuse.' Aḥmad [Ibn Ḥanbal] specified this and Aws al-Thaqafī (may God be pleased with him) said, 'I was in a delegation from [the Banū] Thaqīf when the Messenger of God ﷺ said to us, "Devote yourselves diligently to two portions (*ḥizbayn*)[159] of the Qur'ān." I did not want to leave until I asked him for a judgement, so we asked his Companions how they divided up the Qur'ān. They replied, "We divide it into [groups of] three *sūra*s, seven *sūra*s, nine *sūra*s, eleven, thirteen and the portion of interrupted (*mufaṣṣal*) [*sūra*s, which is] from [*Sūrat*] *Qāf* until [the Qur'ān] reaches [its] end."'[160]

[Being in a state of] ablution (*wuḍūʾ*) is desirable (*mustaḥabb*) for reciting the Qur'ān; [as is the use of] a *miswāk* [beforehand]; [also desirable is] to recite [it] in a clean place; to sit facing the *qibla* with humbleness, tranquillity and dignity, bowing one's head in reverence; to audibly seek refuge in God at the beginning of the recitation; to take one's time; to contemplate; to weep and

وَظَائِفُ تِلاَوَةِ الْقُرْآنِ

يُسْتَحَبُّ الْإِكْثَارُ مِنْهَا فَفِي الْحَدِيثِ: «مَنْ قَرَأَ حَرْفاً مِنْ كِتَابِ اللهِ فَلَهُ بِهِ حَسَنَةٌ، وَالْحَسَنَةُ بِعَشْرِ أَمْثَالِهَا.»

وَقَالَ ﷺ لِعَبْدِ اللهِ بْنِ عَمْرٍو: «إِقْرَإِ الْقُرْآنَ فِي شَهْرٍ.» قَالَ: «إِنِّي أَجِدُ قُوَّةً.» قَالَ ﷺ: «إِقْرَأْهُ فِي خَمْسَةِ عَشَرَ.» قَالَ: «إِنِّي أَقْوَى مِنْ ذٰلِكَ.» قَالَ ﷺ: «إِقْرَأْهُ فِي جُمُعَةٍ.»

وَقَالَ بَعْضُ الْعُلَمَاءِ: «يُكْرَهُ تَأْخِيرُ خَتْمَةٍ أَكْثَرَ مِنْ أَرْبَعِينَ يَوْماً بِلاَ عُذْرٍ.» نَصَّ عَلَيْهِ أَحْمَدُ وَقَالَ أَوْسٌ الثَّقَفِيُّ: «كُنْتُ فِي وَفْدِ ثَقِيفٍ فَقَالَ لَنَا رَسُولُ اللهِ ﷺ: «وَاظِبُوا عَلَى حِزْبَيْنِ مِنَ الْقُرْآنِ.» فَأَرَدْتُ أَنْ لَا أَخْرُجَ حَتَّى أَقْضِيَهُ، فَسَأَلْنَا أَصْحَابَهُ: «كَيْفَ يُحَزِّبُونَ الْقُرْآنَ؟» قَالُوا: «نُخْرِجُ بِهِ ثَلَاثَ سُوَرٍ وَسَبْعَ سُوَرٍ وَتِسْعَ سُوَرٍ، وَإِحْدَى عَشَرَ، وَثَلَاثَ عَشَرَ، وَحِزْبُ الْمُفَصَّلِ مِنْ قٓ حَتَّى يُخْتَمَ.»

وَيُسْتَحَبُّ الْوُضُوءُ لِقِرَاءَةِ الْقُرْآنِ وَالسِّوَاكَ وَأَنْ يَقْرَأَ فِي مَكَانٍ نَظِيفٍ وَيَجْلِسَ مُسْتَقْبِلَ الْقِبْلَةِ بِخُشُوعٍ وَسَكِينَةٍ وَوَقَارٍ مُطْرِقاً رَأْسَهُ وَيَتَعَوَّذَ فِي اِبْتِدَاءِ الْقِرَاءَةِ جَهْراً وَالتَّرَسُّلُ وَالتَّدَبُّرُ وَالْبُكَاءُ وَالتَّبَاكِي وَتَحْسِينُ الصَّوْتِ

cause weeping in others; to beautify one's voice while reciting; [to recite] it in sequence; [to recite] aloud if one does not fear acting ostentatiously and if it will not disturb anyone who is sleeping or praying; to recite from the Qur'ān codex (*muṣḥaf*), because looking upon it is worship; to not speak with anyone during the recitation; to not laugh; to not jest; to not look at anything distracting; to correctly recite each letter according to how a trained reciter (*qāriʾ*) has confirmed it; to recite each complete recitation of the Qur'ān (*khatma*) according to that of [an acknowledged] transmitter (*rāwī*); and [to proceed] in this way until one completes one's recitation, and thus to have fulfilled the full right of the Qur'ān.

[It is also desirable] to prostrate oneself upon the recitation of a verse of prostration (*sajda*) and—in addition to what we have already said above about what should be recited during the prostration in *ṣalāt*—to say: *O God, make it a stored treasure for me with You, make it a great reward for me and remove my burden [of sins] from me through it. Accept it from me just as You accepted it from David* ﵇. *Glory be to our Lord. Truly, the promise of our Lord shall come to pass.*[K]

If one reads a verse of mercy (*raḥma*), one should be happy and ask [for mercy]. [Or if one reads] a verse of punishment (*ʿadhāb*), one should [be] anxious and seek refuge in God. [If one reads a verse] of transcendence (*tanzīh*), then declare [God] to be transcendent and magnify [Him]. [If one reads a verse] of glorification (*tasbīḥ*) or supplication (*duʿāʾ*), then be humble and beseech [God].

At the end of the *Fātiḥa*[161] and [*Sūrat*] *al-Baqara*[162] one should say, *Amen*, and at the end of [*Sūrat*] *al-Baqara*, one should add, *O God, our Lord, praise be to You*, ten times.[163] At the end of [the verse], '*I swear by the Day of Resurrection,*'[164] [in *Sūrat al-Qiyāma*, one should say,] *Of course*. At the end of [*Sūrat*] *al-Mursalāt*[165] [one should say,] *I believe in God*. At the beginning of, '*Glorify the name of your Lord, the Most High,*'[166] [in *Sūrat al-Aʿlā*, one should say,] *Glory be to my Lord, the Most High*. At the end of [the verse], '*And the fig,*'[167]

بِالْقِرَاءَةِ وَتَرْتِيبُهَا، وَالْجَهْرُ إِذَا لَمْ يَخَفْ رِيَاءً وَلَمْ يُؤْذِ نَائِماً أَوْ مُصَلِّياً، وَالْقِرَاءَةُ فِي الْمُصْحَفِ لِأَنَّ النَّظَرَ فِيهِ عِبَادَةٌ، وَأَنْ لَا يَتَكَلَّمَ فِي أَثْنَاءِ الْقِرَاءَةِ مَعَ أَحَدٍ، وَلَا يَضْحَكَ وَلَا يَعْبَثَ وَلَا يَنْظُرَ إِلَى مَا يُلْهِي وَأَنْ يَسْتَوْفِيَ كُلَّ حَرْفٍ أَثْبَتَهُ قَارِئٌ فَيَقْرَأُ كُلَّ خَتْمَةٍ لِرَاوٍ، وَهٰكَذَا إِلَى أَنْ يَسْتَوْفِيَ الْقُرْآنَ لِيَكُونَ قَدْ أَتَى عَلَى جَمِيعِ مَا هُوَ قُرْآنٌ.

وَالسُّجُودُ عِنْدَ قِرَاءَةِ آيَةِ السَّجْدَةِ وَيَقُولُ فِيهِ زِيَادَةً عَلَى مَا تَقَدَّمَ فِي سُجُودِ الصَّلَاةِ: اَللّٰهُمَّ اجْعَلْهَا لِي عِنْدَكَ ذُخْراً وَأَعْظِمْ بِهَا لِي أَجْراً وَضَعْ عَنِّي بِهَا وِزْراً. وَتَقَبَّلْهَا مِنِّي كَمَا قَبِلْتَهَا مِنْ دَاوُدَ ﷺ. سُبْحَانَ رَبِّنَا. إِنْ كَانَ وَعْدُ رَبِّنَا لَمَفْعُولاً.

وَإِذَا مَرَّ بِآيَةِ رَحْمَةٍ، اِسْتَبْشَرَ وَسَأَلَ أَوْ عَذَابٍ، أَشْفَقَ وَتَعَوَّذَ أَوْ تَنْزِيهٍ نَزَّهَ وَعَظَّمَ أَوْ تَسْبِيحٍ أَوْ دُعَاءٍ تَضَرَّعَ وَطَلَبَ.

وَيَقُولُ فِي آخِرِ الْفَاتِحَةِ وَالْبَقَرَةِ: آمِينْ. وَيَزِيدُ فِي آخِرِ الْبَقَرَةِ: اَللّٰهُمَّ رَبَّنَا وَلَكَ الْحَمْدُ (عَشْراً). وَفِي آخِرِ ﴿لَا أُقْسِمُ بِيَوْمِ الْقِيَامَةِ﴾: بَلَى. وَفِي آخِرِ الْمُرْسَلَاتِ: آمَنْتُ بِاللهِ. وَفِي أَوَّلِ ﴿سَبِّحِ اسْمَ رَبِّكَ الْأَعْلَى﴾: سُبْحَانَ رَبِّيَ الْأَعْلَى. وَفِي آخِرِ سُورَةِ ﴿وَالتِّينِ﴾: بَلَى وَأَنَا عَلَى ذٰلِكَ مِنَ الشَّاهِدِينَ. وَفِي

[in *Sūrat al-Tīn*, one should say,] *Of course, and I am one of the witnesses to that*. During [the verse,] '*So which of the favours of your Lord would you deny?*'[168] [in *Sūrat al-Raḥmān*, one should say,] *We do not deny any of your blessings, our Lord; praise be to You*. At [the verse,] '*And [by] the soul and He who fashioned it*,'[169] [in *Sūrat al-Shams*, one should say,] *O God, give my soul its God-fearingness and purify it; You are the Best of those who purify it. You are its Patron and its Guardian*. [In *Sūrat al-Baqara*,] at '*And when My servants ask you concerning Me—indeed I am near [...]*'[170] to the end of the verse, [one should say:] *O God, truly You have commanded us to supplicate to You and have pledged to answer. I am here, O God, I am here. I am here; You have no partner. I am here; truly, Yours is the praise, the blessing and the kingdom. You have no partner. I bear witness that You are Unique, One, Utterly Independent. He neither begets nor is born, nor is there any equivalent to Him. I bear witness that Your promise is true, that meeting You is true, that Paradise is true, that Hellfire is true and that the Hour is coming—there is no doubt about it—and that You will resurrect those in the graves*.

At [the verse,] '*God witnesses [...]*'[171] [in *Sūrat Āl ʿImrān*, one should say,] *And I bear witness to what God witnesses. I entrust this testimony to God and it is stored for me with God as a deposited trust*. If one recites, '*And the Jews say, "The hand of God is chained,"*'[172] [in *Sūrat al-Māʾida*, then] one should lower one's voice.

The best times for reciting the Qurʾān are after the morning prayer (*ṣubḥ* [*fajr*]) and after the sunset (*maghrib*) and evening (*ʿishāʾ*) prayers. [The best] days are Fridays, Mondays, Thursdays and the Day of *ʿArafa*. [The best] ten-day periods are the last ten [nights] of Ramaḍān and the first ten [days] of Dhū'l-Ḥijja. [The best] month is Ramaḍān.

One should choose to begin [the recitation of the Qurʾān] on the day of *Jumʿa* and to finish reciting it completely from beginning to end (*khatm*) on the eve of Thursday [in other words, on Wednesday night]. The best *khatm* of the Qurʾān is [performed]

﴿فَبِأَيِّ آلَاءِ رَبِّكُمَا تُكَذِّبَانِ﴾: وَلَا بِشَيْءٍ مِنْ نِعَمِكَ رَبَّنَا نُكَذِّبُ، فَلَكَ الْحَمْدُ. وَعِنْدَ ﴿وَنَفْسٍ وَمَا سَوَّاهَا﴾ اَلْآيَةُ: اَللّٰهُمَّ آتِ نَفْسِي تَقْوَاهَا وَزَكِّهَا، أَنْتَ خَيْرُ مَنْ زَكَّاهَا أَنْتَ وَلِيُّهَا وَمَوْلَاهَا. وَعِنْدَ ﴿إِذَا سَأَلَكَ عِبَادِي عَنِّي فَإِنِّي قَرِيبٌ﴾ اَلْآيَةُ: اَللّٰهُمَّ إِنَّكَ أَمَرْتَ بِدُعَائِكَ وَتَكَفَّلْتَ بِالْإِجَابَةِ. لَبَّيْكَ اللّٰهُمَّ لَبَّيْكَ لَبَّيْكَ، لَا شَرِيكَ لَكَ لَبَّيْكَ، إِنَّ الْحَمْدَ وَالنِّعْمَةَ لَكَ وَالْمُلْكَ. لَا شَرِيكَ لَكَ. أَشْهَدُ أَنَّكَ فَرْدٌ أَحَدٌ صَمَدٌ. لَمْ يَلِدْ وَلَمْ يُولَدْ وَلَمْ يَكُنْ لَهُ كُفُواً أَحَدٌ. وَأَشْهَدُ أَنَّ وَعْدَكَ حَقٌّ وَلِقَاءَكَ حَقٌّ وَالْجَنَّةَ حَقٌّ وَالنَّارَ حَقٌّ وَالسَّاعَةَ آتِيَةٌ، لَا رَيْبَ فِيهَا، وَأَنَّكَ تَبْعَثُ مَنْ فِي الْقُبُورِ.

وَعِنْدَ ﴿شَهِدَ اللّٰهُ﴾: وَأَنَا أَشْهَدُ بِمَا شَهِدَ اللّٰهُ. وَأَسْتَوْدِعُ اللّٰهَ هٰذِهِ الشَّهَادَةَ وَهِيَ لِي عِنْدَ اللّٰهِ وَدِيعَةٌ. وَإِذَا قَرَأَ ﴿وَقَالَتِ الْيَهُودُ يَدُ اللّٰهِ مَغْلُولَةٌ﴾ خَفَضَ بِهَا صَوْتَهُ.

وَأَفْضَلُ أَوْقَاتِ الْقِرَاءَةِ: بَعْدَ صَلَاةِ الصُّبْحِ وَبَعْدَ الْمَغْرِبِ وَالْعِشَاءِ. وَمِنَ الْأَيَّامِ: اَلْجُمُعَةُ وَالْاِثْنَيْنِ وَالْخَمِيسُ وَعَرَفَةُ. وَمِنَ الْأَعْشَارِ: الْعَشْرُ الْأَخِيرِ مِنْ رَمَضَانَ، وَالْأُوَّلُ مِنْ ذِي الْحِجَّةِ. وَمِنَ الشُّهُورِ: رَمَضَانُ.

وَيَخْتَارُ الْاِبْتِدَاءَ بِهِ يَوْمَ الْجُمُعَةِ وَيَخْتِمُهُ لَيْلَةَ الْخَمِيسِ. وَالْأَفْضَلُ اَلْخَتْمُ أَوَّلَ النَّهَارِ فِي الصَّيْفِ وَأَوَّلَ اللَّيْلِ فِي الشِّتَاءِ. وَيَكُونُ بِرَكْعَتَيِ الْفَجْرِ وَسُنَّتِهِ

at the beginning of the day during summer and at the beginning of the night during winter. It should be done with the two *rakʿas* of dawn (*fajr*) and those of the sunset *sunna* prayer (*maghrib*). It is *Sunna* to fast on the day of the *khatm*, and for one's family and friends to be present because mercy descends upon [its completion]. One should pronounce the *takbīr* from [*Sūrat*] *al-Ḍuḥā*[173] until the end of the Qurʾān.

Upon the completion of each *sūra*, one should say, *There is no god but God; God is most Great*—in the same way that the *takbīr* is recited at the end of Ramaḍān—and one should supplicate, because with every *takbīr*, supplications are accepted.

When the Prophet ﷺ was completing a *khatm* [of the Qurʾān], and recited [the *sūra*,] '*Say, "I seek refuge in the Lord of mankind,"*'[174] he would begin [reciting once more from *Sūrat*] *al-Ḥamd* [the *Fātiḥa*], then he would recite from [the beginning of *Sūrat*] *al-Baqara* until, '*it is those who are the successful.*'[175] Then he ﷺ would supplicate with the *khatma* supplication, which is this: *Praise be to God, Lord of the worlds. Praise be to God Who created the heavens and the earth, and made the darkness and the light. Then those who disbelieve equate [others] with their Lord. There is no god but God. And those who equate [others] with God have lied and gone far astray. There is no god but God. Those who associate [others] with God amongst the Arabs, the Magians, the Jews, the Christians, the Sabians, those who claim that God has a son, wife, rival or someone similar to Him, like Him, or equal to Him—they have lied. For You are our Lord, far be it that You would take a partner in what You have created. Praise be to God Who has not taken a wife or a son. He has no partner in sovereignty and He has no helper from the mundane, so magnify Him greatly. God is utterly the Greatest. Abundant praise be to God. Glory be to God, morning and evening.*[L]

الْمَغْرِبِ. وَيُسَنُّ صَوْمُ يَوْمِ الْخَتْمِ وَأَنْ يَحْضُرَ أَهْلَهُ وَأَصْدِقَاءَهُ لِأَنَّ الرَّحْمَةَ تَنْزِلُ عِنْدَهُ. وَالتَّكْبِيرُ مِنَ الضُّحَى إِلَى آخِرِ الْقُرْآنِ.

فَيَقُولُ عِنْدَ خَتْمِ كُلِّ سُورَةٍ: لَا إِلٰهَ إِلَّا اللّٰهُ وَاللّٰهُ أَكْبَرُ، تَشْبِيهاً لَهُ بِصَوْمِ رَمَضَانَ إِذَا أَكْمَلَ عِدَّتَهُ يُكَبِّرُ، وَالدُّعَاءُ فَمَعَ كُلِّ تَكْبِيرَةٍ دَعْوَةٌ مُسْتَجَابَةٌ.

وَكَانَ النَّبِيُّ ﷺ إِذَا خَتَمَ فَقَرَأَ: ﴿قُلْ أَعُوذُ بِرَبِّ النَّاسِ﴾، اِفْتَتَحَ مِنَ الْحَمْدِ ثُمَّ قَرَأَ مِنَ الْبَقَرَةِ إِلَى: ﴿أُوْلٰئِكَ هُمُ الْمُفْلِحُونَ﴾. ثُمَّ دَعَا بِدُعَاءِ الْخَتْمَةِ وَهُوَ هٰذَا: اَلْحَمْدُ لِلّٰهِ رَبِّ الْعَالَمِينَ. اَلْحَمْدُ لِلّٰهِ الَّذِي خَلَقَ السَّمَاوَاتِ وَالْأَرْضَ وَجَعَلَ الظُّلُمَاتِ وَالنُّورَ. ثُمَّ الَّذِينَ كَفَرُوا بِرَبِّهِمْ يَعْدِلُونَ. لَا إِلٰهَ إِلَّا اللّٰهُ. وَكَذَبَ الْعَادِلُونَ بِاللّٰهِ فَضَلُّوا ضَلَالاً بَعِيداً. لَا إِلٰهَ إِلَّا اللّٰهُ. وَكَذَبَ الْمُشْرِكُونَ بِاللّٰهِ مِنَ الْعَرَبِ وَالْمَجُوسِ وَالْيَهُودِ وَالنَّصَارَى وَالصَّابِئِينَ وَمَنِ ادَّعَى لِلّٰهِ وَلَداً أَوْ صَاحِبَةً أَوَ نِدّاً أَوْ شَبِيهاً أَوْ مَثَلاً أَوْ عَدْلاً. فَأَنْتَ رَبُّنَا أَعْظَمُ مِنْ اَنْ تَتَّخِذَ شَرِيكاً فِيمَا خَلَقْتَ. وَالْحَمْدُ لِلّٰهِ الَّذِي لَمْ يَتَّخِذْ صَاحِبَةً وَلَا وَلَداً وَلَمْ يَكُنْ لَهُ شَرِيكٌ فِي الْمُلْكِ وَلَمْ يَكُنْ لَهُ وَلِيٌّ مِنَ الذُّلِّ وَكَبِّرْهُ تَكْبِيراً. اَللّٰهُ اَكْبَرُ كَبِيْراً وَالْحَمْدُ لِلّٰهِ كَثِيراً وَسُبْحَانَ اللّٰهِ بُكْرَةً وَأَصِيلاً.

[Recite,] '*Praise be to God Who has sent down upon His servant the Book [...]*' until His Words, '*They speak naught but lies.*'[176] *Praise be to God, His is what is in the heavens and the earth. Praise be to Him in the Hereafter.* [Recite] the two verses: '*Praise be to God and peace be upon His servants Whom He has chosen. Is God better or what they associate [with Him]?*'[177] *Say: God is better, more enduring, wiser, more generous and greater than what they associate [with Him]; praise be to God. But most of them do not use their intelligence. God spoke the truth. Your messengers have conveyed [Your messages] and I am amongst the witnesses to that. O God, bless the angels and the messengers. Have mercy upon Your believing servants from amongst the people of the heavens and earth. And conclude [this recitation] for us with goodness and begin [a new recitation] for us with goodness. Bless the Almighty Qur'ān for us. Benefit us through [its] verses and the Wise Remembrance (Dhikr Ḥakīm). Our Lord, accept [it] from us; truly You are the All-Hearing, the All-Knowing.* This is the end of the *khatma* supplication narrated by Bayhaqī in *The Branches of Faith.*[178]

Another transmitted supplication [recited upon completing the Qur'ān]: *O God, keep me company in the loneliness of my grave. O God, show mercy to me through the Qur'ān and make it an imam, a light, a [source of] guidance and a mercy for me. O God, remind me of what I have forgotten from it and teach me what I do not know of it. Provide me with time during the night and at the ends of the day for reciting it, and make it a proof for me, O Lord of the worlds.*

﴿اَلْحَمْدُ لِلّٰهِ الَّذِي أَنْزَلَ عَلَى عَبْدِهِ الْكِتَابَ﴾ إِلَى قَوْلِهِ: ﴿إِنْ يَقُولُونَ إِلَّا كَذِباً﴾. اَلْحَمْدُ لِلّٰهِ الَّذِي لَهُ مَا فِي السَّمَاوَاتِ وَالْأَرْضِ. وَلَهُ الْحَمْدُ فِي الْآخِرَةِ. اَلْآيَتَيْنِ: ﴿اَلْحَمْدُ لِلّٰهِ وَسَلَامٌ عَلَى عِبَادِهِ الَّذِيْنَ اصْطَفَى آللّٰهُ خَيْرٌ أَمَّا يُشْرِكُونَ﴾. قُلْ: اَللّٰهُ خَيْرٌ وَأَبْقَى وَأَحْكَمُ وَأَكْرَمُ وَأَعْظَمُ مِمَّا يُشْرِكُونَ وَالْحَمْدُ لِلّٰهِ. بَلْ أَكْثَرُهُمْ لَا يَعْقِلُونَ. صَدَقَ اللّٰهُ، وَبَلَّغَتْ رُسُلُكَ، وَأَنَا عَلَى ذٰلِكَ مِنَ الشَّاهِدِينَ. اَللّٰهُمَّ صَلِّ عَلَى الْمَلَائِكَةِ وَالْمُرْسَلِينَ، وَارْحَمْ عِبَادَكَ الْمُؤْمِنِينَ مِنْ أَهْلِ السَّمَاوَاتِ وَالْأَرْضِ. وَاخْتِمْ لَنَا بِخَيْرٍ وَافْتَحْ لَنَا بِخَيْرٍ. وَبَارِكْ لَنَا فِي الْقُرْآنِ الْعَظِيمِ. وَانْفَعْنَا بِالْآيَاتِ وَالذِّكْرِ الْحَكِيمِ. رَبَّنَا تَقَبَّلْ مِنَّا إِنَّكَ أَنْتَ السَّمِيعُ الْعَلِيمُ. هٰذَا آخِرُ دُعَاءِ الْخَتْمَةِ رَوَاهُ الْبَيْهَقِيُّ فِي شُعَبِ الْإِيمَانِ.

وَمِنَ الْأَدْعِيَةِ الْمَأْثُورَةِ فِيهِ: اَللّٰهُمَّ آنِسْ وَحْشَتِي فِي قَبْرِي. اَللّٰهُمَّ ارْحَمْنِي بِالْقُرْآنِ وَاجْعَلْهُ لِي إِمَاماً وَنُوراً وَهُدًى وَرَحْمَةً. اَللّٰهُمَّ ذَكِّرْنِي مِنْهُ مَا نَسِيتُ وَعَلِّمْنِي مِنْهُ مَا جَهِلْتُ. وَارْزُقْنِي تِلَاوَتَهُ آنَاءَ اللَّيْلِ وَأَطْرَافَ النَّهَارِ وَاجْعَلْهُ لِي حُجَّةً يَا رَبَّ الْعَالَمِينَ.

DAILY PRACTICES FOR FASTING

Upon seeing the new moon, one should say three times: *O God, may this crescent moon rise over us with good fortune, safety, peace, Islam, success in what our Lord loves and [with which] He is pleased, contentment from the Most Compassionate and protection from Satan. God is my Lord and Your Lord, O crescent moon of goodness and rectitude.* One should say three times, *I believe in He who created you.*

Praise be to God Who caused the month of such-and-such to pass and Who caused the month of such-and-such to begin. God is most Great. God is most Great. Praise be to God Who created you and created everything. God is our Lord and your Lord; we do not worship [anything] save God. We do not associate any partner with Him at all. O God, bless us in Rajab and Shaʿbān, and make us reach Ramaḍān. During the month of Ramaḍān, one should add, *O God, make it good for us and make us good for it in ease and well-being, and accept it from us.*

Upon breaking the fast, you should say: *O God, for You I have fasted and I have broken my fast with Your provision. I have placed my trust in You, so accept [this] from me; truly You are the All-Hearing, the All-Knowing. The thirst has gone, the veins have been moistened and the reward has been secured—if God wills. Praise be to God, Who aided me so I could fast, and Who provided for me so I could break my fast. O God, truly I ask You, by Your mercy that encompasses everything, to forgive me my sin.*[M]

It is *Sunna* to break one's fast before praying the sunset prayer (*maghrib*), even if it be with a sip of water.[179] One should break one's fast with moist dates, but if they cannot be found, then with [regular] dates [or, failing that,] with water. One should eat the pre-dawn meal (*saḥūr*) and use a little perfume.

وَظَائِفُ الصَّوْمِ

إِذَا رَأَى الْهِلَالَ قَالَ: اللّٰهُمَّ أَهِلَّهُ عَلَيْنَا بِالْيُمْنِ وَالْأَمَانِ وَالسَّلَامَةِ وَالْإِسْلَامِ وَالتَّوْفِيقِ لِمَا يُحِبُّ رَبُّنَا وَيَرْضَى وَرِضْوَانٍ مِنَ الرَّحْمٰنِ وَجِوَارٍ مِنَ الشَّيْطَانِ. رَبِّي وَرَبُّكَ اللهُ، هِلَالُ خَيْرٍ وَرُشْدٍ (ثَلَاثاً). آمَنْتُ بِالَّذِي خَلَقَكَ (ثَلَاثاً).

اَلْحَمْدُ لِلّٰهِ الَّذِي ذَهَبَ بِشَهْرِ كَذَا وَجَاءَ بِشَهْرِ كَذَا. اَللهُ أَكْبَرُ اللهُ أَكْبَرُ. اَلْحَمْدُ لِلّٰهِ الَّذِي خَلَقَكَ وَخَلَقَ كُلَّ شَيْءٍ. رَبُّنَا وَرَبُّكَ اللهُ، لَا نَعْبُدُ إِلَّا اللهَ. وَلَا نُشْرِكُ بِهِ شَيْئاً. اَللّٰهُمَّ بَارِكْ لَنَا فِي رَجَبَ وَشَعْبَانَ وَبَلِّغْنَا رَمَضَانَ. وَيَزِيدُ فِي شَهْرِ رَمَضَانَ: اَللّٰهُمَّ سَلِّمْهُ لَنَا وَسَلِّمْنَا لَهُ فِي يُسْرٍ وَعَافِيَةٍ وَتَقَبَّلْهُ مِنَّا.

وَتَقُولُ عِنْدَ فِطْرِكَ: اَللّٰهُمَّ لَكَ صُمْتُ وَعَلَى رِزْقِكَ أَفْطَرْتُ. وَعَلَيْكَ تَوَكَّلْتُ فَتَقَبَّلْ مِنِّي إِنَّكَ أَنْتَ السَّمِيعُ الْعَلِيمُ. ذَهَبَ الظَّمَأُ وَابْتَلَّتِ الْعُرُوقُ وَثَبَتَ الْأَجْرُ إِنْ شَاءَ اللهُ. وَالْحَمْدُ لِلّٰهِ الَّذِي أَعَانَنِي فَصُمْتُ، وَرَزَقَنِي فَأَفْطَرْتُ. اَللّٰهُمَّ إِنِّي أَسْأَلُكَ بِرَحْمَتِكَ الَّتِي وَسِعَتْ كُلَّ شَيْءٍ أَنْ تَغْفِرَ لِي ذَنْبِي.

وَالسُّنَّةُ أَنْ يُفْطِرَ قَبْلَ أَنْ يُصَلِّيَ الْمَغْرِبَ وَلَوْ عَلَى شَرْبَةِ مَاءٍ وَأَنْ يُفْطِرَ عَلَى رُطَبَاتٍ فَإِنْ لَمْ يَجِدْ فَتَمْراً فَالْمَاءُ وَأَنْ يَتَسَحَّرَ وَيَمَسَّ شَيْئاً مِنَ الطِّيبِ.

The specific traits of fasting are protecting the tongue, the hearing and the sight [from sins]. And whoever does not desist from speaking falsehood or acting upon it, God has no need for them to abstain from their food and drink.

The Messenger of God ﷺ never exceeded eleven *rakʿas*, whether during Ramaḍān [when praying the *tarāwīḥ* prayer] or otherwise. The *Sunna* of *tarāwīḥ* was inaugurated during the era of ʿUmar [b. al-Khaṭṭāb] (may God be pleased with him), and it consists of twenty *rakʿas* for anyone other than the people of Medina, and for the people of Medina it is thirty-six *rakʿas*. And they pray *witr* with three [*rakʿas*], reciting ten verses in each *rakʿa*.

Maintaining a period of spiritual retreat in the mosque (*iʿtikāf*) is *Sunna* during Ramaḍān, and is an emphasised *Sunna* (*Sunna muʾakkada*) during the last ten days [of that month]. If one's *iʿtikāf* coincides with the Night of Power (*Laylat al-Qadr*) one should say abundantly, *O God, truly You are Pardoning, Generous. You love to pardon, so pardon [us].*

The best days for fasting are Mondays, Thursdays and the day of *Jumʿa* [when combined] with [Thursday] (not in isolation[180]), the Day of ʿArafa, ʿĀshūrāʾ and Tāsūʿāʾ.[181] The 'white days',[182] which are the thirteenth, fourteenth and fifteenth [of the lunar month].[183] The 'black days',[184] which are the last three days of the [lunar] month. [Also,] Thursdays, the days of *Jumʿa* and Saturdays of each sacred month,[185] and six days in Shawwāl. Amongst the ten-day periods: the first [ten days] of Dhū'l-Ḥijja and Muḥarram amongst the sacred months. [And the whole of] Rajab and Shaʿbān.

وَخَاصِّيَّةُ الصَّوْمِ حِفْظُ اللِّسَانِ وَالسَّمْعِ وَالْبَصَرِ. وَمَنْ لَمْ يَدَعْ قَوْلَ الزُّورِ وَالْعَمَلَ بِهِ فَلَيْسَ لِلّٰهِ حَاجَةٌ فِي أَنْ يَدَعَ طَعَامَهُ وَشَرَابَهُ.

وَكَانَ ﷺ لَا يَزِيدُ فِي رَمَضَانَ وَلَا غَيْرِهِ عَلَى إِحْدَى عَشَرَةَ رَكْعَةً. وَسُنَّةُ التَّرَاوِيحِ مِنْ عَهْدِ عُمَرَ (رَضِيَ اللهُ تَعَالَى عَنْهُ) وَهِيَ عِشْرُونَ رَكْعَةً لِغَيْرِ أَهْلِ الْمَدِينَةِ، وَلِأَهْلِ الْمَدِينَةِ سِتٌّ وَثَلَاثُونَ رَكْعَةً. وَيُوتِرُونَ بِثَلَاثَةٍ وَيَقْرَأُ فِي كُلِّ رَكْعَةٍ عَشْرَ آيَاتٍ.

وَيُسَنُّ الْاِعْتِكَافُ فِي رَمَضَانَ وَيُتَأَكَّدُ فِي الْعَشْرِ الْأَخِيرِ. وَإِذَا صَادَفَ لَيْلَةَ الْقَدْرِ فَلْيُكْثِرْ مِنْ قَوْلِ: اَللّٰهُمَّ إِنَّكَ عَفُوٌّ كَرِيمٌ تُحِبُّ الْعَفْوَ فَاعْفُ عَنَّا.

وَالْأَيَّامُ الْفَاضِلَةُ لِلصَّوْمِ: يَوْمُ الْاِثْنَيْنِ وَالْخَمِيسِ وَالْجُمُعَةُ مَعَهُ، لَا مُنْفَرِداً، وَعَرَفَةُ وَعَاشُورَاءَ وَتَاسُوعَاءَ. وَالْأَيَّامُ الْبِيضُ وَهِيَ الثَّالِثُ عَشَرَ وَتَالِيَاهُ وَالسُّودُ وَهِيَ ثَلَاثُ آخِرِ الشَّهْرِ. وَالْخَمِيسُ وَالْجُمُعَةُ وَالسَّبْتُ مِنْ كُلِّ شَهْرٍ حَرَامٍ وَسِتٌّ مِنْ شَوَّالٍ. وَمِنَ الْأَعْشَارِ: الْأَوَّلُ مِنْ ذِي الْحِجَّةِ وَمِنَ الْمُحَرَّمِ مِنَ الشُّهُورِ الْحُرُمِ. وَرَجَبَ وَشَعْبَانَ.

[It is said] in a *ḥadīth*, 'Whoever fasts Ramaḍān and Shawwāl, and on Wednesdays and Thursdays, shall enter Paradise.'

The Messenger of God ﷺ said, 'Fast on the Day of ʿĀshūrāʾ and act contrary to the Jews [by also] fasting one day before it, or one day after it.'

He ﷺ said, 'Whoever is generous towards their dependents and family on the Day of ʿĀshūrāʾ, God shall be generous towards them for the rest of the year.'

He said ﷺ: 'Whoever applies an eye cosmetic (*kuḥl*) made from lead ore on the Day of ʿĀshūrāʾ will not suffer from inflammation of the eye.'

If someone quarrels or insults one while one is fasting, [then one should] say, *I seek refuge in God from you. Truly, I am fasting*. If one is performing an obligatory (*farḍ*) fast, one should say this [out loud] with one's tongue, or [inaudibly] in one's heart if the fast is supererogatory (*nafl*).[186]

Holding a *Mawlid* celebration out of joy and happiness for the birth of the Prophet ﷺ during the month of Rabīʿ al-Awwal every year is good and praiseworthy.[187]

وَفِي الْحَدِيْثِ: «مَنْ صَامَ رَمَضَانَ وَشَوَّالاً وَالْأَرْبِعَاءَ وَالْخَمِيسَ دَخَلَ الْجَنَّةَ.»

وَقَالَ ﷺ: «صُومُوا يَوْمَ عَاشُورَاءَ وَخَالِفُوا الْيَهُودَ وَصُومُوا قَبْلَهُ يَوْماً وَبَعْدَهُ يَوْماً.»

وَقَالَ ﷺ: «مَنْ وَسَّعَ عَلَى عِيَالِهِ وَأَهْلِهِ يَوْمَ عَاشُورَاءَ وَسَّعَ اللهُ عَلَيْهِ سَائِرَ سَنَتِهِ.»

وَقَالَ ﷺ: «مَنِ اكْتَحَلَ بِالْإِثْمِدِ يَوْمَ عَاشُورَاءَ لَمْ يَرْمَدْ.»

وَإِذَا قَاتَلَهُ أَحَدٌ أَوْ شَاتَمَهُ وَهُوَ صَائِمٌ، قَالَ: أَعُوذُ بِاللهِ مِنْكَ إِنِّي صَائِمٌ. فَإِنْ كَانَ فِي صَوْمِ فَرْضٍ قَالَهُ بِلِسَانِهِ، أَوْ نَفْلٍ بِقَلْبِهِ.

وَعَمَلُ الْمَوْلِدِ كُلَّ سَنَةٍ فِي شَهْرِ رَبِيعِ الْأَوَّلِ اِسْتِبْشَاراً وَسُرُوراً بِمَوْلِدِ النَّبِيِّ ﷺ حَسَنٌ مَحْمُودٌ.

DAILY PRACTICES FOR EATING AND DRINKING

When one is served food one should say, *O God, bless us in what You have provided for us and save us from the punishment of Hellfire.*[N]

When you begin eating, [do so] in the name of God. If one forgets, one should say, *In the name of God at the beginning and the end of it*. If one does not remember [to do this] until [after] one has finished [the meal], one should recite *Sūrat al-Ikhlāṣ*.[188]

When one finishes [the meal] one should say: *Abundant, pure and blessed praise be to God. [He] cannot be recompensed, never holds back, cannot be disregarded and ever needed; [He is] our Lord. Praise be to God Who has fed us, given us drink and has made us Muslims. Praise be to God Who has fed us, given us drink, has allowed it to go down easily and has made an exit for it. Praise be to God Who has fed me this and has provided it to me with no power from me and no might. Praise be to God Who has fed me, satiated me, given me drink and has quenched [my thirst]. O God, You have fed us, You have given us drink, You have given us wealth, You have given us property and You have given us life, so praise be to You for what You have given us. Praise be to God Who feeds and is not fed. He has bestowed un-repayable favours upon us and has showered us with [His] bounty. I ask You, by Your mercy, to save me from Hellfire. Praise be to God Who has fed us with food and given us drink, Who has clothed us from nakedness, guided us from misguidance, caused us to see after blindness and has greatly favoured [us] over many of those He has created.*

وَظَائِفُ الأَكْلِ وَالشُّرْبِ

إِذَا قُرِّبَ إِلَيْهِ الأَكْلُ قَالَ: اَللّٰهُمَّ بَارِكْ لَنَا فِيمَا رَزَقْتَنَا وَقِنَا عَذَابَ النَّارِ.

فَإِذَا شَرَعَ فِي الأَكْلِ يُسَمِّي. فَإِذَا نَسِيَ، قَالَ: بِسْمِ اللهِ أَوَّلَهُ وَآخِرَهُ. فَإِنْ لَمْ يَتَذَكَّرْ حَتَّى فَرَغَ، قَرَأَ سُورَةَ الإِخْلَاصِ.

فَإِذَا فَرَغَ، قَالَ: اَلْحَمْدُ لِلّٰهِ حَمْداً كَثِيْراً طَيِّباً مُبَارَكاً فِيهِ غَيْرَ مَكْفِيٍّ وَلَا مَكْفُوْرٍ وَلَا مُوَدَّعٍ وَلَا مُسْتَغْنىً عَنْهُ رَبَّنَا. اَلْحَمْدُ لِلّٰهِ الَّذِي أَطْعَمَنَا وَأَسْقَانَا وَجَعَلَنَا مِنَ الْمُسْلِمِينَ. اَلْحَمْدُ لِلّٰهِ الَّذِي أَطْعَمَ وَسَقَى وَسَوَّغَ وَجَعَلَ لَهُ مَخْرَجاً. اَلْحَمْدُ لِلّٰهِ الَّذِي أَطْعَمَنِي هٰذا وَرَزَقَنِيهِ مِنْ غَيْرِ حَوْلٍ مِنِّي وَلَا قُوَّةٍ. اَلْحَمْدُ لِلّٰهِ الَّذِي أَطْعَمَنِي وَأَشْبَعَنِي وَسَقَانِي وَأَرْوَانِي. اَللّٰهُمَّ أَطْعَمْتَ وَسَقَيْتَ وَأَغْنَيْتَ وَأَقْنَيْتَ وَأَحْيَيْتَ فَلَكَ الْحَمْدُ عَلَى مَا أَعْطَيْتَ. اَلْحَمْدُ لِلّٰهِ الَّذِي يُطْعِمُ وَلَا يُطْعَمُ. مَنَّ عَلَيْنَا وَأَفْضَلَ. أَسْأَلُكَ بِرَحْمَتِكَ أَنْ تُجِيرَنَا مِنَ النَّارِ. اَلْحَمْدُ لِلّٰهِ الَّذِي أَطْعَمَ مِنَ الطَّعَامِ وَسَقَى مِنَ الشَّرَابِ وَكَسَى مِنَ الْعُرْيِ وَهَدَى مِنَ الضَّلَالَةِ وَبَصَّرَ مِنَ الْعَمَايَةِ وَفَضَّلَ عَلَى كَثِيرٍ مِمَّنْ خَلَقَ تَفْضِيلاً.

When one sees the first fruit [of the season] one should say, *O God, bless our fruit for us. O God, just as You have granted us the beginning of it, grant us the end of it.*

When one drinks milk one should say, *O God, bless it for us and increase us from it.*

For all other food one should say, *O God, bless it for us and feed us [with what is] even better than it.*

When one drinks water one should say, *Praise be to God Who has given us drink with fresh sweet water through His mercy, and Who has not made it salty or bitter through our sins.*

It is *Sunna* to wash both hands before a meal, and [doing so] after it is emphasised (*muʾakkad*). One should not spend the night with the foul smell of meat on one's hands. One should remove one's shoes when eating, and eat with the right hand [using] three fingers. One should [take] what is closest to one (except for fruit) and eat from the outer part of the dish and its sides, not from its highest part or from its middle. One should not cut meat or bread with a knife. One should lick one's fingers before wiping them with a napkin, lick the bowl [using one's fingers] and pick up what has fallen from the eating mat. When a morsel falls, do not leave it; rather remove any harm [dirt] from it and eat it.

One should not eat while leaning on one's side, lying on one's front or while standing. Rather, one should eat while kneeling or sitting on one's thighs or heels, or by raising the right knee up [near one's stomach] and sitting on the left foot. One should not to eat on a table (*khiwān*),[189] but rather upon an eating mat (*sufra*). One should not find fault with the food, sniff it or eat it while it is piping hot. One should gather together the people of the house for eating; they should not eat separately.

وَإِذَا رَأَى أَوَّلَ الْفَاكِهَةِ قَالَ: اَللّٰهُمَّ بَارِكْ لَنَا فِي ثِمَارِنَا. اَللّٰهُمَّ كَمَا أَرَيْتَنَا أَوَّلَهُ فَأَرِنَا آخِرَهُ.

وَإِذَا شَرِبَ لَبَناً قَالَ: اَللّٰهُمَّ بَارِكْ لَنَا فِيهِ وَزِدْنَا مِنْهُ.

وَفِي سَائِرِ الطَّعَامِ يَقُولُ: اَللّٰهُمَّ بَارِكْ لَنَا فِيهِ وَأَطْعِمْنَا خَيْراً مِنْهُ.

وَإِذَا شَرِبَ الْمَاءَ قَالَ: اَلْحَمْدُ لِلّٰهِ الَّذِي سَقَانَا عَذْباً فُرَاتاً بِرَحْمَتِهِ وَلَمْ يَجْعَلْهُ مِلْحاً أُجَاجاً بِذُنُوبِنَا.

وَيُسَنُّ غَسْلُ الْيَدَيْنِ قَبْلَ الطَّعَامِ وَبَعْدَهُ مُؤَكَّد. وَلَا يَبِيتُ وَفِي يَدِهِ غَمَرٌ. وَيَنْزِعُ النَّعْلَيْنِ عِنْدَ الْأَكْلِ وَالْأَكْلُ بِالْيَمِينِ وَبِثَلَاثِ أَصَابِعَ. وَمِمَّا يَلِيهِ إِلَّا فِي الْفَوَاكِهَ وَمِنْ أَسْفَلِ الصَّفْحَةِ وَجَوَانِبِهَا، لَا مِنْ أَعْلَاهَا وَلَا وَسْطِهَا. وَأَنْ لَا يَقْطَعَ اللَّحْمَ وَلَا الْخُبْزَ بِالسِّكِّينِ. وَأَنْ يَلْعَقَ أَصَابِعَهُ قَبْلَ مَسْحِهَا بِالْمِنْدِيلِ وَيَلْعَقُ الْقَصْعَةَ وَيَتَتَبَّعُ مَا سَقَطَ مِنَ السُّفْرَةِ. وَإِذَا وَقَعَتْ مِنْهُ لُقْمَةٌ فَلَا يَتْرُكُهَا بَلْ يُمِيطُ مَا أَصَابَهَا مِنْ أَذًى وَيَأْكُلُهَا.

وَلَا يَأْكُلُ مُتَّكِئاً وَلَا مُنْبَسِطاً عَلَى وَجْهِهِ وَلَا قَائِماً. بَلْ يَأْكُلُ جَاثِياً عَلَى رُكْبَتَيْهِ أَوْ مُقْعِياً أَوْ عَلَى قَدَمَيْهِ أَوْ يُقِيمُ رُكْبَتَهُ الْيُمْنَى وَيَقْعُدُ عَلَى الْيُسْرَى. وَلَا يَأْكُلُ عَلَى خِوَانٍ بَلْ عَلَى سُفْرَةٍ. وَلَا يُعِيبُ الطَّعَامَ وَلَا يَشُمُّهُ وَلَا يَأْكُلُهُ حَارّاً. وَيَجْمَعُ أَهْلَ الْبَيْتِ عَلَى الْأَكْلِ وَلَا يَأْكُلُوا مُتَفَرِّقِينَ.

If food comes to one from someone with whom one does not feel safe eating, then one should not eat until they have begun to eat from it. This is what the Prophet ﷺ did due to the poisoned sheep that was given to him at Khaybar. He ﷺ did not eat [finely ground] bread or grilled meat until he met God, and he did not reject sweets or milk.

It is *Sunna* to prop up a waterskin, to cover the vessels of food and cooking pots, to close the doors at night and to mention the name of God three times during all of that. If a fly should fall into any food or drink, one should fully submerge it and then remove it. When potash is brought, one takes it with the right hand. It is *Sunna* to use a toothpick to remove food that sticks [to the teeth], and to not clean [the teeth] with potash.[190]

وَإِذَا أَتَاهُ مَنْ لَمْ يَأْمَنْهُ بِأَكْلٍ، لَمْ يَأْكُلْ حَتَّى يَبْدَأَهُ بِأَنْ يَأْكُلَ مِنْهُ. هٰكَذَا كَانَ النَّبِيُّ ﷺ مِنْ أَجْلِ الشَّاةِ الَّتِي أُهْدِيَتْ لَهُ بِخَيْبَرَ وَهِيَ مَسْمُومَةٌ. وَلَمْ يَأْكُلْ ﷺ خُبْزاً وَلَا شَيْئاً سَمِيطاً حَتَّى لَحِقَ اللّٰهَ وَلَا يَرُدُّ الْحَلْوَى وَلَا اللَّبَنَ.

وَيُسَنُّ إِيْكَاءُ السِّقَاءِ وَتَغْطِيَةُ الْآنِيَةِ وَغَلْقُ الْأَبْوَابِ بِاللَّيْلِ وَيَذْكُرُ اِسْمَ اللّٰهِ فِي كُلٍّ مِنَ الثَّلَاثِ. وَإِذَا وَقَعَ الذُّبَابُ فِي الطَّعَامِ وَالشَّرَابِ يُغْمِسُهُ كُلَّهُ ثُمَّ يُنْزِعُهُ. وَإِذَا أَتَى بِالْأُشْنَانِ تُنَاوِلُهُ مِنْهُ بِالْيَمِينِ. وَيُسَنُّ التَّخَلُّلُ مِنَ الطَّعَامِ بِمَا لَانَ، وَلَا يَتَخَلَّلُ بِالْأُشْنَانِ.

DAILY PRACTICES FOR CLOTHING AND ADORNMENT

When putting on clothes one should say, *O God, truly I ask You for the good of it and for the good of that for which [it has been made] and I seek refuge in You from its evil and from the evil of that for which [it has been made]. Praise be to God Who has clothed me with this and Who has provided it to me with neither power from me, nor might.*[○]

When putting on new clothes one should say: *O God, praise be to You. You are the One Who has clothed me with it. I ask You for the good of it and for the good of that for which it has been made and I seek refuge in You from its evil and from the evil of that for which it has been made. Praise be to God Who has clothed me with what hides my nakedness and with which I adorn myself in my life. Praise be to God Who has provided me with attire with which I adorn myself amongst the people.*

The Messenger of God ﷺ commanded us to wear the best of what we could find, to perfume ourselves with the best of what we could find and to wear white, because it is the cleanest and purest [of colours], and [because] it was his a favourite colour after green.[191]

He ﷺ had two garments that he would wear on the day of *Jumʿa* and if they became worn out, he would incline towards something similar to them. He prohibited [the wearing of] any garment conspicuous in its beauty or vileness, and he prohibited making the shirt, loincloth or turban excessively long. He ﷺ said, 'The believer's loincloth (*izār*) should [come as far as] the middle of his shin, and there is no harm in what is between his shin and his ankles, but what [comes] below that is in Hellfire.'

وَظَائِفُ اللِّبَاسِ وَالزِّينَةِ

إِذَا لَبِسَ ثَوْبَهُ قَالَ: اَللّٰهُمَّ إِنِّي أَسْأَلُكَ مِنْ خَيْرِهِ وَخَيْرِ مَا هُوَ لَهُ. وَأَعُوذُ بِكَ مِنْ شَرِّهِ وَشَرِّ مَا هُوَ لَهُ. اَلْحَمْدُ لِلّٰهِ الَّذِي كَسَانِي هٰذا وَرَزَقَنِيهِ مِنْ غَيْرِ حَوْلٍ مِنِّي وَلَا قُوَّةٍ.

وَإِذَا لَبِسَ جَدِيداً قَالَ: اَللّٰهُمَّ لَكَ الْحَمْدُ. أَنْتَ كَسَوْتَنِيهِ. أَسْأَلُكَ خَيْرَهُ وَخَيْرَ مَا صُنِعَ لَهُ وَأَعُوذُ بِكَ مِنْ شَرِّهِ وَشَرِّ مَا صُنِعَ لَهُ. اَلْحَمْدُ لِلّٰهِ الَّذِي كَسَانِي مَا أُوَارِي بِهِ عَوْرَتِي وَأَتَجَمَّلُ بِهِ فِي حَيَاتِي. اَلْحَمْدُ لِلّٰهِ الَّذِي رَزَقَنِي مِنَ الرِّيَاشِ مَا أَتَجَمَّلُ بِهِ بَيْنَ النَّاسِ.

وَقَدْ أَمَرَنَا رَسُولُ اللهِ ﷺ أَنْ نَلْبَسَ أَجْوَدَ مَا يُوجَدُ وَنَتَطَيَّبَ بِأَجْوَدِ مَا نَجِدُ وَأَنْ نَلْبَسَ الْبَيَاضَ، فَإِنَّهُ أَنْظَفُ وَأَطْيَبُ وَكَانَ أَحَبُّ الْأَلْوَانِ إِلَيْهِ بَعْدَهُ اَلْخُضْرَةُ.

وَكَانَ لَهُ ثَوْبَانِ يَلْبَسُهُمَا فِي جُمُعَتِهِ فَإِذَا انْصَرَفَ طُوِيَا إِلَى مِثْلِهِ. وَيَنْهَى عَنْ ثَوْبِ شُهْرَةٍ فِي الْحُسْنِ وَالدَّنَاءَةِ، وَعَنِ الْإِسْبَالِ فِي الْقَمِيصِ وَالْإِزَارِ وَالْعِمَامَةِ. وَقَالَ: «أُزْرَةُ الْمُؤْمِنِ إِلَى أَنْصَافِ سَاقَيْهِ وَلَا جُنَاحَ عَلَيْهِ فِيمَا بَيْنَهُ وَبَيْنَ الْكَعْبَيْنِ، وَمَا كَانَ أَسْفَلَ مِنْ ذٰلِكَ فِي النَّارِ.»

He ﷺ would wear a [long] shirt made of cotton [that hung] above his ankles, and his sleeves [reached just before] his fingers and he would cut the excess. The Prophet ﷺ would not part from [his] *ṭaylasān*[192] and would say, 'This garment cannot be thanked enough.' The length of his *ṭaylasān* was six *dhirā*ʿs (cubits) and its width was three *dhirā*ʿs.

[Once,] the Prophet ﷺ saw a dishevelled man wearing dirty clothes and said, 'Can he not find something with which to wash his hair and his clothes?'

ʿĀʾisha (may God be pleased with her) said, 'I never saw the Messenger of God ﷺ dirty.'

He ﷺ used to say, 'God loathes the dishevelled and the dirty.'

The Prophet ﷺ liked the wearing of a shirt (*qamīṣ*), he would loosen his loincloth and he liked wearing a Yemenī shawl (*ḥibra*). He ﷺ would wear a white cap [under his turban] (*qalansuwa*), circle the turban around his head, tuck it in at the back, and let a section [of cloth] hang between his shoulders. It has been related, that the minimum length of this section was four fingers. It has also been related that the maximum was two *dhirā*ʿs, with a hand span between them.

The Prophet ﷺ said, 'When one of you puts on shoes one should start [putting them on] from the right [foot] and when one takes them off one should start from the left.' The imams extended this rule by analogy to the putting on and removing one's clothes, and to rolling up one's sleeves. The Prophet ﷺ prohibited individuals from taking off their shoes while standing and from walking with only one shoe on. One should not be unkempt, wear [only] one leather sock (*khuff*) or sit [on the floor] with one's shoes on; he ﷺ [also] commanded us to occasionally walk barefoot.[193]

وَكَانَ ﷺ يَلْبَسُ قَمِيصاً مِنْ قُطْنٍ فَوْقَ الْكَعْبَيْنِ وَكُمَّاهُ مَعَ الأَصَابِعِ وَيَقْطَعُ مَا فَضُلَ. وَكَانَ ﷺ لَا يُفَارِقُ الطَّيْلَسَانَ وَيَقُولُ: «هٰذا ثَوْبٌ لَا يُؤَدَّى شُكْرُهُ.» وَكَانَ طُولُ طَيْلَسَانِهِ سِتَّةُ أَذْرُعٍ وَعَرْضُهُ ثَلاثَةُ أَذْرُعٍ.

وَرَأَى ﷺ رَجُلاً شَعِثاً وَسِخَ الثِّيَابِ، فَقَالَ: «أَمَا كَانَ هٰذا يَجِدُ مَا يَغْسِلُ بِهِ رَأْسَهُ وَيَغْسِلُ بِهِ ثِيَابَهُ؟»

وَقَالَتْ عَائِشَةُ (رَضِيَ اللهُ عَنْهَا): «مَا رَأَيْتُ رَسُولَ اللهِ ﷺ وَسِخاً قَطُّ.»

وَكَانَ يَقُولُ: «اَللهُ يُبْغِضُ الشَّعِثَ الْوَسِخَ.»

وَكَانَ ﷺ يُحِبُّ لُبْسَ الْقَمِيصِ وَكَانَ يُطْلِقُ إِزَارَهُ وَيُحِبُّ لُبْسَ الْحِبَرَةِ. وَكَانَ ﷺ يَلْبَسُ قَلَنْسُوَةً بَيْضَاءَ وَكَانَ يُدِيرُ الْعِمَامَةَ عَلَى رَأْسِهِ وَيُكَوِّرُهَا مِنْ وَرَائِهِ وَيُرْسِلُ لَهَا ذُؤَابَةً بَيْنَ كَتِفَيْهِ. وَأَقَلُّ مَا وَرَدَ فِي قَدْرِ الْعَذْبَةِ أَرْبَعُ أَصَابِعَ وَأَكْثَرُ مَا وَرَدَ ذِرَاعٌ، وَبَيْنَهُمَا شِبْرٌ.

وَقَالَ ﷺ: «إِذَا انْتَعَلَ أَحَدُكُمْ فَلْيَبْدَأْ بِالْيَمِينِ وَإِذَا نَزَعَ فَلْيَبْدَأْ بِالشِّمَالِ.» وَقَاسَ الْأَئِمَّةُ عَلَى ذٰلِكَ الثَّوْبِ لُبْساً وَنَزْعاً وَتَشْمِيراً. وَنَهَى أَنْ يَنْتَعِلَ الرَّجُلُ قَائِماً وَأَنْ يَمْشِيَ فِي نَعْلٍ وَاحِدَةٍ إِذَا انْقَطَعَ شِعْثُهُ، أَوْ خُفٍّ وَاحِدٍ، وَأَنْ يَجْلِسَ وَنَعْلَاهُ فِي رِجْلَيْهِ. وَأَمَرَ أَنْ يَحْتَفِيَ أَحْيَاناً.

He ﷺ used to wear a ring of silver with a stone set therein. He would wear it on his smallest finger with the stone turned towards his palm. He ﷺ would wear a ring on his right hand and, [at other times,] on his left. He ﷺ prohibited wearing it on the middle finger or index finger, and prohibited the wearing of a ring made of gold, iron or copper.[194] He ﷺ said, 'Wear a ring of *ʿaqīq*,[195] for truly it is blessed.'

He ﷺ would lean on his left side, and upon a pillow made of animal skin stuffed with palm fibres.

The Prophet ﷺ prohibited shaving part of the hair and leaving the rest. He also prohibited the plucking of grey hairs and said they were the light of a Muslim and of Islam. For the believers, there is a reward, increase in status and light on the Day of Resurrection for each grey hair [that one has], as long as one does not dye it—meaning, [as long as one does not dye it] black—or pluck it.[196]

The Prophet ﷺ would make the width of his beard and its length balanced. Once, Abū Ayyūb (may God be pleased with him) trimmed some of his beard and the Prophet ﷺ said to him, 'May no harm come to you, O Abū Ayyūb.'

Ibn ʿUmar (may God be pleased with him) would grab his beard [with his hand] then trim what exceeded his fist, and he would trim the sides of his beard so they were balanced; and Abū Hurayra (may God be pleased with him) did likewise.[197]

The Prophet ﷺ would regularly rub his head with oil and comb his beard. He prohibited any one of us from combing our hair every day.

He ﷺ would never leave his mosque [to embark on a journey] without his *miswāk*, his comb, his eye cosmetic (*kuḥl*), his mirror or his scissors.

وَكَانَ ﷺ يَلْبَسُ خَاتِماً مِنْ فِضَّةٍ وَفَصُّهُ مِنْهُ. وَيلْبَسُهُ فِي خِنْصَرِهِ وَفَصُّهُ فِي بَاطِنِ كَفِّهِ. وَيَخْتَتِمُ فِي الْيُمْنَى وَفِي الْيَسَارِ. وَنَهَى عَنْهُ فِي الْوُسْطَى وَالْمُسَبَّحَةِ وَعَنْ خَاتَمِ الذَّهَبِ وَالْحَدِيْدِ الشِّبْهِ. وَقَالَ: «تَخَتَّمُوا بِالْعَقِيقِ فَإِنَّهُ مُبَارَكٌ.»

وَكَانَ يَتَّكِئُ عَلَى يَسَارِهِ وَعَلَى وِسَادَةٍ مِنْ أُدُمٍ حَشْوُهَا لِيفٌ.

وَنَهَى ﷺ عَنِ الْقَزَعِ وَنَتْفِ الشَّيْبِ. وَقَالَ هُوَ نُورُ الْمُسْلِمِ وَالْإِسْلَامِ وَلِلْمُؤْمِنِينَ بِكُلِّ شَيْبَةٍ حَسَنَةٌ وَرُفْعُ دَرَجَةٍ وَنُورٌ الْقِيَامَةَ مَا لَمْ يَخْضَبْهَا (يَعْنِي بِالسَّوَادِ) وَيَنْتِفْهَا.

كَانَ ﷺ يَأْخُذُ مِنْ عَرْضِ لِحْيَتِهِ وَطُوْلِهَا بِالسَّوِيَّةِ. وَأَخَذَ أَبُو أَيُّوبَ مِنْ لِحْيَتِهِ شَيْئاً، فَقَالَ ﷺ: «لَا يُصِبْكَ السَّوْءُ يَا أَبَا أَيُّوبَ.»

وَكَانَ اِبْنُ عُمَرَ يَقْبِضُ عَلَى لِحِيَتِهِ ثُمَّ يَأْخُذُ مَا زَادَ عَلَى الْقُبْضَةِ وَيَأْخُذُ مِنْ عَارِضَيْهِ وَيُسَوِّي أَطْرَافَ لِحْيَتِهِ، وَكَذٰلِكَ أَبُو هُرَيْرَةَ.

وَكَانَ ﷺ يُكْثِرُ دَهْنَ رَأْسِهِ وَتَسْرِيحَ لِحْيَتِهِ. وَنَهَى أَنْ يَمْتَشِطَ أَحَدُنَا كُلَّ يَوْمٍ.

وَكَانَ لَا يُفَارِقُ مَسْجِدَهُ سِوَاكُهُ وَمَشْطَهُ وَالْمُكْحَلَةَ وَالْمِرْآةَ وَالْمِدْرَاةَ.

He ﷺ would occasionally look in the mirror and ordered the same. When he looked into one, he ﷺ would say: *Praise be to God Who beautified my appearance and my character, and Who adorned in me what He made repulsive in others. Praise be to God Who made my appearance proportionate through His justice and Who fashioned the shape of my character and beautified it, and Who made me one of the Muslims.*

If his shoe strap broke, he ﷺ would retrieve it.

He ﷺ would apply an eye cosmetic (*kuḥl*) every night, three times to each of his eyes.

He ﷺ would not refuse perfume or scent. The most beloved of scents to him ﷺ was henna flower (*fāghiya*).

[Concerning] the natural sense of personal hygiene (*sunan al-fiṭra*), one should: trim the moustache, pare the nails, pluck the underarm hairs, shave the pubic region and wash the finger joints. The time for this is the day of *Jumʿa* before the prayer, or on Thursday; and there is severe reprehensibility in delaying it beyond forty days. The custom regarding the pubic region of a woman is to pluck, not to shave; Nawawī called attention to this in his *Revision* (Tahdhīb [al-asmāʾ wa'l-lughāt]).

The Prophet ﷺ used to enter the public bath with a light, and when he reached his pubic region, he would shine the light on himself. He ﷺ would cut his nails every fifteen days, and he would shine the light on himself every month.[198] It [was related] thus in a weakly authenticated *ḥadīth* in the *History* (Tārīkh) of Ibn ʿAsākir.

The Prophet ﷺ commanded that hair, nails and the blood from cupping should be buried.

He ﷺ forbade sitting upon the skins of predatory animals.[199]

وَكَانَ يَنْظُرُ فِي الْمِرْآةِ أَحْيَاناً وَيَأْمُرُ بِهِ. وَيَقُولُ إِذَا نَظَرَ فِيهَا: اَلْحَمْدُ لِلّٰهِ الَّذِي حَسَّنَ خَلْقِي وَخُلُقِي وَزَانَ مِنِّي مَا شَانَ مِنْ غَيْرِي. اَلْحَمْدُ لِلّٰهِ الَّذِي سَوَّى خَلْقِي بِعَدْلِهِ وَصَوَّرَ صُورَةَ خُلُقِي فَأَحْسَنَهَا وَجَعَلَنِي مِنَ الْمُسْلِمِينَ.

وَكَانَ ﷺ إِذَا انْقَطَعَ شِسْعُهُ اِسْتَرْجَعَ.

وَكَانَ يَتَكَحَّلُ فِي كُلِّ لَيْلَةٍ ثَلَاثاً فِي هٰذِهِ وَثَلَاثاً فِي هٰذِهِ.

وَكَانَ لَا يَرُدُّ الطِّيبَ وَالرَّيْحَانَ. وَكَانَ أَحَبُّ الرَّيَاحِينِ إِلَيْهِ اَلْفَاغِيَةُ.

وَسُنَنُ الْفِطْرَةِ: قَصُّ الشَّارِبِ وَقَلْمُ الْأَظَافِرِ وَنَتْفُ الْإِبِطِ وَحَلْقُ الْعَانَةِ وَغَسْلُ الْبَرَاجِمِ. وَوَقْتُ ذٰلِكَ: يَوْمَ الْجُمُعَةِ قَبْلَ الصَّلَاةِ أَوْ يَوْمَ الْخَمِيسِ وَيُكْرَهُ كَرَاهَةً شَدِيدَةً تَأْخِيرُهَا عَنْ أَرْبَعِينَ يَوْماً. وَالسُّنَّةُ فِي عَانَةِ الْمَرْأَةِ اَلنَّتْفُ، لَا الْحَلْقُ، نَبَّهَ عَلَيْهِ النَّوَوِيُّ فِي تَهْذِيبِهِ.

وَكَانَ ﷺ يَدْخُلُ الْحَمَّامَ وَيَتَنَوَّرُ فَإِذَا بَلَغَ الْعَانَةَ، نَوَّرَ نَفْسَهُ. وَكَانَ يَقْلِمُ أَظْفَارَهُ كُلَّ خَمْسَةَ عَشَرَ يَوْماً، وَيَتَنَوَّرُ كُلَّ شَهْرٍ. كَذَا فِي حَدِيثٍ ضَعِيفٍ فِي تَارِيخِ ابْنِ عَسَاكِرَ.

وَأَمَرَ أَنْ يُدْفَنَ الشَّعْرُ وَالْأَظْفَارُ وَدَمُ الْحِجَامَةِ.

وَنَهَى عَنِ الْجُلُوسِ عَلَى جُلُودِ السِّبَاعِ.

DAILY PRACTICES FOR SITTING AND STANDING

The Prophet ﷺ would squat on his heels, raising his knees; he would sit with his legs drawn up, clasping [them] with his hands or wrapping [them] in his cloak; and he would cross his hands over. This was the way he sat most of the time, but sometimes he sat cross-legged. He ﷺ forbade a person to sit with the legs drawn up [while dressed] in a single garment without wearing any undergarments, or to sit by leaning back with one's hands [supporting one] behind one's back.[200] He ﷺ [also] forbade sitting partly in the sun and partly in the shade because it is the sitting place of Satan; instead, he commanded sitting in the shade, because it is truly blessed.

He ﷺ said, 'The most honourable place to sit is that which faces the *qibla*.'

He ﷺ prohibited a person from standing by planting their right leg and standing up off of it; he said [that] this was a step that God (Exalted is He) loathes.[201]

It is *Sunna* that a person should never be in a place without remembering God (*dhikr*) or praying for the Prophet ﷺ in it, because one will certainly be responsible for that on the Day of Resurrection. When one stands from where one is sitting, one should say: *Glory be to You, O God, and praise be to You. I bear witness there is no god but You. I seek Your forgiveness, and I turn to You in repentance. Turn towards me and forgive me.*[P] [Saying this three times.] *Glory be to your Lord, the Lord of Honour, [He is] above what they ascribe [to Him]. May peace be upon the messengers. Praise be to God, Lord of the worlds.*

وَظَائِفُ الْجُلُوسِ وَالْقِيَامِ

كَانَ ﷺ يَجْلِسُ الْقُرْفُصَاءَ يَنْصُبُ رُكْبَتَيْهِ وَيَحْتَبِي بِيَدَيْهِ أَوْ بِشَمْلَتِهِ وَيُشَبِّكُ بِيَدَيْهِ. فَهٰذا أَكْثَرُ جُلُوسِهِ وَرُبَّمَا جَلَسَ مُتَرَبِّعاً. وَنَهَى أَنْ يَحْتَبِيَ الرَّجُلُ فِي ثَوْبٍ وَاحِدٍ لَيْسَ عَلَى فَرجِهِ مِنْهُ شَيْءٌ وَأَنْ يَقْعُدَ وَيَتَّكِئَ عَلَى أَلْيَتِهِ وَيَدُهُ خَلْفَ ظَهْرِهِ. وَأَنْ يَقْعُدَ فِي الشَّمْسِ وَبَعْضُهُ فِي الظِّلِّ وَبَعْضُهُ فِي الشَّمْسِ فَإِنَّهُ مَقْعَدُ الشَّيْطَانِ، وَأَمَرَ بِالْقُعُودِ فِي الظِّلِّ فَإِنَّهُ مُبَارَكٌ.

وَقَالَ: «أَكْرَمُ الْمَجَالِسِ مَا اسْتَقْبَلَ بِهِ الْقِبْلَةَ.»

وَنَهَى الرَّجُلَ إِذَا قَامَ أَنْ يَمُدَّ رِجْلَهُ الْيُمْنَى وَيُثَبِّتَ، وَقَالَ هٰذِهِ خُطْوَةٌ يُبْغِضُهَا اللّٰهُ تَعَالَى.

وَالسُّنَّةُ أَنْ لَا يُخَلِّيَ الْإِنْسَانُ مَجْلِساً جَلَسَهُ عَنْ ذِكْرِ اللّٰهِ وَالصَّلَاةِ عَلَى النَّبِيِّ ﷺ فَإِنَّهُ يَكُونُ عَلَيْهِ تَبِعَةً يَوْمَ الْقِيَامَةِ. وَإِذَا قَامَ مِنْ مَجْلِسِهِ قَالَ: سُبْحَانَكَ اللّٰهُمَّ وَبِحَمْدِكَ أَشْهَدُ أَنْ لَا إِلٰهَ إِلَّا أَنْتَ. أَسْتَغْفِرُكَ وَأَتُوبُ إِلَيْكَ. تُبْ عَلَيَّ وَاغْفِرْ لِي (ثَلَاثاً). سُبْحَانَ رَبِّكَ، رَبِّ الْعِزَّةِ عَمَّا يَصِفُونَ. وَسَلَامٌ عَلَى الْمُرْسَلِينَ. وَالْحَمْدُ لِلّٰهِ رَبِّ الْعَالَمِينَ.

The Prophet ﷺ prohibited sitting by pathways, but if it is unavoidable, then its rights must be observed. This [includes]: lowering the gaze; preventing harm; returning greetings; commanding right and forbidding wrong; giving directions; helping the oppressed; helping with carrying [things]; responding to someone who sneezes [by saying, May God have mercy upon you (*yarḥamuka Allāh*)]; and helping the blind.

The Prophet ﷺ said, 'Gatherings [should be conducted] in good faith; whatever happens during them should not be repeated [to others]—provided that this does not harm you.'

It is humble to be content to sit anywhere [in a gathering] with [no concern for] the honour of the gathering [meaning, to not desire to sit at the front], and to sit at the edge of the gathering.

He ﷺ prohibited one from making one's brother stand up [for one to] then sit in their place. He ﷺ [also] prohibited sitting between a person and their child, between two people speaking (except with their permission), and sitting in a circle (*ḥalqa*) or walking across it (except with their permission).

It is *Sunna* for one to stand for a scholar, for a righteous person, for [one's] father or for a ruler.[202]

[Once,] a man entered upon the Messenger of God ﷺ while he was in the mosque, and he ﷺ made space for him and said, 'Truly a Muslim has rights. If his brother sees him [coming to sit down], he should make space for him.'

The Prophet ﷺ would not sit in a dark house without having a lamp in it.

وَنَهَى ﷺ عَنِ الْجُلُوسِ بِالطُّرُقَاتِ فَإِنْ كَانَ لَا بُدَّ مِنْهَا فَقِيَامٌ بِحَقِّهَا. وَذٰلِكَ: غَضُّ الْبَصَرِ، وَكَفُّ الْأَذَى، وَرَدُّ السَّلَامِ، وَالْأَمْرُ بِالْمَعْرُوفِ وَالنَّهْيُ عَنِ الْمُنْكَرِ، وَهِدَايَةُ السَّبِيلِ، وَنَصْرُ الْمَظْلُومِ، وَالْإِعَانَةُ فِي الْحَمْلِ، وَتَشْمِيتُ الْعَاطِسِ، وَإِرْشَادُ الْأَعْمَى.

قَالَ ﷺ: «اَلْمَجَالِسُ بِالْأَمَانَةِ، مَا حَدَثَ بِهِ فِيهَا لَا يُنْقَلُ إِنْ لَمْ يَسُؤْكُمْ.»

مِنَ التَّوَاضُعِ اَلرِّضَى بِالدُّونِ مِنْ شَرَفِ الْمَجَالِسِ وَأَنْ يَجْلِسَ حَيْثُ اِنْتَهَى بِهِ الْمَجْلِسُ.

وَنَهَى أَنْ يُقِيمَ الرَّجُلُ أَخَاهُ مِنْ مَجْلِسِهِ ثُمَّ يَجْلِسُ فِيهِ وَعَنِ الْجُلُوسِ فِيهِ بَيْنَ الرَّجُلِ وَابْنِهِ وَبَيْنَ اِثْنَيْنِ يَتَحَدَّثَانِ إِلَّا بِإِذْنِهِمَا وَعَنِ الْجُلُوسِ فِي الْحَلْقَةِ وَعَنْ تَخَطِّي حَلْقَةٍ إِلَّا بِإِذْنِهِمْ.

وَيُسَنُّ الْقِيَامُ لِلْعَالِمِ وَالصَّالِحِ وَالْوَالِدِ وَالسُّلْطَانِ.

وَدَخَلَ عَلَى النَّبِيِّ ﷺ رَجُلٌ وَهُوَ فِي الْمَسْجِدِ فَتَزَحْزَحَ لَهُ وَقَالَ: «إِنَّ لِلْمُسْلِمِ حَقّاً. إِذَا رَآهُ أَخُوهُ يَتَزَحْزَحُ لَهُ.»

كَانَ لَا يَجْلِسُ فِي بَيْتٍ مُظْلِمٍ إِلَّا أَنْ يُسْرَجَ لَهُ فِيهِ سِرَاجٌ.

DAILY PRACTICES UPON SLEEPING

It is custom for youths not to share the same bed;[203] to lock the doors at the time of sunset; to pronounce the name of God (Exalted is He); to extinguish the lamp and every fire before sleeping; for a person to sleep in a state of ritual purity (*ṭahāra*), but if this is difficult then one may perform the dry ablution (*tayammum*); to face the *qibla*; to [sleep with] one's written will, *miswāk* and ablution vessel at one's head; to repent of every sin; and to intend to stand [in prayer] during the night (*qiyām al-layl*).

When one retires to one's bed, one should wipe it with the inside of one's loincloth for one does not know what may have happened there during the day. Then one should use a *miswāk* and lie down on one's right side with one's right hand under one's cheek. Then one should say: *In the name of God, the Most Compassionate, the Most Merciful. I seek refuge in God from Satan the accursed. In Your name, O God, I live and I die. In Your name, my Lord, I have laid down on my side and in Your name I raise it. If You seize my soul [while I sleep], then forgive it, and if You release it, then protect it with that which You have protected the righteous. O God, truly I have submitted my soul to You, I have consigned my affair to You and have entrusted my back to You out of desire for You and fear of You. There is no place of refuge and no safe haven except in You. I believe in Your Book, which You revealed, and in Your Prophet ﷺ, who You sent.*[Q]

And one should say three times, *O God, save me [from] Your punishment on the day You resurrect Your servants.*

وَظَائِفُ النَّوْمِ

يُسَنُّ كَفُّ الصِّبْيَانِ وَغَلْقُ الأَبْوَابِ عِنْدَ غُرُوبِ الشَّمْسِ وَيُسَمِّي اللّٰهَ تَعَالَى وَيُطْفِئُ الْمِصْبَاحَ وَكُلَّ نَارٍ قَبْلَ النَّوْمِ، وَأَنْ يَنَامَ الْإِنْسَانُ عَلَى طَهَارَةٍ فَإِنْ تَعَذَّرَ تَيَمَّمَ، وَيَسْتَقْبِلُ الْقِبْلَةَ، وَوَصِيَّتُهُ مَكْتُوبَةٌ عِنْدَ رَأْسِهِ وَسِوَاكُهُ وَطَهُورُهُ، وَيَعْقِدُ التَّوْبَةَ مِنْ كُلِّ ذَنْبٍ وَيَنْوِي الْقِيَامَ مِنَ اللَّيْلِ.

فَإِذَا آوَى إِلَى فِرَاشِهِ نَفَضَهُ بِدَاخِلَةِ إِزَارِهِ فَإِنَّهُ لَا يَدْرِي مَا خَلَفَهُ عَلَيْهِ. ثُمَّ يَسْتَاكُ ثُمَّ يَضْطَجِعُ عَلَى شِقِّهِ الأَيْمَنِ وَيَدُهُ الْيُمْنَى تَحْتَ خَدِّهِ. ثُمَّ يَقُولُ: بِسْمِ اللهِ الرَّحْمٰنِ الرَّحِيمِ. أَعُوذُ بِاللهِ مِنَ الشَّيْطَانِ الرَّجِيمِ. بِاسْمِكَ اللّٰهُمَّ أَحْيَا وَأَمُوتُ. بِاسْمِكَ رَبِّي وَضَعْتُ جَنْبِي وَبِاسْمِكَ أَرْفَعُهُ. إِنْ أَمْسَكْتَ نَفْسِي فَاغْفِرْ لَهَا وَإِنْ أَرْسَلْتَهَا فَاحْفَظْهَا بِمَا تَحْفَظُ بِهِ الصَّالِحِينَ. اَللّٰهُمَّ إِنِّي أَسْلَمْتُ نَفْسِي إِلَيْكَ وَفَوَّضْتُ أَمْرِي إِلَيْكَ وَأَلْجَأْتُ ظَهْرِي إِلَيْكَ رَغْبَةً وَرَهْبَةً إِلَيْكَ. لَا مَلْجَأَ وَلَا مَنْجَا إِلَّا إِلَيْكَ. آمَنْتُ بِكِتَابِكَ الَّذِي أَنْزَلْتَ وَبِنَبِيِّكَ الَّذِي أَرْسَلْتَ.

وَيَقُولُ: اَللّٰهُمَّ قِنِي عَذَابَكَ يَوْمَ تَبْعَثُ عِبَادَكَ (ثَلَاثاً).

O God, Lord of the seven heavens, Lord of the earth and Lord of the almighty Throne. Our Lord, Lord of everything, splitter of the grain and the date stone, sender of the Torah, the Bible, the Psalms and the Qur'ān. I seek refuge in You from the evil of every [thing] possessed of evil that You take by its forelock. You are the First; there was nothing before You. You are the Last; there is nothing after You. You are the Manifest; there is nothing that surpasses You. You are the Hidden; there is nothing beyond You. Discharge for us our debt and spare us from poverty.

O God, truly I seek refuge in Your noble Face and in Your perfect Words from the evil that You take by its forelock. O God, truly You expose debt and crime, and Your army is not defeated. Your promise is not broken, and before You [on the Day of Judgement] the wealth of the wealthy will be of no benefit. Glory be to You and praise be to You. Praise be to God Who has fed us, has given us drink, has given us satisfaction and has sheltered us; for how many are those who have no one to give them satisfaction or to shelter them.

O God, forgive me my sins, chase away my satan, dismantle the proof [against me] and make me be in the highest height [of Heaven]. Praise be to God Who has given me satisfaction; Who has sheltered me, fed me and given me drink; Who has bestowed favours upon me and has showered [me] with bounty; Who has given to me and has given generously. Praise be to God in every situation, Lord of each thing and its Proprietor, God of each thing. I seek refuge in You from Hellfire. I seek refuge in the perfect Words of God from the evil of what He has created. O God, You have created my soul and You will cause it to die, so to You belongs its dying and its living. If You seize it [while I sleep], have mercy on it, and if you grant respite to it, protect it by means of the protection of belief.

اَللّٰهُمَّ رَبَّ السَّمَاوَاتِ السَّبْعِ وَرَبَّ الْأَرْضِ وَرَبَّ الْعَرْشِ الْعَظِيمِ. رَبَّنَا وَرَبَّ كُلِّ شَيْءٍ، فَالِقَ الْحَبِّ وَالنَّوَى، مُنْزِلَ التَّوْرَاةِ وَالْإِنْجِيلِ وَالزَّبُورِ وَالْفُرْقَانِ. أَعُوذُ بِكَ مِنْ شَرِّ كُلِّ ذِي شَرٍّ أَنْتَ آخِذٌ بِنَاصِيَتِهِ. أَنْتَ الْأَوَّلُ فَلَيْسَ قَبْلَكَ شَيْءٌ وَأَنْتَ الْآخِرُ فَلَيْسَ بَعْدَكَ شَيْءٌ وَأَنْتَ الظَّاهِرُ فَلَيْسَ فَوْقَكَ شَيْءٌ وَأَنْتَ الْبَاطِنُ فَلَيْسَ دُونَكَ شَيْءٌ. اِقْضِ عَنَّا الدَّيْنَ وَأَغْنِنَا مِنَ الْفَقْرِ.

اَللّٰهُمَّ إِنِّي أَعُوذُ بِوَجْهِكَ الْكَرِيمِ وَكَلِمَاتِكَ التَّامَّةِ وَمِنْ شَرِّ مَا أَنْتَ آخِذٌ بِنَاصِيَتِهِ. اَللّٰهُمَّ إِنَّكَ تَكْشِفُ الْمَغْرَمَ وَالْمَأْثَمَ لَا يُهْزَمُ جُنْدُكَ وَلَا يُخْلَفُ وَعْدُكَ وَلَا يَنْفَعُ ذَا الْجَدِّ مِنْكَ الْجَدُّ. سُبْحَانَكَ وَبِحَمْدِكَ. اَلْحَمْدُ لِلّٰهِ الَّذِي أَطْعَمَنَا وَسَقَانَا وَكَفَانَا، وَآوَانَا، فَكَمْ مِمَّنْ لَا كَافِيَ لَهُ وَلَا مُؤْوِيَ.

اَللّٰهُمَّ اغْفِرْ لِي ذَنْبِي وَاخْسَأْ شَيْطَانِي وَفُكَّ بُرْهَانِي وَاجْعَلْنِي فِي الْعُلَى الْأَعْلَى. اَلْحَمْدُ لِلّٰهِ الَّذِي كَفَانِي وَآوَانِي وَأَطْعَمَنِي وَسَقَانِي وَالَّذِي مَنَّ عَلَيَّ فَأَفْضَلَ وَالَّذِي أَعْطَانِي فَأَجْزَلَ. اَلْحَمْدُ لِلّٰهِ عَلَى كُلِّ حَالٍ. رَبَّ كُلِّ شَيْءٍ وَمَلِيكَهِ وَإِلٰهَ كُلِّ شَيْءٍ أَعُوذُ بِكَ مِنَ النَّارِ. وَأَعُوذُ بِكَلِمَاتِ اللّٰهِ التَّامَّاتِ مِنْ شَرِّ مَا خَلَقَ. اَللّٰهُمَّ أَنْتَ خَلَقْتَ نَفْسِي وَأَنْتَ تَتَوَفَّاهَا فَلَكَ مَمَاتُهَا وَمَحْيَاهَا. إِنْ قَبَضْتَهَا فَارْحَمْهَا وَإِنْ أَخَّرْتَهَا فَاحْفَظْهَا بِحِفْظِ الْإِيمَانِ.

O God, I ask You for well-being. O God, Originator of the heavens and earth, Knower of the unseen and the seen, Lord of each thing and its Proprietor. I bear witness that there is no god but You alone—You have no partner with You—and that Muḥammad is Your servant and Your messenger; and the angels bear witness. O God, truly I seek refuge in You from the evil of my soul, from the evil of Satan and his associating partners with You. I seek refuge in You from perpetrating evil upon myself, or bringing it upon a Muslim. Praise be to God Who is Lofty and Dominating. Praise be to God Who is Hidden and All-Aware. Praise be to God Who is Sovereign and All-Powerful. Praise be to God who gives life to the dead; He has power over all things.

O God, allow me to enjoy my hearing and my sight, and make them both inheritors from me. Give me victory over my enemy and allow me to take revenge on them. O God, I seek refuge in You from overwhelming debt and from hunger, for truly it is the worst companion.

One should say three times, *I seek forgiveness from God; there is no god but He, the Living, the Self-Subsisting, and I turn to Him in repentance.* Then one should pronounce the *taḥmīd*, the *tasbīḥ* and the *takbīr* one hundred times. One should recite the *Fātiḥa*,[204] the *Āyat al-Kursī* (the 'Throne Verse'),[205] the end of [*Sūrat*] *al-Baqara*[206] and of [*Sūrat*] *al-Isrā'*,[207] the end of [*Sūrat*] *al-Kahf*,[208] [*Sūrat*] *al-Sajda*,[209] [*Sūrat*] *Yāsīn*,[210] [*Sūrat*] *al-Zukhruf*,[211] [*Sūrat*] *al-Dukhān*,[212] [*Sūrat*] *al-Wāqi'a*,[213] the *musabbiḥāt*,[214] [*Sūrat*] *Tabārak*,[215] '*Competition in [worldly] increase diverts you*' [*Sūrat al-Takāthur*][216] and [*Sūrat*] *al-Ikhlāṣ*,[217] [to be recited] once or one hundred times, [then] the *mu'awwadhatayn*,[218] and one should conclude with *Sūrat al-Kāfirūn*.[219] One should sleep upon completing [the latter], for truly it confers immunity against associating partners with God (*shirk*).

اَللّٰهُمَّ إِنِّي أَسْأَلُكَ الْعَافِيَةَ. اَللّٰهُمَّ فَاطِرَ السَّمَاوَاتِ وَالْأَرْضِ، عَالِمَ الْغَيْبِ وَالشَّهَادَةِ، رَبَّ كُلِّ شَيْءٍ وَمَلِيكَهِ. أَشْهَدُ أَنْ لَا إِلٰهَ إِلَّا أَنْتَ وَحْدَكَ لَا شَرِيكَ لَكَ، وَأَنَّ مُحَمَّداً عَبْدُكَ وَرَسُولُكَ، وَالْمَلَائِكَةُ يَشْهَدُونَ. اَللّٰهُمَّ إِنِّي أَعُوذُ بِكَ مِنْ شَرِّ نَفْسِي وَمِنْ شَرِّ الشَّيْطَانِ وَشِرْكِهِ. وَأَعُوذُ بِكَ أَنْ أَقْتَرِفَ عَلَى نَفْسِي سُوءاً أَوْ أَجُرَّهُ عَلَى مُسْلِمٍ. اَلْحَمْدُ لِلّٰهِ الَّذِي عَلَا فَقَهَرَ. وَالْحَمْدُ لِلّٰهِ الَّذِي بَطَنَ فَخَبَرَ. وَالْحَمْدُ لِلّٰهِ الَّذِي مَلَكَ فَقَدَرَ. وَالْحَمْدُ لِلّٰهِ الَّذِي يُحْيِي الْمَوْتَى وَهُوَ عَلَى كُلِّ شَيْءٍ قَدِيرٌ.

اَللّٰهُمَّ مَتِّعْنِي بِسَمْعِي وَبَصَرِي وَاجْعَلْهُمَا الْوَارِثَ مِنِّي. وَانْصُرْنِي عَلَى عَدُوِّي وَأَرِنِي مِنْهُ ثَأْرِي. اَللّٰهُمَّ إِنِّي أَعُوذُ بِكَ مِنْ غَلَبَةِ الدَّيْنِ وَمِنَ الْجُوعِ فَإِنَّهُ بِئْسَ الضَّجِيعَ.

وَيَقُولُ: أَسْتَغْفِرُ اللهَ الَّذِي لَا إِلٰهَ إِلَّا هُوَ الْحَيُّ الْقَيُّومُ وَأَتُوبُ إِلَيْهِ، ثَلَاثاً. ثُمَّ يُحَمِّدُ وَيُسَبِّحُ وَيُكَبِّرُ مِائَةَ مَرَّةٍ. وَيَقْرَأُ الْفَاتِحَةَ وَآيَةَ الْكُرْسِيِّ وَآخِرَ الْبَقَرَةِ وَالْإِسْرَاءَ وَآخِرَ الْكَهْفِ وَالسَّجْدَةَ، وَيس وَالزُّخْرُفَ وَالدُّخَانَ وَالْوَاقِعَةَ وَالْمُسَبِّحَاتِ وَتَبَارَكَ وَأَلْهَاكُمُ وَالْإِخْلَاصَ مَرَّةً أَوْ مِائَةَ مَرَّةٍ وَالْمُعَوِّذَتَيْنِ وَيَخْتِمُ بِسُورَةِ الْكَافِرِينَ. وَيَنَامُ عَلَى خَتْمِهَا فَإِنَّهَا بَرَاءَةٌ مِنَ الشِّرْكِ.

It is disliked (*makrūh*) for one to sleep in a house alone; on a roof that has no walls around it; in the middle of the road; amongst people; while naked; in a saffron-coloured blanket; while wrapped in one's garment without allowing space for one's arms (*mushtamil al-ṣammāʾ*); while [lying] on one's stomach, because truly it is a posture that God (Exalted is He) loathes; sleeping after the afternoon prayer (*ʿaṣr*), after the morning prayer (*ṣubḥ* [*fajr*]) and before the evening prayer (*ʿishāʾ*); and speaking after the evening prayer except about good things. In a *ḥadīth*, [it is said,] 'Whoever writes a verse of poetry after the evening prayer shall not have the prayer that night accepted from them.'[220]

It is recommended (*mustaḥabb*) to take an afternoon nap (*qaylūla*), because truly the evil spirits (*shayāṭīn*) do not take an afternoon nap.

If one is worried, one should say: *O God, Lord of the seven heavens and what they cover, Lord of the earth and what is carried upon it, and Lord of the evil spirits and what they have misguided. Be a Protector for me from the evil of Your creation—all of them collectively—lest one of them hastily act upon me with evil, or lest one of them overcome me. Great is Your protection and magnificent is Your praise; there is no god beside You. I seek refuge in You, Lord, lest the evil spirits be present. O God, the stars have disappeared, eyes have become tranquil and You are the Living, the Self-Subsisting. Neither slumber nor sleep overcomes Him. O Living, O Self-Subsisting, grant sleep to my night and guide my night.*

When one finishes sleeping, one should say: *I seek refuge in the perfect Words of God that neither the virtuous nor the corrupt can transgress. I seek refuge from the evil of what has been sent down from the heavens and what has been raised into them. I seek refuge from the evil of what has spread in the earth and what emerges from it. I seek refuge from the evil of the trials of the night and the day, and from the evil of events occurring during the night and during the day, unless it is a nocturnal event that brings good, O Most Compassionate.*

وَيُكْرَهُ أَنْ يَنَامَ فِي بَيْتٍ وَحْدَهُ أَوْ عَلَى سَطْحٍ لَيْسَ لَهُ جِدَارٌ أَوْ عَلَى قَارِعَةِ الطَّرِيقِ أَوْ بَيْنَ الْقَوْمِ أَوْ عَارِياً أَوْ فِي مِلْحَفَةٍ مُعَصْفَرَةٍ أَوْ مُشْتَمِلِ الصَّمَّاءِ أَوْ عَلَى بَطْنِهِ فَإِنَّهَا ضِجْعَةٌ يُبْغِضُهَا اللهُ تَعَالَى، وَالنَّوْمُ بَعْدَ الْعَصْرِ وَبَعْدَ الصُّبْحِ وَقَبْلَ الْعِشَاءِ، وَالْحَدِيثُ بَعْدَهَا إِلَّا فِي خَيْرٍ. وَفِي الْحَدِيثِ: «مَنْ قَرَضَ بَيْتَ شِعْرٍ بَعْدَ الْعِشَاءِ الْآخِرَةِ لَمْ تُقْبَلْ لَهُ صَلَاةٌ تِلْكَ اللَّيْلَةَ.»

وَيُسْتَحَبُّ الْقَيْلُولَةُ فَإِنَّ الشَّيَاطِينَ لَا تَقِيلُ.

فَإِنْ قَلِقَ قَالَ: اَللّٰهُمَّ رَبَّ السَّمَاوَاتِ السَّبْعِ وَمَا أَظَلَّتْ وَرَبَّ الْأَرْضِ وَمَا أَقَلَّتْ وَرَبَّ الشَّيَاطِينِ وَمَا أَضَلَّتْ كُنْ لِي جَائِراً مِنْ شَرِّ خَلْقِكَ كُلِّهِمْ جَمِيعًا أَنْ يَفْرُطَ عَلَيَّ أَحَدٌ مِنْهُمْ أَوْ أَنْ يَطْغَى عَلَيَّ. عَزَّ جَارُكَ وَجَلَّ ثَنَاؤُكَ وَلَا إِلٰهَ غَيْرُكَ. أَعُوذُ بِكَ رَبِّ أَنْ يَحْضُرُونِ. اَللّٰهُمَّ غَارَتِ النُّجُومُ وَهَدَأَتِ الْعُيُونُ وَأَنْتَ حَيٌّ قَيُّومٌ. لَا تَأْخُذُهُ سِنَةٌ وَلَا نَوْمٌ. يَا حَيُّ يَا قَيُّومُ، أَنِمْ لَيْلِي وَأَهْدِ لَيْلِي.

فَإِذَا كَانَ يَفْزَعُ مِنْ نَوْمِهِ قَالَ: أَعُوذُ بِكَلِمَاتِ اللهِ التَّامَّاتِ الَّتِي لَا يُجَاوِزُهُنَّ بَرٌّ وَلَا فَاجِرٌ مِنْ شَرِّ مَا يُنْزَلُ مِنَ السَّمَاءِ وَمَا يُعْرَجُ فِيهَا، وَمِنْ شَرِّ مَا ذَرَأَ فِي الْأَرْضِ وَمَا يَخْرُجُ مِنْهَا، وَمِنْ شَرِّ فِتَنِ اللَّيْلِ وَالنَّهَارِ، وَمِنْ شَرِّ طَوَارِقِ اللَّيْلِ وَالنَّهَارِ إِلَّا طَارِقاً يَطْرُقُ بِخَيْرٍ يَارَحْمٰنُ.

If one feels lonely, one should say, *Glory be to the King, the Most Holy, Lord of the angels and the spirit.*

If one has seen a dream that one likes, one should praise God. Or, if one dislikes it, one should spit to one's left three times, change the side that one is [sleeping] on and say, *O God, I seek refuge in You from the evil of Satan and evil dreams*, three times. *I seek refuge in God from that which God's angels and His Messenger have sought refuge from, and from the evil of my dream tonight lest it harm me in my religion or my worldly life, O Most Compassionate.* And one should not speak about [evil dreams] for they will not harm one.

If one has awoken and desires [to go back] to sleep, one should say: *There is no god but God alone; He has no partner. To Him is the dominion, to Him is all praise and He has power over all things. Praise be to God; glory be to God. There is no god but God; God is most Great. There is no power and no might save in God. O God, forgive me; there is no god but You. Glory be to You. O God, I seek Your forgiveness for my sins. I ask You for Your mercy. O God, increase me in knowledge, do not mislead my heart after having guided me and bestow mercy upon me from Your presence. Truly, You are the Bestower. There is no god but God, the Unique, the Dominator. Lord of the heavens and the earth, and of what is between them, the Eminent, the Ever-Forgiving.*

If one sees a shooting star one should say, [*This is*] *what God has willed; there is no power and no might save in God.*

If a rooster crows, one should ask for God's bounty. [If one hears] a dog or a donkey, one should seek refuge from Satan. It is disliked (*makrūh*) [for one] to curse a rooster or fleas.

فَإِذَا اسْتَوْحَشَ قَالَ: سُبْحَانَ الْمَلِكِ الْقُدُّوسِ، رَبِّ الْمَلَائِكَةِ وَالرُّوحِ.

فَإِنْ رَأَى رُؤْيَاً يُحِبُّهَا، يَحْمَدُ اللّٰهَ، أَوْ يَكْرَهُهَا بَصَقَ عَنْ يَسَارِهِ ثَلَاثاً وَتَحَوَّلَ عَنْ جَنْبِهِ الَّذِي كَانَ عَلَيْهِ وَقَالَ: اَللّٰهُمَّ إِنِّي أَعُوذُ بِكَ مِنْ شَرِّ الشَّيْطَانِ وَسَيِّئَاتِ الْأَحْلَامِ (ثَلَاثاً). أَعُوذُ بِاللّٰهِ مِمَّا عَاذَتْ بِهِ مَلَائِكَةُ اللّٰهِ وَرَسُولُهُ وَمِنْ شَرِّ رُؤْيَايَ اللَّيْلَةَ أَنْ تَضُرَّنِي فِي دِينِي أَوْ دُنْيَايَ يَا رَحْمٰنُ. وَلَا يُحَدِّثُ بِهَا فَإِنَّهَا لَنْ تَضُرَّهُ.

فَإِذَا اسْتَيْقَظَ وَأَرَادَ النَّوْمَ قَالَ: لَا إِلٰهَ إِلَّا اللّٰهُ وَحْدَهُ، لَا شَرِيكَ لَهُ، لَهُ الْمُلْكُ وَلَهُ الْحَمْدُ وَهُوَ عَلَى كُلِّ شَيْءٍ قَدِيرٌ. وَالْحَمْدُ لِلّٰهِ، وَسُبْحَانَ اللّٰهِ وَلَا إِلٰهَ إِلَّا اللّٰهُ، وَاللّٰهُ أَكْبَرُ. وَلَا حَوْلَ وَلَا قُوَّةَ إِلَّا بِاللّٰهِ. اللّٰهُمَّ اغْفِرْ لِي، لَا إِلٰهَ إِلَّا أَنْتَ سُبْحَانَكَ. اَللّٰهُمَّ أَسْتَغْفِرُ لِذَنْبِي. أَسْأَلُكَ رَحْمَتَكَ. اَللّٰهُمَّ زِدْنِي عِلْماً وَلَا تُزِغْ قَلْبِي بَعْدَ أَنْ هَدَيْتَنِي وَهَبْ لِي مِنْ لَدُنْكَ رَحْمَةً. إِنَّكَ أَنْتَ الْوَهَّابُ. لَا إِلٰهَ أَلَّا اللّٰهُ الْوَاحِدُ الْقَهَّارُ، رَبُّ السَّمَاوَاتِ وَالْأَرْضِ وَمَا بَيْنَهُمَا الْعَزِيزُ الْغَفَّارُ.

فَإِنْ رَأَى كَوْكَباً انْقَضَّ قَالَ: مَا شَاءَ اللّٰهُ، لَا قُوَّةَ إِلَّا بِاللّٰهِ.

فَإِنْ صَاحَ الدِّيكُ سَأَلَ مِنْ فَضْلِ اللّٰهِ، وَالْكَلْبُ وَالْحِمَارُ تَعَوَّذَ مِنَ الشَّيْطَانِ. وَيُكْرَهُ سَبُّ الدِّيكِ وَالْبَرَاغِيثِ.

If one gets up to pray in the middle of the night, one should sit up, wipe the sleep from one's eyes with one's hands, then recite the end of [*Sūrat*] *Āl ʿImrān*,[221] then pray.

The *Sunna* for anyone who leaves their house at night to go to the toilet is to lock the door of their house, because that blocks Satan from entering. Then one should use *a miswāk* and seek forgiveness from God three times, for Satan sleeps on his snout.

One should say: *O God, praise be to You; You are the Lord of the heavens and all that is in them. Praise be to You; You are the Light of the heavens and the earth, and all that is in them. You are the Truth, Your promise is true, meeting You is true, Paradise is true, Hellfire is true, the Hour is true, the Prophets are true and Muḥammad is true. O God, to You I have submitted, in You I believe, in You I place my trust, to You I turn and for You I dispute. So forgive me for what I have sent ahead and for what I have yet to commit; for what I have performed secretly and for what I have performed publicly. You are the Expediter and You are the Delayer. There is no god but You, my God. There is no power and no might save in You*. And one may add after this whatever God wills.

One should commence one's prayer with two short *rakʿas* and pronounce the *takbīr*, the *taḥmīd*, the *tahlīl*, the *istighfār* and say ten times: *Glory be to God and praise be to Him, Glory be to the King, the Most Holy. O God, truly I seek refuge in You from longing for the world and from the constriction of the Day of Resurrection. O God, forgive me, guide me, provide for me and grant me well-being.*

فَإِنْ قَامَ إِلَى الصَّلَاةِ مِنْ جَوْفِ اللَّيْلِ جَلَسَ فَمَسَحَ النَّوْمَ عَنْ عَيْنَيْهِ بِيَدَيْهِ ثُمَّ قَرَأَ خَوَاتِيمَ آلِ عِمْرَانَ ثُمَّ صَلَّى.

وَالسُّنَّةُ لِمَنْ خَرَجَ بِاللَّيْلِ لِحَاجَتِهِ أَنْ يُغْلِقَ بَابَ بَيْتِهِ فَإِنَّ ذٰلِكَ يَمْنَعُ الشَّيْطَانَ. ثُمَّ اسْتَاكَ ثُمَّ اسْتَغْفَرَ ثَلَاثَ مَرَّاتٍ فَإِنَّ الشَّيْطَانَ يَبِيتُ عَلَى خَيَاشِيمِهِ.

وَيَقُولُ: اَللّٰهُمَّ لَكَ الْحَمْدُ، أَنْتَ رَبُّ السَّمَاوَاتِ وَمَنْ فِيهِنَّ. وَلَكَ الْحَمْدُ، أَنْتَ نُورُ السَّمَاوَاتِ وَالْأَرْضِ وَمَنْ فِيهِنَّ. أَنْتَ الْحَقُّ وَوَعْدُكَ الْحَقُّ وَلِقَاؤُكَ حَقٌّ وَالْجَنَّةُ حَقٌّ وَالنَّارُ حَقٌّ وَالسَّاعَةُ حَقٌّ وَالنَّبِيُّونَ حَقٌّ وَمُحَمَّدٌ حَقٌّ. اَللّٰهُمَّ لَكَ أَسْلَمْتُ وَبِكَ آمَنْتُ وَعَلَيْكَ تَوَكَّلْتُ وَإِلَيْكَ أَنَبْتُ وَبِكَ خَاصَمْتُ. فَاغْفِرْ لِي مَا قَدَّمْتُ وَمَا أَخَّرْتُ وَمَا أَسْرَرْتُ وَمَا أَعْلَنْتُ. أَنْتَ الْمُقَدِّمُ وَأَنْتَ الْمُؤَخِّرُ. لَا إِلٰهَ إِلَّا أَنْتَ إِلٰهِي. وَلَا حَوْلَ وَلَا قُوَّةَ إِلَّا بِكَ. وَيَطُولُ بَعْدُ مَا شَاءَ اللّٰهُ.

وَيَفْتَتِحُ صَلَاتَهُ بِرَكْعَتَيْنِ خَفِيفَتَيْنِ، وَيُكَبِّرُ وَيَحْمَدُ وَيُهَلِّلُ وَيَسْتَغْفِرُ وَيَقُولُ: سُبْحَانَ اللهِ وَبِحَمْدِهِ. سُبْحَانَ الْمَلِكِ الْقُدُّوسِ. اَللّٰهُمَّ إِنِّي أَعُوذُ بِكَ مِنْ ضِيقِ الدُّنْيَا وَضِيقِ يَوْمِ الْقِيَامَةِ. اَللّٰهُمَّ اغْفِرْ لِي وَاهْدِنِي وَارْزُقْنِي وَعَافِنِي (عَشْراً عَشْراً).

One should say at the beginning of the prayer: *O God, Lord of Gabriel, Michael and Isrāfīl, Originator of the heavens and the earth, You shall decide between Your servants [and pass judgement] concerning what they differed in. Guide me to the truth of what has been differed in, by Your permission. Truly, You guide on a straight path whom You please.*

You should say after the night vigil (*ṣalāt al-layl*[222]): *O God, truly I ask You for mercy from Your presence that will guide my heart, collect my affairs, put my affairs in order, restore my absent ones, raise my witnessing and protect me from every evil. O God, grant me sincere belief, certainty that does not have disbelief after it and mercy through which to obtain the honour of Your generosity in this world and the Hereafter.*

O God, I ask You for success in the Divine Decree (qaḍāʾ), *for the lodging of the martyrs, for the life of the felicitous and for victory over enemies. O God, I lodge my need with You—even if my knowledge falls short and my work slackens—in my desperate need of Your mercy. I ask You, O Judge of affairs, O Curer of breasts, to separate me from the punishment of the Inferno, from being summoned to destruction and from the trial of the grave, just as You have separated the oceans. O God, despite the shortcomings of my knowledge, what my intention* (niyya) *and my affair did not reach from amongst the goodness [that] You have promised any one from Your creation, or [from amongst] the goodness [that] You give to anyone from amongst Your servants—truly I ask You for it and beseech You for it by Your mercy, O Most Merciful of those who show mercy, O Lord of the worlds.*

O God, Yours is the severe power and the guided affair. I ask You for safety on the Day of the Threat (Yawm al-Waʿīd) *and for Paradise on the Day of Eternity* (Yawm al-Khulūd), *with a seat amongst the martyrs, those who bow, those who prostrate and those who fulfil their covenants.*

يَقُولُ عِنْدَ الصَّلَاةِ: اَللّٰهُمَّ رَبَّ جِبْرِيلَ وَمِيكَائِيلَ وَإِسْرَافِيلَ، فَاطِرَ السَّمَاوَاتِ وَالْأَرْضِ، أَنْتَ تَحْكُمُ بَيْنَ عِبَادِكَ فِيمَا كَانُوا فِيهِ يَخْتَلِفُونَ. اِهْدِنِي لِمَا اخْتُلِفَ فِيهِ مِنَ الْحَقِّ بِإِذْنِكَ. إِنَّكَ تَهْدِي مَنْ تَشَاءُ إِلَى صِرَاطٍ مُّسْتَقِيمٍ.

وَتَقُولُ بَعْدَ صَلَاةِ اللَّيْلِ: اَللّٰهُمَّ إِنِّي أَسْأَلُكَ رَحْمَةً مِنْ عِنْدِكَ تَهْدِي بِهَا قَلْبِي وَتَجْمَعُ بِهَا أَمْرِي وَتَلِمُّ بِهَا شَعِثِي وَتُصْلِحُ بِهَا غَائِبِي وَتَرْفَعُ بِهَا شَاهِدِي وَتَعْصِمُنِي بِهَا مِنْ كُلِّ سُوءٍ. اَللّٰهُمَّ أَعْطِنِي إِيمَاناً صَادِقاً وَيَقِيناً لَيْسَ بَعْدَهُ كُفْرٌ وَرَحْمَةً أَنَالُ بِهَا شَرَفَ كَرَامَتِكَ فِي الدُّنْيَا وَالْآخِرَةِ.

اَللّٰهُمَّ إِنِّي أَسْأَلُكَ الْفَوْزَ فِي الْقَضَاءِ وَنُزُلَ الشُّهَدَاءِ وَعَيْشَ السُّعَدَاءِ وَالنَّصْرَ عَلَى الْأَعْدَاءِ. اَللّٰهُمَّ إِنِّي أَنْزِلُ بِكَ حَاجَتِي وَإِنْ قَصُرَ رَأْيِي وَضَعُفَ عَمَلِي وَافْتَقَرْتُ إِلَى رَحْمَتِكَ. فَأَسْأَلُكَ يَا قَاضِيَ الْأُمُورِ وَيَا شَافِيَ الصُّدُورِ كَمَا تُجِيرُ بَيْنَ الْبُحُورِ أَنْ تُجِيرَنِي مِنْ عَذَابِ السَّعِيرِ وَمِنْ دَعْوَةِ الثُّبُورِ وَمِنْ فِتْنَةِ الْقُبُورِ. اللّٰهُمَّ مَا قَصُرَ عَنْهُ رَأْيِي وَلَمْ تَبْلُغْهُ نِيَّتِي وَلَمْ تَبْلُغْهُ مَسْأَلَتِي مِنْ خَيْرٍ وَعَدْتَهُ أَحَداً مِنْ خَلْقِكَ، أَوْ خَيْرٍ أَنْتَ مُعْطِيهِ أَحَداً مِنْ عِبَادِكَ، فَإِنِي أَرْغَبُ إِلَيْكَ فِيهِ وَأَسْأَلُكَهُ بِرَحْمَتِكَ يَا أَرْحَمَ الرَّاحِمِينَ يَا رَبَّ الْعَالَمِينَ.

اَللّٰهُمَّ ذَا الْحَوْلِ الشَّدِيدِ وَالْأَمْرِ الرَّشِيدِ أَسْأَلُكَ الْأَمْنَ يَوْمَ الْوَعِيدِ وَالْجَنَّةَ يَوْمَ الْخُلُودِ مَعَ الْمُقَرَّبِينَ الشُّهُودِ، اَلرُّكَّعِ السُّجُودِ، الْمُوفِينَ بِالْعُهُودِ. إِنَّكَ

Truly, You are Kind and Loving. Truly, You do whatsoever You wish. O God, make us guiding and guided, not misguiding and misguided. Make us be peaceful to Your friends and hostile to Your enemies. Through Your Love, we love whoever loves You. Through Your enmity, we show enmity to whoever shows enmity to You and opposes You. O God, this is the supplication and the answer is Yours; this is the effort and upon You I depend.

O God, make a light for me in my heart and in my grave; light in front of me, light before me and light behind me; light on my right and light on my left; light above me and light beneath me; light in my hearing and light in my sight; light in my hair and light in my skin; light in my flesh, light in my blood and light in my bones.

O God, grant me a great light, give me light and make me light. Glory be to He Who is gentle in [His] exaltedness and speaks through it. Glory be to He Who is cloaked in majesty and acts generously through it. Glory be to He Who has no need of glorification other than His own. Glory be to the Lord of grace and blessing. Glory be to the Lord of magnificence and magnanimity. Glory be to the Lord of majesty and generosity. One should seek forgiveness seventy times.

If a person falls asleep during the prayer, then let them lie down until their [need for] sleep goes away.[223] It is desirable (*mustaḥabb*) to lie down between the night vigil (*ṣalāt al-layl*) and the time of the early morning meal (*saḥar*), until the traces of sleep leave one.[224] Whoever sleeps through [their time allocated to reciting] a portion of the Qurʾān (*ḥizb*), or part of it, should recite it during the time between the dawn prayer (*fajr*) and the midday prayer (*ẓuhr*); it will be recorded for them as if they had recited it at night.

رَؤُوفٌ وَدُودٌ. وَإِنَّكَ تَفْعَلُ مَا تُرِيدُ. اَللّٰهُمَّ اجْعَلْنَا هَادِينَ مَهْدِيِّينَ غَيْرَ ضَالِّينَ وَلَا مُضِلِّينَ، سِلْماً لِأَوْلِيَائِكَ وَعَدُوّاً لِأَعْدَائِكَ. نُحِبُّ بِحُبِّكَ مَنْ أَحَبَّكَ وَنُعَادِي بِعَدَاوَتِكَ مَنْ عَادَاكَ وَخَالَفَكَ. اَللّٰهُمَّ هٰذَا الدُّعَاءُ وَعَلَيْكَ الْإِجَابَةُ، وَهٰذَا الْجُهْدُ وَعَلَيْكَ التُّكْلَانُ.

اَللّٰهُمَّ اجْعَلْ لِي نُوراً فِي قَلْبِي وَقَبْرِي وَنُوراً أَمَامِي وَنُوراً مِنْ بَيْنِ يَدَيَّ وَنُوراً مِنْ خَلْفِي وَنوراً عَنْ يَمِينِي وَنُوراً عَنْ شِمَالِي وَنُوراً مِنْ فَوْقِي وَنُوراً مِنْ تَحْتِي وَنُوراً فِي سَمْعِي وَنُوراً فِي بَصَرِي وَنُوراً فِي شَعْرِي وَنُوراً فِي بَشَرِي وَنُوراً فِي لَحْمِي وَنُوراً فِي دَمِي وَنُوراً فِي عِظَامِي.

اَللّٰهُمَّ أَعْظِمْ لِي نُوراً وَأَعْطِنِي نُوراً وَاجْعَلْ لِي نُوراً. سُبْحَانَ الَّذِي تَعَطَّفَ بِالْعِزِّ وَقَالَ بِهِ. سُبْحَانَ الَّذِي لَبِسَ الْمَجْدَ وَتَكَرَّمَ بِهِ. سُبْحَانَ الَّذِي لَا يَنْبَغِي التَّسْبِيحُ إِلَّا لَهُ. سُبْحَانَ ذِي الْفَضْلِ وَالنِّعَمِ. وَسُبْحَانَ ذِي الْمَجْدِ وَالْكَرَمِ. وَسُبْحَانَ ذِي الْجَلَالِ وَالْإِكْرَامِ. وَيَسْتَغْفِرُ سَبْعِينَ مَرَّةً.

وَإِذَا نَعِسَ فِي الصَّلَاةِ فَلْيَرْقُدْ حَتَّى يَذْهَبَ عَنْهُ النَّوْمُ. وَيَسْتَحِبُّ ضِجْعَةً بَيْنَ صَلَاةِ اللَّيْلِ وَالسَّحرِ حَتَّى يَذْهَبَ عَنْهُ أَثَرُ السَّهَرِ. وَمَنْ نَامَ عَنْ حِزْبِهِ أَوْ عَنْ شَيْءٍ مِنْهُ فَقَرَأَهُ فِيمَا بَيْنَ صَلَاةِ الْفَجْرِ وَصَلَاةِ الظُّهْرِ، كُتِبَ لَهُ كَأَنَّمَا قَرَأَهُ مِنَ اللَّيْلِ.

VARIOUS PRACTICES DURING THE NIGHT AND THE DAY

The *Sunna* for anyone leaving their house is to greet their family before leaving, and to say upon leaving the house, *In the name of God. I have placed my trust in God; there is no power and no might save in God.*[R]

One should raise one's head to the heavens and say, *O God, I seek refuge in You lest I misguide or am misguided; lest I disgrace or am disgraced; lest I oppress or am oppressed; or lest I show ignorance or ignorance is shown to me. I believe in God and I seek protection in God. What God wills; God is sufficient for me and what a blessed Trustee.*[S]

One should greet everyone one meets; [both] those that one knows and those that one does not know. One should avidly desire to greet ten people from amongst the Muslims every day, and to be the first one [to give the greeting (*salām*)], for truly [the one who greets first] is better than the responder. Its wording is, 'Peace be upon you, and the mercy of God and His blessings' (*al-salām ʿalaykum wa-raḥmat Allāh wa-barakātuhu*). The responder should add, 'His forgiveness and His pleasure' (*wa-maghfiratuhu wa-riḍwānuhu*).[225]

It is *Sunna* for someone riding to greet someone who is walking, for someone walking to [greet] someone who is sitting and for the few to [greet] the many. If one is with a friend and a tree or obstruction happens to come between them, when they meet [again] they should greet [one another]. Gesturing with one finger during the greeting is disliked (*makrūh*), because it is an action of the Jewish people.

وَظَائِفُ شَتَّى فِي اللَّيْلِ وَالنَّهَارِ

اَلسُّنَّةُ لِمَنْ خَرَجَ مِنْ بَيْتِهِ أَنْ يُسَلِّمَ عَلَى أَهْلِهِ قَبْلَ أَنْ يَخْرُجَ وَأَنْ يَقُولَ عِنْدَ خُرُوجِهِ مِنَ الْبَيْتِ: بِسْمِ اللهِ. تَوَكَّلْتُ عَلَى اللهِ. لَا حَوْلَ وَلَا قُوَّةَ إِلَّا بِاللهِ.

وَيَرْفَعُ رَأْسَهُ إِلَى السَّمَاءِ وَيَقُولُ: اَللّٰهُمَّ إِنِّي أَعُوذُ بِكَ أَنْ أَضِلَّ أَوْ أُضَلَّ، أَوْ أَذِلَّ أَوْ أُذَلَّ، أَوْ أَظْلِمَ أَوْ أُظْلَمَ، أَوْ أَجْهَلَ أَوْ يُجْهَلَ عَلَيَّ. آمَنْتُ بِاللهِ، اِعْتَصَمْتُ بِاللهِ. مَا شَاءَ اللهُ، حَسْبِيَ اللهُ وَنِعْمَ الْوَكِيلُ.

وَيُسَلِّمُ عَلَى كُلِّ مَنْ لَقِيَهُ، عَرَفَهُ أَوْ لَمْ يَعْرِفْهُ. وَيَحْرِصُ أَنْ يُسَلِّمَ كُلَّ يَوْمٍ عَلَى عَشْرَةٍ مِنَ الْمُسْلِمِينَ وَأَنْ يَكُونَ هُوَ الْمُبْتَدِي فَإِنَّهُ أَفْضَلُ مِنَ الرَّادِّ. وَصِيغَتُهُ: «اَلسَّلَامُ عَلَيْكُمْ وَرَحْمَةُ اللهِ وَبَرَكَاتُهُ.» وَيَزِيدُ الرَّادُّ: «وَمَغْفِرَتُهُ وَرِضْوَانُهُ.»

وَالسُّنَّةُ أَنْ يُسَلِّمَ الرَّاكِبُ عَلَى الْمَاشِي وَالْمَاشِي عَلَى الْقَاعِدِ وَالْقَلِيلُ عَلَى الْكَثِيرِ. وَإِذَا كَانَ مَعَهُ رَفِيقٌ وَحَالَتْ بَيْنَهُمَا شَجَرَةٌ أَوْ أَكَمَةٌ ثُمَّ الْتَقَيَا سَلَّمَ عَلَيْهِ. وَتُكْرَهُ الْإِشَارَةُ فِي السَّلَامِ بِإِصْبَعٍ وَاحِدَةٍ فَإِنَّهُ فِعْلُ الْيَهُودِ.

[Once,] the Prophet ﷺ passed by a [group of] youths, so he said, 'Peace be upon you, and the mercy of God, O youths.'

In a *ḥadīth* it was said, 'If two Muslims meet and they shake hands, praise God, bless the Prophet ﷺ, seek forgiveness and each of them smiles in the face of his companion, they are forgiven and one hundred mercies descend upon them; for the one who initiates [the greeting], ninety [mercies] and for the one who shakes hands, ten [mercies].' The greeting should precede the handshake.

The *Sunna* for whoever is asked about how they are is for them to say, '[My response] to you is to praise.'

When the Prophet ﷺ walked, he would lean on a staff or on a palm branch. He used to love palm branches and his hand would never be without one. He ﷺ would not turn [his head] to look behind him when [walking] on his way, and if he did turn for some reason, he would turn [his body] entirely. He ﷺ would not let any of his Companions walk behind him. He forbade walking to the mosque and markets in a shirt without a loincloth beneath it—meaning that the shirt on its own is not sufficient to cover the private parts.

He ﷺ said, 'Those who are barefoot have more right to the middle of the road than those wearing shoes, and women do not have a right to the middle of the road, but rather to its sides.'

The *Sunna* for anyone riding an animal is to say, *In the name of God. Praise be to God 'Who has subjected this to us, though we were unable to subdue it...,'* [and recite] these two verses.[226]

وَمَرَّ النَّبِيُّ ﷺ عَلَى صِبْيَانٍ فَقَالَ: «اَلسَّلَامُ عَلَيْكُمْ وَرَحْمَةُ اللهِ يَا صِبْيَانُ.»

وَفِي الْحَدِيثِ: «إِذَا الْتَقَى الْمُسْلِمَانِ فَتَصَافَحَا وَحَمِدَا اللهَ وَصَلَّيَا عَلَى النَّبِيِّ ﷺ وَاسْتَغْفَرَا وَضَحِكَ كُلٌّ وَاحِدٍ مِنْهُمَا فِي وَجْهِ صَاحِبِهِ، غُفِرَ لَهُمَا وَنَزَلَ عَلَيْهِمَا مِائَةُ رَحْمَةٍ لِلْبَادِي تِسْعُونَ وَلِلْمُصَافِحِ عَشْرٌ.» وَيُقَدِّمُ السَّلَامَ عَلَى الْمُصَافَحَةِ.

وَالسُّنَّةُ لِمَنْ سُئِلَ عَنْ حَالِهِ أَنْ يَقُولَ: «أَحْمَدُ اللهَ إِلَيْكَ.»

وَكَانَ ﷺ إِذَا مَشَى تَوَكَّأَ عَلَى عَصًى أَوْ عُرْجُونٍ. وَكَانَ يُحِبُّ الْعَرَاجِينَ وَلَا يَزَالُ فِي يَدِهِ مِنْهَا. وَكَانَ لَا يَلْتَفِتُ فِي طَرِيقِهِ وَرَاءَهُ وَإِذَا الْتَفَتَ لِحَاجَةٍ الْتَفَتَ جَمِيعاً. وَلَا يَدَعُ أَحَداً مِنَ الصَّحَابَةِ يَمْشِي خَلْفَهُ. وَنَهَى عَنِ الْمَشْيِ فِي الْمَسَاجِدِ وَالْأَسْوَاقِ فِي الْقُمُصِ إِلَّا وَتَحْتَهَا الْإِزَارُ، وَالْمَعْنَى فِيهِ أَنَّ الْقَمِيصَ وَحْدَهُ يَصِفُ حَجْمَ الْعَوْرَةِ.

وَقَالَ: «اَلْحَافِي أَحَقُّ بِصَدْرِ الطَّرِيقِ مِنَ الْمُنْتَعِلِ وَلَيْسَ لِلنِّسَاءِ حَقٌّ وَسْطَ الطَّرِيقِ بَلْ جَوَانِبَهَا.»

وَالسُّنَّةُ لِمَنْ رَكِبَ الدَّابَّةَ أَنْ يَقُولَ: بِسْمِ اللهِ. اَلْحَمْدُ لِلهِ ﴿الَّذِي سَخَّرَ لَنَا هٰذَا وَمَا كُنَّا لَهُ مُقْرِنِينَ﴾ الْآيَتَيْنِ.

Glory be to You, I truly have oppressed myself and have committed evil, so forgive me. For truly, no one forgives sins except You. Praise be to God Who has carried us on the land and in the sea, Who has provided for us of the good things and Who has preferred us over much of what He has created, with [definite] preference. One should pronounce the *takbīr* three times, the *taḥmīd* three times, the *tasbīḥ* three times and the *tahlīl* once.

If one's [animal] stumbles one should say, *In the name of God*, and it is disliked for one to say, 'May you be destroyed, you Satan,' or, 'Curse you, you donkey,' or, 'May God disgrace you.'

The Messenger of God ﷺ prohibited hitting the faces of animals, branding them on the face[227] or their being used as chairs [for sitting on] on the road and in the markets. [He ﷺ prohibited] three people riding on one animal.[228] If two people are riding, then the owner of the animal has the right to [sit] at the front. He ﷺ ordered that loads be placed behind [the rider] so that the feet can sit [in the stirrups] and the hands can hold [the reins].

He ﷺ said, 'Were you to be forgiven for what you do to the beasts [that you own], then you would be much forgiven.'

[As for] any of one's animals, slaves or adolescent children that are behaving badly, one should recite in their ear, '*Is it other than the religion of God they seek...*'[229]

The Prophet ﷺ prohibited hitting the face of a servant, insulting them to their face or saying, 'May God disfigure your face and the face of those who look like you.' One should neither rush [one's servant] in their prayer, nor delay them from their food and drink. One should satisfy their appetite completely and one should sell

سُبْحَانَكَ إِنِّي ظَلَمْتُ نَفْسِي وَعَمِلْتُ سُوءاً فَاغْفِرْ لِي إِنَّهُ لَا يَغْفِرُ الذُّنُوبَ إِلَّا أَنْتَ. اَلْحَمْدُ لِلّٰهِ الَّذِي حَمَلَنَا فِي الْبَرِّ وَالْبَحْرِ وَرَزَقَنَا مِنَ الطَّيِّبَاتِ، وَفَضَّلَنَا عَلَى كَثِيرٍ مِمَّنْ خَلَقَ تَفْضِيلاً. وَيُكَبِّرُ ثَلَاثاً وَيُحَمِّدُ ثَلَاثاً وَيُسَبِّحُ ثَلَاثاً وَيُهَلِّلُ مَرَّةً.

فَإِذَا عَثَرَتْ، قَالَ: بِسْمِ اللّٰهِ. وَيُكْرَهُ أَنْ يَقُولَ: «تَعِسَ الشَّيْطَانُ» أَوْ «لُعِنَتْ يَا حِمَارُ» أَوْ «أَخْزَاكَ اللّٰهُ.»

وَنَهَى رَسُولُ اللّٰهِ ﷺ عَنْ ضَرْبِ وُجُوهِ الدَّوَابِّ وَوَسْمِهَا فِي الْوَجْهِ وَأَنْ تُتَّخَذَ كَرَاسِيَ فِي الطَّرِيقِ وَالْأَسْوَاقِ. وَأَنْ يَرْكَبَ ثَلَاثَةٌ عَلَى دَابَّةٍ. وَإِذَا رَكِبَ اثْنَانِ فَصَاحِبُ الدَّابَّةِ أَحَقُّ بِصَدْرِهَا. وَأَمَرَ بِتَأْخِيرِ الْحَمْلِ فَإِنَّ الرِّجْلَ مُوثَقَةٌ وَالْيَدُ مُعَلَّقَةٌ.

وَقَالَ: «لَوْ غُفِرَ لَكُمْ مَا تَأْتُونَ مِنَ الْبَهَائِمِ لَغُفِرَ لَكُمْ كَثِيراً.»

وَمَنْ سَاءَ خُلُقُهُ مِنَ الدَّوَابِّ وَالرَّقِيقِ وَالصِّبْيَانِ يَقْرَأُ فِي أُذُنِهِ: ﴿أَفَغَيْرَ دِينِ اللّٰهِ يَبْغُونَ﴾ اَلْآيَة.

وَنَهَى ﷺ عَنْ ضَرْبِ وَجْهِ الْخَادِمِ وَسَبِّ وَجْهِهِ وَأَنْ يَقُولَ: «مَسَخَ اللّٰهُ وَجْهَكَ وَوَجْهَ مَنْ يُشْبِهُكَ.» وَلَا يُعْجِلُهُ عَنْ صَلَاتِهِ وَلَا يُقِيمُهُ عَنْ طَعَامِهِ وَشَرَابِهِ. وَيُشْبِعُهُ كُلَّ الْإِشْبَاعِ وَيَبِيعُهُ إِذَا اسْتَبَاعَ. وَلَا يَقُولُ:

[one's slave] if they ask to be sold. One should not say, 'My male servant and my female servant,' but rather, 'My male youth and my female youth.' And the servant should not say, 'My lord and my lady,' but rather, 'My master and my mistress.'

The Prophet ﷺ said, 'Whoever is pleased when a person walks behind them while they are riding is increased in nothing but distance from God.'

He ﷺ [also] said, 'If one of you strikes their servant and remembers God, then do not lay hands on him.'

It is *Sunna* to call an individual by the names that are most beloved to them and to refer to them by it. If one calls to someone they do not know, they should say, 'O ʿAbd Allāh,' or, 'O son of ʿAbd Allāh.'

One should never insult anyone, but if it is absolutely necessary, one should restrict oneself to something like the words, 'Truly you are miserly, or, cowardly, or, always sleeping, or, a liar.'[230]

The Messenger of God ﷺ prohibited arguing, quarrelling, telling witty stories that men tell and mentioning them (unless it is done with goodness) and cursing the night, day, sun, moon, the planet Mars, the wind, roosters and fleas. [He ﷺ also prohibited] one from saying, 'I feel bad,' if one is nauseous; instead, one should say, 'I feel upset.'

He ﷺ prohibited referring to grapes as *karam*; instead, one should say *ʿinab* [another name for grapes], and gardens of *aʿnāb* [the plural form].[231]

«عَبْدِي وَأَمَتِي» بَلْ يَقُولُ: «فَتَايَ وَفَتَاتِي.» وَلَا يَقُولُ الـمَمْلُوكُ: «رَبِّي وَرَبَّتِي» بَلْ «سَيِّدِي وَسَيِّدَتِي.»

وَقَالَ ﷺ: «مَنْ سَعَى خَلْفَهُ إِنْسَانٌ وَهُوَ رَاكِبٌ لَمْ يَزْدَدْ مِنَ اللهِ إِلَّا بُعْداً.»

وَقَالَ: «إِذَا ضَرَبَ أَحَدُكُمْ خَادِمَهُ فَذَكَرَ اللهَ فَارْفَعُوا أَيْدِيَكُمْ عَنْهُ.»

وَالسُّنَّةُ أَنْ يُدْعَى الرَّجُلُ بِأَحَبِّ أَسْمَائِهِ وَكُنَاهُ إِلَيْهِ. وَإِذَا دَعَا مَنْ لَا يَعْرِفُ، قَالَ: «يَاعَبْدَ اللهِ» أَوْ «يَا ابْنَ عَبْدِ اللهِ.»

وَأَنْ لَا يَسُبَّ أَحداً فَإِنْ كَانَ وَلَا بُدَّ فَلْيَقْتَصِرْ عَلَى مِثْلِ قَوْلٍ: «إِنَّكَ بَخِيلٌ» أَوْ «جُبَانٌ» أَوْ «نَئُومٌ» أَوْ «كَذُوبٌ.»

وَنَهَى رَسُولُ اللهِ ﷺ عَنِ الْجِدَالِ وَالْمُمَارَاةِ وَمُلَاحَاةِ الرِّجَالِ وَذِكْرِهِمْ إِلَّا بِخَيْرٍ، وَسَبِّ اللَّيْلِ وَالنَّهَارِ وَالشَّمْسِ وَالْقَمَرِ وَالمِرِّيخِ وَالرِّيحِ وَالدِّيكِ وَالْبَرْغُوثِ. وَأَنْ يَقُولَ إِنْ حَصَلَ لَهُ غِثْيَانٌ: «خَبُثَتْ نَفْسِي» وَلْيَقُلْ: «لَقِسَتْ نَفْسِي.»

وَأَنْ يَقُولَ لِلْعِنَبِ: «اَلْكَرَم» بَلْ يَقُولُ: «اَلْعِنَبُ» وَحَدَائِقُ «الْأَعْنَابُ.»

[He ﷺ also prohibited] saying, 'I grew [such-and-such a crop]', and instead one should say, 'I cultivated'; and not, 'What God wills and what so-and-so wills', but rather, 'What God wills', and then, 'What so-and-so wills'.

[He ﷺ also prohibited] saying, 'I am your ransom', or, 'May my mother and father be a ransom for you', but rather, that is said exclusively to the Prophet [232].ﷺ

[He ﷺ also prohibited] saying, 'Blessed morning,' or, 'May God's blessings be through you.'[233]

Nor should one say to a newly-wed person, 'Live in harmony and beget sons,' as was said during the Age of Ignorance (*Jāhiliyya*); instead, it should be said to them, *May God bless you, may God's blessings be upon you and may He join you two in goodness.*

He ﷺ prohibited speaking about the intimacy that occurs between spouses, boasting about intimacy. [He ﷺ also prohibited] two people whispering while a third person is with them, because it would distress them.[234]

The *Sunna* for someone who is angry while standing is to sit. If their anger subsides, [then good]; if not, let them lie down, or be silent and say, *I seek refuge in God from Satan the accursed*, and perform the ablution (*wuḍū'*).

It is *Sunna* for one who spits out phlegm to hide their phlegm [in the dirt] in order for it not to touch the skin of a believer, or their clothes. One should not spit to one's right but to one's left, if no one is there; otherwise below one's feet.

وَأَنْ يَقُولَ: «زَرَعْتُ» بَلْ: «حَرَثْتُ.» وَأَنْ يَقُولَ: «مَا شَاءَ اللّٰهُ وَشَاءَ فُلَانٌ» بَلْ يَقُولُ ثُمَّ «شَاءَ فُلَانٌ.»

وَأَنْ يَقُولَ: «جَعَلْتُ فِدَاكَ» أَوْ «فِدَاكَ أَبِي وَأُمِّي» وَإِنَّمَا يُقَالُ ذٰلِكَ لِلنَّبِيِّ ﷺ خَاصَّةً.

وَأَنْ يَقُولَ: «أَنْعِمْ صَبَاحاً» «وَأَنْعَمَ اللّٰهُ بِكَ.»

وَلَا لِلْمُتَزَوِّجِ: «بِالرِّفَاءِ وَالْبَنِينَ» كَمَا كَانَ فِي الْجَاهِلِيَّةِ أَيْضاً بَلْ يُقَالُ لَهُ: «بَارَكَ اللّٰهُ لَكَ وَبَارَكَ عَلَيْكَ وَجَمَعَ بَيْنَكُمَا فِي خَيْرٍ.»

وَنَهَى ﷺ عَنِ التَّحَدُّثِ بِمَا يَجْرِي بَيْنَ الزَّوْجَيْنِ فِي الْجِمَاعِ وَعَنِ الْمُفَاخَرَةِ فِي الْجِمَاعِ وَعَنْ تَنَاجِي اِثْنَيْنِ وَمَعَهُمَا ثَالِثٌ مِنْ أَجْلِ أَنَّهُ يُحْزِنُهُ.

وَالسُّنَّةُ لِمَنْ غَضِبَ وَهُوَ قَائِمٌ أَنْ يَجْلِسَ. فَإِنْ ذَهَبَ عَنْهُ الْغَضَبُ وَإِلَّا فَلْيَضْطَجِعْ أَوْ يَسْكُتْ وَيَقُولُ: أَعُوذُ بِاللهِ مِنَ الشَّيْطَانِ الرَّجِيمِ، وَيَتَوَضَّأُ.

وَالسُّنَّةُ لِمَنْ يَتَنَخَّمُ أَنْ يَغِيبَ نُخَامَتَهُ لِئَلَّا تُصِيبَ جِلْدَ مُؤْمِنٍ أَوْ ثَوْبَهُ. وَأَنْ لَا يَبْصُقَ عَنْ يَمِينِهِ بَلْ عَنْ يَسَارِهِ إِنْ كَانَ فَارِغاً وَإِلَّا تَحْتَ قَدَمَيْهِ.

The Prophet ﷺ used to dislike seeing an individual raise their voice loudly and preferred seeing them use a lowered voice.

The *Sunna* for whoever loves another is to inform them.

The *Sunna* for whoever is writing is to begin by [introducing] themselves and declaring God's transcendence—for this is the most successful [way]—and nobility is the [true] seal of a letter. Responding to a letter is a duty; in the same way as returning a greeting [is a duty].

The *Sunna* for whoever sneezes is to cover their face with their hand or garment to muffle the sound, and say, *Praise be to God, Lord of the worlds in every state*. It is said to [the one who sneezed], *May God show you mercy*, and they should reply, *May God forgive you and me*, or, *May God guide you and make good your condition*. The one who hears the sneeze should initiate it by saying, *Praise be to God*. If one sneezes when one is on one's own, then say, *Praise be to God, may God forgive me*, for truly the angels who are with them shall offer a prayer for the one who sneezed.

The *Sunna* for whoever sees something that pleases him from another is to supplicate for blessings (*baraka*) for them and to say, *What God wills; there is no power save in God*. If he afflicts him with the evil eye, he is compelled to take a purificatory bath (*ghusl*). A bowl of water should be brought; one should lower one's hand into the bowl, gargle and spit [the water] out into the bowl and wash one's face from the bowl. Then one should pour water with one's left hand upon one's right; then, with one's right hand upon one's left. Then one lowers one's left hand into the bowl and pours water on the right elbow; then with the right hand one pours it on one's

وَكَانَ ﷺ يَكْرَهُ أَنْ يَرَى الرَّجُلَ جَهِيراً رَفِيعَ الصَّوْتِ وَيُحِبُّ أَنْ يَرَاهُ خَفِيضَ الصَّوْتِ.

وَالسُّنَّةُ لِمَنْ أَحَبَّ أَحَداً أَنْ يُعْلِمَهُ.

وَالسُّنَّةُ لِمَنْ كَتَبَ أَنْ يَبْدَأَ بِنَفْسِهِ وَبِتَنْزِيهِ اللهِ فَهُوَ أَنْجَحُ وَكَرَامَةُ الْكِتَابِ خَتْمُهُ. وَجَوَابُ الْكِتَابِ حَقٌّ كَرَدِّ السَّلَامِ.

وَالسُّنَّةُ لِمَنْ عَطَسَ أَنْ يُغَطِّيَ وَجْهَهُ بِيَدِهِ أَوْ ثَوْبِهِ وَيُخَفِّضُ صَوْتَهُ وَيَقُولُ: اَلْحَمْدُ لِلّٰهِ رَبِّ الْعَالَمِينَ عَلَى كُلِّ حَالٍ. وَيُقَالُ لَهُ: يَرْحَمُكَ اللهُ. وَيَقُولُ هُوَ: يَغْفِرُ اللهُ لِي وَلَكُمْ أَوْ يَهْدِيكُمُ اللهُ وَيُصْلِحُ بَالَكُمْ. وَيَبْدَؤُهُ السَّامِعُ بِالْحَمْدِ. وَإِذَا عَطَسَ وَحْدَهُ يَقُولُ: اَلْحَمْدُ لِلّٰهِ يَغْفِرُ اللهُ لِي، فَإِنَّ الْمَلَائِكَةَ الَّذِينَ مَعَهُ يُشَمِّتُونَهُ.

وَالسُّنَّةُ لِمَنْ رَأَى مِنْ أَحَدٍ مَا يُعْجِبُهُ أَنْ يَدْعُوَ لَهُ بِالْبَرَكَةِ وَأَنْ يَقُولَ: مَا شَاءَ اللهُ، لَا قُوَّةَ إِلَّا بِاللهِ. فَإِذَا أَصَابَهُ بِالْعَيْنِ جُبِرَ عَلَى الْاِغْتِسَالِ. فَيُؤْتَى بِقَدَحٍ مِنْ مَاءٍ فَيَدْخُلُ يَدَهُ فِي الْقَدْحِ فَيَتَمَضْمَضُ وَيَمُجُّهُ فِي الْقَدْحِ وَيَغْسِلُ وَجْهَهُ فِي الْقَدْحِ. ثُمَّ يَصُبُّ بِيَدِهِ الْيُسْرَى عَلَى كَفِّهِ الْيُمْنَى ثُمَّ بِكَفِّهِ الْيُمْنَى عَلَى كَفِّهِ الْيُسْرَى. ثُمَّ يَدْخُلُ يَدَهُ الْيُسْرَى فَيَصُبُّ عَلَى مِرْفَقِ يَدِهِ الْيُمْنِ

left elbow. Then one washes the right foot, then the left. Then one should wash one's two knees, then beneath one's loincloth. Then one pours water on one's head in one go, and one should not put the bowl down until it is empty. One should turn over the bowl for whoever comes afterwards.

It is *Sunna* to clean houses, the courtyards of dwellings and to remove the refuse from them, for truly God (Exalted is He) is pure and loves cleanliness, and [refuse] is the seat of evil spirits. One should not wipe the house with a napkin used for the face, for it is used to sleep on.

Whoever is satiated with [food] that they were not given is like someone donning two wrongfully-gained garments.

Whoever listens to a conversation [between] people who do not wish [to be overheard] shall have boiling lead poured into their ears [on the Day of Resurrection].

It is not permitted for anyone to take the goods of one's friend, or of a neighbour, even if it were [only] a staff. [It is not permitted] to frighten a Muslim.

It is desirable (*mustaḥabb*) to kill scorpions, venomous lizards and snakes after they have been notified.[235] If they are seen in a dwelling, it should be said to them, *I ask you by the covenant of Noah and Solomon son of David*, and [the] owner should say, *Leave! By God and the Last Day, you must not appear to us again or harm us.*[236]

The *Sunna* for whoever boards a ship is to say, '*In the name of God be its course and its anchorage...*'[237] [to the end of] the verse, and, '*They did not afford God His due respect...*'[238]

ثُمَّ بِيَدِهِ الْيُمْنَى عَلَى مِرْفَقِ يَدِهِ الْيُسْرَى. ثُمَّ يَغْسِلُ قَدَمَهُ الْيُمْنَى ثُمَّ قَدَمَهُ الْيُسْرَى. ثُمَّ يَغْسِلُ رُكْبَتَيْهِ ثُمَّ دَاخِلَ إِزَارِهِ. ثُمَّ يَصُبُّ عَلَى رَأْسِهِ صُبَّةً وَاحِدَةً وَلَا يَضَعُ الْقِدْحَ حَتَّى يَفْرُغَ. وَيَكْفِئُ الْإِنَاءَ مَنْ خَلْفَهُ.

وَالسُّنَّةُ تَنْظِيفُ الْبُيُوتِ وَأَفْنِيَةُ الدُّورِ وَإِخْرَاجُ الْقُمَامَاتِ مِنْهَا فَإِنَّ اللهَ تَعَالَى نَظِيفٌ يُحِبُّ النَّظَافَةَ، وَهِيَ مَقْعَدُ الشَّيَاطِينِ. وَلَا يَكْنِسُ بِمِنْدِيلِ الْفَمِ فِي الْبَيْتِ فَإِنَّهُ مَضْجِعُهُ.

وَالـمُتَشَبِّعُ بِمَا لَمْ يُعْطَ كَلَابِسِ ثَوْبَيْ زُورٍ.

وَمَنِ اسْتَمَعَ إِلَى حَدِيثِ قَوْمٍ يَكْرَهُونَهُ، صُبَّ فِي أُذُنَيْهِ الْآنُكُ.

وَلَا يَحِلُّ لِأَحَدٍ أَنْ يَأْخُذَ مَتَاعَ صَاحِبِهِ وَلَوْ عَصاً وَلَا جَارٍ. وَأَنْ لَا يُرَوِّعَ مُسْلِماً.

وَيُسْتَحَبُّ قَتْلُ الْعَقْرَبِ وَالْوَزَغِ وَالْحَيَّةِ بَعْدَ أَنْ تُؤْذَنَ. وَيُقَالُ لَهَا إِذَا ظَهَرَتْ فِي الْمَسْكَنِ: أَسْأَلُكَ بِعَهْدِ نُوحٍ وَسُلَيْمَانَ بْنِ دَاوُدَ. وَقَالَ مَالِكٌ: أُخْرُجْ عَلَيْكَ بِاللهِ وَالْيَوْمِ الْآخِرِ أَنْ لَا تَبْدُوا لَنَا وَلَا تُؤْذُونَا.

وَالسُّنَّةُ لِمَنْ رَكِبَ السَّفِينَةَ أَنْ يَقُولَ: ﴿بِسْمِ اللهِ مَجْرَاهَا وَمُرْسَاهَا﴾ اَلْآيَة، ﴿وَمَا قَدَرُوا اللهَ حَقَّ قَدْرِهِ﴾ اَلْآيَة.

It is prohibited to travel by sea when it is rough. An individual should not look at their shadow in the water.

The *Sunna* when one returns to one's house at the end of the day is to give a greeting when one reaches the door of one's abode, for truly it repels the demon (*qarīn*) that is with one. Then one gives a greeting when one enters, for truly it expels the evil spirits from the inhabitants [of the house]. So one should say: *Peace be upon us from our Lord. Blessed greetings and pure prayers be to God. Peace be upon you*. One should say: *In the name of God. O God, truly I ask You for a goodly entrance and for a goodly exit. In the name of God we have entered, in the name of God we have exited and in God we have placed our trust. Praise be to God Who has fed me and given me drink. Praise be to God Who has bestowed un-repayable favours upon me. I ask you to save me from Hellfire.*[T] One should recite *Sūrat al-Ikhlāṣ*[239] and the *Āyat al-Kursī* (the 'Throne Verse').[240] If one enters an empty house, one should say, *In the name of God. Praise be to God. Peace be upon us and upon the righteous servants of God*.

وَيَنْهَى عَنْ رُكُوبِ الْبَحْرِ عِنْدَ ارْتِجَاجِهِ وَأَنْ يَنْظُرَ الرَّجُلُ إِلَى ظِلِّهِ فِي الْمَاءِ.

وَالسُّنَّةُ إِذَا رَجَعَ آخِرَ النَّهَارِ إِلَى بَيْتِهِ أَنْ يُسَلِّمَ إِذَا بَلَغَ بَابَ حُجْرَتِهِ فَإِنَّهُ يُرَجِّعُ قَرِينَهُ الَّذِي مَعَهُ. ثُمَّ يُسَلِّمُ إِذَا دَخَلَ فَإِنَّهُ يُخَرِّجُ سَاكِنَهَا مِنَ الشَّيَاطِينِ. فَيَقُولُ: اَلسَّلَامُ عَلَيْنَا مِنْ رَبِّنَا. اَلتَّحِيَّاتُ الطَّيِّبَاتُ الْمُبَارَكَاتُ لِلّٰهِ. سَلَامٌ عَلَيْكُمْ. وَيَقُولُ: بِسْمِ اللهِ. اَللّٰهُمَّ إِنِّي أَسْأَلُكَ خَيْرَ الْمَوْلَجِ وَخَيْرَ الْمَخْرَجِ. بِسْمِ اللهِ وَلَجْنَا وَبِسْمِ اللهِ خَرَجْنَا وَعَلَى اللهِ تَوَكَّلْنَا. اَلْحَمْدُ لِلّٰهِ الَّذِي أَطْعَمَنِي وَسَقَانِي. وَالْحَمْدُ لِلّٰهِ الَّذِي مَنَّ عَلَيَّ. أَسْأَلُكَ أَنْ تُجِيرَنِي مِنَ النَّارِ. وَيَقْرَأُ سُورَةَ الْإِخْلَاصِ وَآيَةَ الْكُرْسِيِّ. فَإِذَا دَخَلَ بَيْتاً خَالِياً قَالَ: بِسْمِ اللهِ. وَالْحَمْدُ لِلّٰهِ. اَلسَّلَامُ عَلَيْنَا وَعَلَى عِبَادِ اللهِ الصَّالِحِينَ.

INVOCATIONS DURING TIMES OF NEED

At times of distress it is said: *There is no god but God Almighty, Lord of the almighty Throne. There is no god but God, Lord of the heavens, Lord of the earths and Lord of the generous Throne. There is no god but God, the Indulgent, the Generous. Glory be to God, Most Holy God, Lord of the almighty Throne. Praise be to God, Lord of the worlds. O Living, O Self-Subsisting, through Your mercy I desperately seek help. O God, it is Your mercy [that] I hope for, so do not leave me to myself for [even] the blink of an eye. Rectify for me all of my affairs. There is no god but You, my Lord; I do not associate [any partner] with You. There is no god but You. Glory be to You; truly I am one of the wrongdoers. I have placed my trust in the Living, Who does not die. Praise be to God Who has not taken a son, Who has no partner in sovereignty and Who has no helper from the mundane, so magnify Him greatly.*[U] One should recite the *Āyat al-Kursī* (the 'Throne Verse')[241] and the end of [*Sūrat*] *al-Baqara*.[242]

At times of worry and sadness it is said: *O God, I am Your servant, the son of Your male servant and the son of Your female servant; I am in Your grasp, my forelock is in Your Hand. Your judgement is exercised in me and Your Divine Decree over me is just. I ask You—in every name of Yours with which You have named Yourself, sent down in Your Book, taught to anyone amongst Your creation or which You have taken unto Yourself in knowledge of the unseen—that You make the magnificent Qur'ān the light of my sight, light of my breast, spring of my heart, eliminator of my sorrow and remover of my worries. There [was] no god but God before everything; there [shall be] no god but God after everything. There is no god but God; Our Lord abides and everything else perishes. There is no power and no might save in God.*

أَذْكَارُ أُمُورٍ عَارِضَةٍ

يُقَالُ عِنْدَ الْكَرْبِ: لَا إِلٰهَ إِلَّا اللّٰهُ الْعَظِيمُ رَبُّ الْعَرْشِ الْعَظِيمِ. لَا إِلٰهَ إِلَّا اللّٰهُ رَبُّ السَّمَوَاتِ وَرَبُّ الْأَرْضِينَ وَرَبُّ الْعَرْشِ الْكَرِيمِ. لَا إِلٰهَ إِلَّا اللّٰهُ الْحَلِيمُ الْكَرِيمُ. سُبْحَانَ اللهِ وَتَبَارَكَ اللّٰهُ رَبُّ الْعَرْشِ الْعَظِيمِ. وَالْحَمْدُ لِلّٰهِ رَبِّ الْعَالَمِينَ. يَا حَيُّ يَا قَيُّومُ بِرَحْمَتِكَ أَسْتَغِيثُ. اَللّٰهُمَّ رَحْمَتَكَ أَرْجُو فَلَا تَكِلْنِي إِلَى نَفْسِي طَرْفَةَ عَيْنٍ. وَأَصْلِحْ لِي شَأْنِي كُلَّهُ. لَا إِلٰهَ إِلَّا أَنْتَ رَبِّيْ، لَا أُشْرِكُ بِكَ شَيْئاً. لَا إِلٰهَ إِلَّا أَنْتَ سُبْحَانَكَ إِنِّي كُنْتُ مِنَ الظَّالِمِينَ. تَوَكَّلْتُ عَلَى الْحَيِّ الَّذِي لَا يَمُوتُ. وَالْحَمْدُ لِلّٰهِ الَّذِي لَمْ يَتَّخِذْ وَلَداً وَلَمْ يَكُنْ لَهُ شَرِيكٌ فِي الْمُلْكِ وَلَمْ يَكُنْ لَهُ وَلِيٌّ مِنَ الذُّلِّ، وَكَبِّرْهُ تَكْبِيراً. وَيَقْرَأُ آيَةَ الْكُرْسِيِّ بِخَوَاتِيمِ الْبَقَرَةِ.

وَيُقَالُ عِنْدَ الْهَمِّ وَالْحُزْنِ: اَللّٰهُمَّ إِنِّي عَبْدُكَ، ابْنُ عَبْدِكَ، ابْنُ أَمَتِكَ فِي قَبْضَتِكَ، نَاصِيَتِي بِيَدِكَ. مَاضٍ فِيَّ حُكْمُكَ عَدْلٌ فِيَّ قَضَاؤُكَ. أَسْأَلُكَ بِكُلِّ اسْمٍ هُوَ لَكَ سَمَّيْتَ بِهِ نَفْسَكَ أَوْ أَنْزَلْتَهُ فِي كِتَابِكَ أَوْ عَلَّمْتَهُ أَحَداً مِنْ خَلْقِكَ أَوِ اسْتَأْثَرْتَ بِهِ فِي عِلْمِ الْغَيْبِ عِنْدَكَ أَنْ تَجْعَلَ الْقُرْآنَ الْعَظِيمَ نُورَ بَصَرِي وَنُورَ صَدْرِي وَرَبِيعَ قَلْبِي وَجَلَاءَ حُزْنِي وَذَهَابَ هَمِّي. لَا إِلٰهَ إِلَّا اللّٰهُ قَبْلَ كُلِّ شَيْءٍ، لَا إِلٰهَ إِلَّا اللّٰهُ بَعْدَ كُلِّ شَيْءٍ. لَا إِلٰهَ إِلَّا اللّٰهُ، يَبْقَى رَبُّنَا وَيَفْنَى كُلُّ شَيْءٍ. لَا حَوْلَ وَلَا قُوَّةَ إِلَّا بِاللّٰهِ.

At times of loneliness it is said: *I seek refuge in the perfect Words of God from His anger, from His punishment, from the evil of His servants and from the whisperings of evil spirits lest they be present. Glory be to the Lord of sovereignty and power. Lord of the angels and the spirit. You have enveloped the heavens and the earth with honour and force.*

Upon [experiencing] satanic whisperings about belief, it is said: *He is the First, the Last, the Manifest, the Hidden and He has knowledge of all things. God is most Great. God is most Great. God is most Great. God is most Great.*

Upon seeing someone who is afflicted with some tribulation, it is said: *Praise be to God, Who has protected me from that with which he has afflicted you and Who has preferred me over much of what He has created, with [definite] preference.* It is disliked *(makrūh)* for the person who is afflicted to be made to hear [someone else's] seeking refuge in God from their tribulation.

During illness it is said: *There is no god but God. God is most Great. There is no god but God. To Him is the Dominion and to Him is all Praise. There is no god but God. There is no power and no might save in God. He gives life and He gives death. He is Living; He does not die. Glory be to God, Lord of the servants, Lord of the lands. Abundant, pure and blessed praise be to God in every situation. God is utterly the Greatest. O our Lord. His majesty and His power are in every place. O God, if you have caused an illness to befall me in order to take my soul during this sickness of mine, then place my soul amongst the souls of those for whom You have already decreed goodness, and distance me from Hellfire just as You distanced those for whom You have already decreed goodness. O God, if You have decreed death for me in it, forgive me, rid me of my sins and make me reside in the Garden of Eden* (Jannat ʿAdn). *There is no god but God, the Indulgent, the Generous. Glory be to God, blessed be God, Lord of the almighty Throne. Praise be to God, Lord of the worlds. O God, truly I ask You to hasten Your bestowal of well-being, [I ask You] for patience [in the face of] Your tribulation and to depart from the world towards Your mercy.*[V]

وِيُقَالُ عِنْدَ الْوَحْشَةِ: أَعُوذُ بِكَلِمَاتِ اللهِ التَّامَّاتِ مِنْ غَضَبِهِ وَعِقَابِهِ وَشَرِّ عِبَادِهِ وَمِنْ هَمَزَاتِ الشَّيَاطِينِ وَأَنْ يَحْضُرُونَ. سُبْحَانَ ذِي الْمُلْكِ وَالْقُدْرَةِ، رَبُّ الْمَلَائِكَةِ وَالرُّوحِ. جَلَّلْتَ السَّمٰوَاتِ وَالْأَرْضَ بِالْعِزِّ وَالْجَبَرُوتِ.

وَيقَالُ عِنْدَ الْوَسْوَسَةِ فِي الْإِيمَانِ: هُوَ الْأَوَّلُ وَالْآخِرُ وَالظَّاهِرُ وَالْبَاطِنُ وَهُوَ بِكُلِّ شَيْءٍ عَلِيمٌ. اَللّٰهُ أَكْبَرُ. اللّٰهُ أَكْبَرُ. اللّٰهُ أَكْبَرُ. اَللّٰهُ أَكْبَرُ.

وَيُقَالُ عِنْدَ رُؤْيَةِ مُبْتَلَي: اَلْحَمْدُ لِلّٰهِ الَّذِي عَافَانِي مِمَّا ابْتَلَاكَ بِهِ وَفَضَّلَنِي عَلَى كَثِيرٍ مِمَّا خَلَقَ تَفْضِيلاً. وَيُكْرَهُ أَنْ يَسْمَعَ الْمُبْتَلِي اَلتَّعَوُّذَ مِنَ الْبَلَاءِ.

وَ يُقَالُ فِي الْمَرَضِ: لَا إِلٰهَ إِلَّا اللّٰهُ وَاللّٰهُ أَكْبَرُ. لَا إِلٰهَ إِلَّا اللّٰهُ لَهُ الْمُلْكُ وَلَهُ الْحَمْدُ. لَا إِلٰهَ إِلَّا اللّٰهُ وَلَا حَوْلَ وَلَا قُوَّةَ إِلَا بِاللّٰهِ. يُحْيِي وَيُمِيتُ وَهُوَ حَيٌّ لَا يَمُوتُ. سُبْحَانَ اللهِ رَبِّ الْعِبَادِ وَرَبِّ الْبِلَادِ. اَلْحَمْدُ لِلّٰهِ حَمْداً كَثِيراً طَيِّباً مُبَارَكاً عَلَى كُلِّ حَالٍ. اَللّٰهُ أَكْبَرُ كَبِيراً. يَا رَبَّنَا، وَجَلَالُهُ وَقُدْرَتُهُ فِي كُلِّ مَكَانٍ. اَللّٰهُمَّ إِنْ كُنْتَ أَمْرَضْتَنِي لِتَقْبِضَ رُوحِي فِي مَرَضِي هٰذا فَاجْعَلْ رُوحِي فِي أَرْوَاحِ مَنْ سَبَقَتْ لَهُمْ مِنْكَ الْحُسْنَى وَبَاعِدْنِي مِنَ النَّارِ كَمَا بَاعَدْتَ أُولٰئِكَ الَّذِينَ سَبَقَتْ لَهُمْ مِنْكَ الْحُسْنَى. اَللّٰهُمَّ إِنْ كُنْتَ كَتَبْتَ عَلَيَّ فِيهِ الْمَوْتَ فَاغْفِرْ لِي وَأَخْرِجْنِي مِنْ ذُنُوبِي وَأَسْكِنِّي جَنَّةَ عَدْنٍ. لَا إِلٰهَ إِلَّا اللّٰهُ الْحَلِيمُ الْكَرِيمُ. سُبْحَانَ اللهِ وَتَبَارَكَ اللّٰهُ رَبُّ الْعَرْشِ الْعَظِيمِ. وَالْحَمْدُ لِلّٰهِ رَبِّ الْعَالَمِينَ. اَللّٰهُمَّ إِنِّي أَسْأَلُكَ تَعْجِيلَ عَافِيَتِكَ وَصَبْراً عَلَى بَلَائِكَ وَخُرُوجاً مِنَ الدُّنْيَا إِلَى رَحْمَتِكَ.

One should recite the *Fātiḥa*[243] and the *mu'awwadhāt*,[244] [then] spit [without saliva] on one's hands and then wipe one's face and say, *There is no god besides You, glory be to You; truly I have been one of the wrongdoers*, forty times.

Upon the place of pain it is said seven times: *In the name of God, in the name of God, in the name of God. I seek refuge in God, His might and His power from the evil that I find, and of which I am cautious.*

During a fever it is said: *In the name of God, the Great. We seek refuge in God Almighty from the evil of everything that is repulsive and from the evil of the heat of Hellfire. O God, show mercy to my brittle bones and my soft skin. I seek refuge in You from the intensity of the Inferno. O mother of Mildam,*[245] *if I have believed in God and the Last Day, then do not consume my flesh, do not devour my blood, do not gouge my mouth, do not split my head and do not group me with those who claim that there is another god with God, because truly I bear witness that there is no god but God and that Muḥammad is His servant and His messenger. O Living, O Self-Subsisting, through Your mercy I desperately seek aid. Rectify for me all of my affairs, do not leave me to myself for [even] the blink of an eye or to anyone amongst people.*

It is disliked (*makrūh*) to insult the fever, to wish for death because of the harm that has descended upon one, as a temptation in religion. If the wish [to die] is overwhelming, let him say, *O God, grant me life, as long as You know life is better for me, or give me death, if death would be better for me.*

When one is dying, say: *Praise be to God, there is no god but God; God is most Great, there is no power and no might save in God. O God, truly You take out the soul from between the sinews and the finger joints. O God, aid me in death and make it easy for me.* One should recite *Sūrat al-Ikhlāṣ*.[246]

وَيَقْرَأُ الْفَاتِحَةَ وَالْمُعَوِّذَاتِ وَيَنْفُثُ عَلَى يَدَيْهِ ثُمَّ يَمْسَحُ بِهِمَا وَجْهَهُ وَيَقُولُ: لَا إِلٰهَ إِلَّا أَنْتَ سُبْحَانَكَ. إِنِّي كُنْتُ مِنَ الظَّالِمِينَ (أَرْبَعِينَ مَرَّةً).

وَيُقَالُ عَلَى مَوْضِعِ الْأَلَمِ: بِسْمِ اللّٰهِ، بِسْمِ اللّٰهِ، بِسْمِ اللّٰهِ. أَعُوذُ بِاللّٰهِ وَعِزَّتِهِ وَقُدْرَتِهِ مِنْ شَرِّ مَا أَجِدُ وَأُحَاذِرُ (سَبْعاً).

وَ يُقَالُ فِي الْحُمَى: بِسْمِ اللّٰهِ الْكَبِيرِ. نَعُوذُ بِاللّٰهِ الْعَظِيمِ مِنْ شَرِّ كُلِّ نَفَّارٍ وَمِنْ شَرِّ حَرِّ النَّارِ. اَللّٰهُمَّ ارْحَمْ عَظْمِيَ الدَّقِيقَ وَجِلْدِيَ الرَّقِيقَ. وَأَعُوذُ بِكَ مِنْ قُوَّةِ الْحَرِيقِ. يَا أُمَّ مِلْدَمٍ إِنْ كُنْتِ آمَنْتِ بِاللّٰهِ وَالْيَوْمِ الْآخِرِ فَلَا تَأْكُلِي اللَّحْمَ وَلَا تَشْرَبِي الدَّمَ وَلَا تَفَوَّرِي عَلَى الْفَمِ وَلَا تَصْدَعِي الرَّأْسَ وَانْتَقِلِي إِلَى مَنْ زَعَمَ مَعَ اللّٰهِ إِلٰهاً آخَرَ، فَإِنِّي أَشْهَدُ أَنْ لَا إِلٰهَ إِلَّا اللّٰهُ وَأَنَّ مُحَمَّداً عَبْدُهُ وَرَسُولُهُ. يَا حَيُّ يَا قَيُّومُ بِرَحْمَتِكَ أَسْتَغِيثُ. أَصْلِحْ لِي شَأْنِي كُلَّهُ وَلَا تَكِلْنِي إِلَى نَفْسِي طَرْفَةَ عَيْنٍ وَلَا إِلَى أَحَدٍ مِنَ النَّاسِ.

وَيُكْرَهُ سَبُّ الْحُمَى وَتَمَنِّيَ الْمَوْتِ لِضُرٍّ نَزَلَ بِهِ لَا لِفِتْنَةِ دِينٍ. فَإِنْ كَانَ لَا بُدَّ مُتَمَنِّياً فَلْيَقُلْ: اَللّٰهَ أَحْيِنِي مَا رَأَيْتَ الْحَيَاةَ خَيْراً لِي وَتَوَفَّنِي إِذَا كَانَتِ الْوَفَاةُ خَيْراً لِي.

وَيُقَالُ فِي النَّزَعِ: اَلْحَمْدُ لِلّٰهِ، لَا إِلٰهَ إِلَّا اللّٰهُ وَاللّٰهُ أَكْبَرُ وَلَا حَوْلَ وَلَا قُوَّةَ إِلَّا بِاللّٰهِ. اَللّٰهُمَّ إِنَّكَ تَأْخُذُ الرُّوحَ مِنْ بَيْنِ الْعَصَبِ وَالْأَنَامِلِ. اَللّٰهُمَّ فَأَعِنِّي عَلَى الْمَوْتِ وَهَوِّنْهُ عَلَيَّ. وَيَقْرَأُ سُورَةَ الْإِخْلَاصِ.

It is *Sunna* to say if one has a difficult livelihood: *[I invoke] the name of God upon myself, my wealth and my religion. O God, make me satisfied with Your decree, and bless me in what You have apportioned for me so that I do not love delaying what you have hastened, or hastening what You have delayed.*

When provisions are slow to come by, it is said, *O God, truly I ask You from Your bounty because no one controls it except You*, and one should say abundantly, *There is no power and no might save in God.*

If an affair becomes difficult, one should say, *O God, there is no ease except what You have made easy; may you make sadness easy—if You so will.*

And if an affair overwhelms one, say: *God has decreed, and that which He wills is done. God is sufficient for me and what a blessed Trustee.*

If an affair worries one, say, *Glory be to God Almighty.*

If debt overwhelms one, say: *O God, through what You have made lawful* (ḥalāl), *spare me from what You have made unlawful* (ḥarām). *Through Your bounty, make me independent of all besides You. O God, reliever of worry, remover of distress, answerer of the call of one in need, Most Compassionate of this world and the Hereafter, and the Most Merciful of them both. You show mercy to me, so show mercy to me with a mercy that makes me independent of all besides You. 'King of All Sovereignty, You give sovereignty to whom You will and You take sovereignty away from whom You will…'* [Recite this] to His Words, '*…without account.*'[247] *O Most Compassionate of this world and the Hereafter and Most Merciful of them both. You give to whom You please in them*[248] *and withhold from whom You please in them. Repay my debt and have mercy upon me, a mercy that makes me independent of the mercy of all besides You.*

وَيُسَنُّ أَنْ يُقَالَ عِنْدَ تَعَذُّرِ الْمَعِيشَةِ: بِسْمِ اللهِ عَلَى نَفْسِي وَمَالِي وَدِينِي. اَللّٰهُمَّ ارْضِنِي بِقَضَائِكَ وَبَارِكْ لِي فِيمَا قُدِّرَ لِي حَتَّى لَا أُحِبَّ تَأْخِيرَ مَا عَجَّلْتَ وَلَا تَعْجِيلَ مَا أَخَّرْتَ.

وَيُقَالُ عِنْدَ اِسْتِبْطَاءِ الرِّزْقِ: اَللّٰهُمَّ إِنِّي أَسْأَلُكَ مِنْ فَضْلِكَ فَإِنَّهُ لَا يَمْلِكُهُ إِلَّا أَنْتَ. وَيُكْثِرُ مِنْ: لَا حَوْلَ وَلَا قُوَّةَ إِلَّا بِاللهِ.

وَيَقُولُ إِذَا صَعُبَ عَلَيْهِ أَمْرٌ: اَللّٰهُمَّ لَا سَهْلَ إِلَّا مَا جَعَلْتَهُ سَهْلاً وَأَنْ تَجْعَلَ الْحُزْنَ إِذَا شِئْتَ سَهْلاً.

وَإِذَا غَلَبَهُ أَمْرٌ يَقُولُ: قَدَّرَ اللهُ وَمَا شَاءَ فَعَلَ. حَسْبِيَ اللهُ وَنِعْمَ الْوَكِيلُ.

وَإِذَا أَهَمَّهُ الْأَمْرُ يَقُولُ: سُبْحَانَ اللهِ الْعَظِيمِ.

وَإِذَا غَلَبَهُ الدَّيْنُ قَالَ: اَللّٰهُمَّ اكْفِنِي بِحَلَالِكَ عَنْ حَرَامِكَ. وَاغْنِنِي بِفَضْلِكَ عَمَّنْ سِوَاكَ. اَللّٰهُمَّ فَارِجَ الْهَمِّ، كَاشِفَ الْكَرْبِ، مُجِيبَ دَعْوَةِ الْمُضْطَرِّ، رَحْمٰنَ الدُّنْيَا وَالْآخِرَةِ وَرَحِيمَهُمَا. أَنْتَ تَرْحَمُنِي فَارْحَمْنِي بِرَحْمَةٍ تُغْنِينِي بِهَا عَمَّنْ سِوَاكَ. ﴿اَللّٰهُمَّ مَالِكَ الْمُلْكِ، تُؤْتِي الْمُلْكَ مَنْ تَشَاءُ وَتَنْزِعُ الْمُلْكَ مِمَّنْ تَشَاءُ﴾ إِلَى قَوْلِهِ: ﴿بِغَيْرِ حِسَابٍ﴾. يَا رَحْمٰنَ الدُّنْيَا وَالْآخِرَةِ وَرَحِيمَهُمَا، تُعْطِي مَنْ تَشَاءُ مِنْهُمَا وَتَمْنَعُ مَنْ تَشَاءُ مِنْهُمَا. اِقْضِ عَنِّي الدَّيْنَ وَارْحَمْنِي رَحْمَةً تُغْنِينِي بِهَا عَنْ رَحْمَةِ سِوَاكَ.

When entering the market it is said: *There is no god but God alone; He has no partner. To Him is the Dominion and to Him is all praise. He gives life and he gives death; He is Living and does not die. In His Hand is all good and He has power over all things. In the name of God, O God, truly I ask You for the good of this market and for the good of what is in it, and I seek refuge in You from the evil of it and from the evil of what is in it. O God, I seek refuge in You lest I suffer an unprofitable transaction, or a dishonest promise.*

When purchasing an animal or a servant, or when wedding a woman, say, *O God, I truly ask You for the good of them and for the good which You created them. I seek refuge in You from their evil and from the evil for which You created them.*

One says at the time of intimacy with one's spouse, *In the name of God. O God, avert us from Satan and avert Satan from what You give us.*

When one sees what one loves, one should say, *Praise be to God, through Whose blessing good actions are completed.*

When one sees what one loathes, one should say, *Praise be to God in every situation.*

If one hears ringing in the ears, one should say, *May God mention the one who has mentioned me with goodness*; then one should invoke God's blessing upon the Prophet ﷺ.

If one's foot falls asleep, one should mention the person who is most beloved to them.[249]

وَيُقَالُ عِنْدَ دُخُولِ السُّوقِ: لَا إِلٰهَ إِلَّا اللهُ وَحْدَهُ لَا شَرِيكَ لَهُ لَهُ الْمُلْكُ وَلَهُ الْحَمْدُ. يُحْيِي وَيُمِيتُ، وَهُوَ حَيٌّ لَا يَمُوتُ. بِيَدِهِ الْخَيْرُ وَهُوَ عَلَى كُلِّ شَيْءٍ قَدِيرٌ. بِسْمِ اللهِ. اَللّٰهُمَّ إِنِّي أَسْأَلُكَ خَيْرَ هٰذا السُّوقِ وَخَيْرَ مَا فِيهِ وَأَعُوذُ بِكَ مِنْ شَرِّهِ وَشَرِّ مَا فِيهِ. اَللّٰهُمَّ إِنِّي أَعُوذُ بِكَ أَنْ أُصِيبَ فِيهِ صَفْقَةً خَاسِرَةً أَوْ يَمِيناً فَاجِرَةً.

وَيَقُولُ إِذَا اشْتَرَى بَهِيمَةً أَوْ خَادِماً أَوْ تَزَوَّجَ اِمْرَأَةً وَيَأْخُذُ بِنَاصِيَتِهَا: اَللّٰهُمَّ إِنِّي أَسْأَلُكَ خَيْرَهَا وَخَيْرَ مَا جَلَبْتَهَا عَلَيْهِ. وَأَعُوذُ بِكَ مِنْ شَرِّهَا وَشَرِّ مَا جَلَبْتَهَا عَلَيْهِ.

وَيُقَالُ عِنْدَ الْجِمَاعِ: بِسْمِ اللهِ. اَللّٰهُمَّ جَنِّبْنَا الشَّيْطَانَ وَجَنِّبِ الشَّيْطَانَ مَا رَزَقْتَنَا.

وَيَقُولُ إِذَا رَأَى مَا يُحِبُّ: اَلْحَمْدُ لِلّٰهِ الَّذِي بِنِعْمَتِهِ تَتِمُّ الصَّالِحَاتُ.

وَإِذَا رَأَى مَا يَكْرَهُ، قَالَ: اَلْحَمْدُ لِلّٰهِ عَلَى كُلِّ حَالٍ.

وَإِذَا طَنَّتْ أُذُنُهُ قَالَ: ذَكَرَ اللهُ مَنْ ذَكَرَنِي بِخَيْرٍ. وَيُصَلِّي وَيُسَلِّمُ عَلَى النَّبِيِّ ﷺ.

وَإِذَا خَدِرَتْ رِجْلُهُ ذَكَرَ أَحَبَّ النَّاسِ إِلَيْهِ.

When someone does something good for one, one should say, *May God reward you with good*, and when harm is removed from one, one should say, *May God avert what you dislike from you.*

If one sees an evil omen one should say: *O God, no one brings good things except You, and no one can take away evil except You. There is no power and no might save in God, the Most High, the Almighty.*

If one fears a ruler, one should say: *There is no god but God, the Forbearing, the Generous. Glory be to God, Lord of the seven heavens, Lord of the almighty Throne. Elevated is he who is close to You and great is Your praise. O God, Lord of the seven heavens and Lord of the almighty Throne, be a protector for me from the evil of so-and-so, from the* jinn, *humankind and their followers, lest one of them hasten to act unjustly towards me or exceed the bounds. Elevated is he who is close to You and great is Your praise. There is no god besides You.*

One should say: *God is most Great; God is greater than His entire creation. God is more powerful than what I fear, and of which I am cautious. I seek refuge in God; there is no god but He. [He is] the One Who holds up the seven heavens lest they fall upon the earth, except by His permission. And I seek refuge from the evil of Your servant so-and-so, their army, their groups and their followers amongst the* jinn *and humankind. O God, be a protector for me from their evil. Great is Your praise and powerful is Your protection. Blessed be Your Name; there is no god besides You. O God, protect me with Your Eye that never sleeps, protect me with Your support that does not desire [anything] and show me mercy through the power that You have over me. I will not be destroyed while You are my hope. How many blessings have You blessed me with that I have offered few thanks for, and how many tribulations have you tested me with that I have shown little patience in. O He Who, [despite] my few thanks upon His bestowal of blessing, has not denied me, and Who, [despite] my paltry patience upon*

وَإِذَا صَنَعَ إِلَيْهِ أَحَدٌ مَعْرُوفاً قَالَ: جَزَاكَ اللّٰهُ خَيْراً. وَإِذَا أَزَالَ عَنْهُ أَذًى قَالَ: صَرَفَ اللّٰهُ عَنْكَ مَا تَكْرَهُ.

وَإِذَا تَطَيَّرَ قَالَ: اَللّٰهُمَّ لَا يَأْتِي بِالْحَسَنَاتِ إِلَّا أَنْتَ وَلَا يَذْهَبُ بِالسَّيِّئَاتِ إِلَّا أَنْتَ. وَلَا حَوْلَ وَلَا قُوَّةَ إِلَّا بِاللّٰهِ، الْعَلِيِّ الْعَظِيمِ.

وَإِذَا خَافَ سُلْطَاناً قَالَ: لَا إِلٰهَ إِلَّا اللّٰهُ الْحَلِيمُ الْكَرِيمُ. سُبْحَانَ اللّٰهِ رَبِّ السَّمٰوَاتِ السَّبْعِ وَرَبِّ الْعَرْشِ الْعَظِيمِ. عَزَّ جَارُكَ وَجَلَّ ثَنَاؤُكَ. اَللّٰهُمَّ رَبَّ السَّمٰوَاتِ السَّبْعِ وَرَبَّ الْعَرْشِ الْعَظِيمِ، كُنْ لِي جَاراً مِنْ شَرِّ فُلَانِ ابْنِ فُلَانٍ وَشَرِّ الْجِنِّ وَالْإِنْسِ وَأَتْبَاعِهِمْ أَنْ يُفْرِطَ عَلَيَّ أَحَدٌ مِنْهُمْ، أَوْ أَنْ يَطْغَى. عَزَّ جَارُكَ وَجَلَّ ثَنَاؤُكَ وَلَا إِلٰهَ إِلَّا أَنْتَ.

وَيَقُولُ: اَللّٰهُ أَكْبَرُ، اللّٰهُ أَكْبَرُ مِنْ خَلْقِهِ جَمِيعاً. اَللّٰهُ أَعَزُّ مِمَّا أَخَافُ وَأَحْذَرُ. أَعُوذُ بِاللّٰهِ الَّذِي لَا إِلٰهَ إِلَّا هُوَ الْمُمْسِكُ السَّمٰوَاتِ السَّبْعِ أَنْ تَقَعَ عَلَى الْأَرْضِ إِلَّا بِإِذْنِهِ، مِنْ شَرِّ عَبْدِكَ فُلَانٍ وَجُنُودِهِ وَأَشْيَاعِهِ وَأَتْبَاعِهِ مِنَ الْجِنِّ وَالْإِنْسِ. اَللّٰهُمَّ كُنْ لِي جَاراً مِنْ شَرِّهِمْ. جَلَّ ثَنَاؤُكَ وَعَزَّ جَارُكَ وَتَبَارَكَ اسْمُكَ وَلَا إِلٰهَ غَيْرُكَ. اَللّٰهُمَّ أَحْرِسْنِي بِعَيْنِكَ الَّتِي لَا تَنَامُ وَاكْنِفْنِي بِرُكْنِكَ الَّذِي لَا يُرَامُ وَارْحَمْنِي بِقُدْرَتِكَ عَلَيَّ فَلَا أَهْلِكُ وَأَنْتَ رَجَائِي. فَكَمْ مِنْ نِعْمَةٍ أَنْعَمْتَهَا عَلَيَّ قَلَّ لَكَ بِهَا شُكْرِي وَكَمْ مِنْ بَلِيَّةٍ اِبْتَلَيْتَنِي بِهَا قَلَّ لَكَ بِهَا صَبْرِي. فَيَا مَنْ قَلَّ عِنْدَ نِعَمِهِ شُكْرِي فَلَمْ

His afflicting [me], has not humiliated me. O He Who sees me persisting in sins and does not expose me, I ask You to bless Muḥammad and his family.

O God, aid me in my religion with [the things of the] world and in my Hereafter with God-fearingness. Protect me from what I am unaware of, and do not leave me to myself in what I know of. O He Whom sins do not hurt and Whom forgiveness does not decrease, bestow upon me what does not decrease You. Forgive me for that which does not harm You; truly You are the Bestower. I ask You for imminent relief, for beautiful patience, for expansive provisions and for well-being from all tribulations. I ask You for complete well-being, continuous well-being and thankfulness for well-being. I ask you for independence from people. There is no power and no might save in God, the Most High, the Almighty.

One should say: *[I invoke] the name of God upon my religion and myself. [I invoke] the name of God upon my family and my wealth. [I invoke] the name of God upon what God has granted me. God, God, my Lord, I do not associate anything with You at all. God is most Great. God is most Great. God is more powerful and more majestic than what I fear, and of which I am cautious. Elevated is he who is close to You and great is Your praise.* [And repeat this] three times. *There is no god besides You. Protect me from every accursed Satan and from every violent tyrant. Truly God is my Patron, Who has revealed the Book, and He protects the righteous. But if they turn back, say: God is sufficient for me, there is no god but He. I have placed my trust in Him and He is the Lord of the almighty Throne.*

يَحْرِمْنِي وَيَا مَنْ قَلَّ عِنْدَ بَلِيَّتِهِ صَبْرِي فَلَمْ يَخْذُلْنِي. وَيَا مَنْ رَآنِي عَلَى الْخَطَايَا فَلَمْ يُفْضِحْنِي، أَسْأَلُكَ أَنْ تُصَلِّيَ عَلَى مُحَمَّدٍ وَعَلَى آلِ مُحَمَّدٍ.

اَللّٰهُمَّ أَعِنِّي عَلَى دِينِي بِالدُّنْيَا وَعَلَى آخِرَتِي بِالتَّقْوَى. وَاحْفَظْنِي فِيمَا غِبْتُ عَنْهُ وَلَا تَكِلْنِي إِلَى نَفْسِي فِيمَا حَضَرْتُهُ. يَا مَنْ لَا تَضُرُّهُ الذُّنُوبُ وَلَا تَنْقُصُهُ الْمَغْفِرَةُ، هَبْ لِي مَا لَا يَنْقُصُكَ. وَاغْفِرْ لِي مَا لَا يَضُرُّكَ إِنَّكَ أَنْتَ الْوَهَّابُ. أَسْأَلُكَ فَرَجاً قَرِيباً وَصَبْراً جَمِيلاً وَرِزْقاً وَاسِعاً وَالْعَافِيَةَ مِنْ جَمِيعِ الْبَلَاءِ. وَأَسْأَلُكَ تَمَامَ الْعَافِيَةِ وَدَوَامَ الْعَافِيَةِ وَالشُّكْرَ عَلَى الْعَافِيَةِ. وَأَسْأَلُكَ الْغِنَى عَنِ النَّاسِ. وَلَا حَوْلَ وَلَا قُوَّةَ إِلَّا بِاللّٰهِ الْعَلِيِّ الْعَظِيمِ.

وَيَقُولُ: بِسْمِ اللّٰهِ عَلَى دِينِي وَنَفْسِي. بِسْمِ اللّٰهِ عَلَى أَهْلِي وَمَالِي. بِسْمِ اللّٰهِ عَلَى مَا أَعْطَانِيَ اللّٰهُ. اَللّٰهَ اَللّٰهَ رَبِّي، لَا أُشْرِكُ بِهِ شَيْئاً. اَللّٰهُ أَكْبَرُ اللّٰهُ أَكْبَرُ. اَللّٰهُ أَعَزُّ وَأَجَلُّ مِمَّا أَخَافُ وَأَحْذَرُ. عَزَّ جَارُكَ وَجَلَّ ثَنَاؤُكَ (ثَلَاثَ مَرَّاتٍ). لَا إِلٰهَ إِلَّا أَنْتَ. أَعِذْنِي مِنْ كُلِّ شَيْطَانٍ رَجِيمٍ وَمِنْ كُلِّ جَبَّارٍ عَنِيدٍ. ﴿إِنَّ وَلِيِّيَ اللّٰهُ الَّذِي نَزَّلَ الْكِتَابَ وَهُوَ يَتَوَلَّى الصَّالِحِينَ﴾. ﴿فَإِنْ تَوَلَّوْا فَقُلْ حَسْبِيَ اللّٰهُ، لَا إِلٰهَ إِلَّا هُوَ عَلَيْهِ تَوَكَّلْتُ وَهُوَ رَبُّ الْعَرْشِ الْعَظِيمِ﴾.

One should say when someone enters upon one: *O God, truly I ask You for Your goodness from the good of [this person]. I seek refuge in You from their evil. I place between you and me: there is no god but God alone, He has no partner. I seek help over you through: there is no power and no might save in God, the Most High, the Almighty. But if they turn back, say: God is sufficient for me, there is no god but He. I have placed my trust in Him and He is the Lord of the almighty Throne. So if they turn back, then they are only in extreme hardship, so God will be sufficient for them, and He is the All-Hearing and the All-Knowing. I am pleased with God as a Lord, with Islam as a religion, with Muḥammad* ﷺ *as a messenger and with the Qurʾān as an imam and a judge. O God, Lord of Gabriel, Michael and Isrāfīl, Lord of Abraham, Ishmael and the tribes of Israel, sender of the Torah, the Bible, the Psalms and the glorious Qurʾān, divert the evil of so-and-so from me.*

If one sees a lion one should say: *God is most Great, God is most Great, God is most Great. God is more powerful than everything and is greater. I seek refuge in God from the evil of what I fear, and of which I am cautious.*

If a dog barks at one, one should say, '*O company of jinn and humankind...*'[250] [and recite until the end of] the verse.

When one sees their enemy, one should say: *O Master of the Day of Judgement, it is You we worship and You we ask for help. Guide us to the straight path.*

When someone becomes burdensome upon one, say, *O God, forgive them and relieve us from them.*

وَيقُولُ إِذَا دَخَلَ عَلَيْهِ أَحَدٌ: اَللّٰهُمَّ إِنِّي أَسْأَلُكَ بِخَيْرِكَ مِنْ خَيْرِهِ وَأَعُوذُ بِكَ مِنْ شَرِّهِ. رَمَيْتُكَ بِلَا إِلَهَ إِلَّا اللهُ وَحْدَهُ لَا شَرِيكَ لَهُ. وَأَسْتَعِينُ عَلَيْكَ بِلَا حَوْلَ وَلَا قُوَّةَ إِلَّا بِاللهِ الْعَلِيِّ الْعَظِيمِ. ﴿فَإِنْ تَوَلَّوْا فَقُلْ حَسْبِيَ اللهُ، لَا إِلٰهَ إِلَّا هُوَ عَلَيْهِ تَوَكَّلْتُ وَهُوَ رَبُّ الْعَرْشِ الْعَظِيمِ﴾. ﴿فَإِنْ تَوَلَّوْا فَإِنَّمَا هُمْ فِي شِقَاقٍ فَسَيَكْفِيكَهُمُ اللهُ وَهُوَ السَّمِيعُ الْعَلِيمُ﴾. رَضِيتُ بِاللهِ رَبّاً وَبِالْإِسْلَامِ دِيناً وَبِمُحَمَّدٍ ﷺ رَسُولاً وَبِالْقُرْآنِ إِمَاماً وَحَكَماً. اَللّٰهُمَّ رَبَّ جِبْرِيلَ وَمِيكَائِيلَ وَإِسْرَافِيلَ وَرَبَّ إِبْرَاهِيمَ وَإِسْمَعِيلَ وَالْأَسْبَاطِ، مُنْزِلَ التَّوْرَاةِ وَالْإِنْجِيلِ وَالزَّبُورِ وَالْقُرْآنِ الْعَظِيمِ، اِدْرَأْ عَنِّي شَرَّ فُلَانٍ.

وَإِذَا رَأَى الْأَسَدَ قَالَ: اَللهُ أَكْبَرُ، اَللهُ أَكْبَرُ، اَللهُ أَكْبَرُ. اَللهُ أَعَزُّ مِنْ كُلِّ شَيْءٍ وَأَكْبَرُ. أَعُوذُ بِاللهِ مِنْ شَرِّ مَا أَخَافُ وَأَحْذَرُ.

وَإِذَا هَوْهَوَ عَلَيْهِ الْكَلْبُ، قَالَ: ﴿يَا مَعْشَرَ الْجِنِّ وَالْإِنْسِ﴾ الآيَة.

وَإِذَا رَأَى عَدُوَّهُ قَالَ: يَا ﴿مَالِكِ يَوْمِ الدِّينِ، إِيَّاكَ نَعْبُدُ وَإِيَّاكَ نَسْتَعِينُ، اِهْدِنَا الصِّرَاطَ الْمُسْتَقِيمَ.﴾

وَإِذَا اسْتَثْقَلَ أَحَداً قَالَ: اَللّٰهُمَّ اغْفِرْ لَهُ وَأَرِحْنَا مِنْهُ.

If one sees a blazing fire, or if strong gusts of wind blow, pronounce the *takbīr*, for truly pronouncing the *takbīr* extinguishes raging fires and clears the clouds of dust.

When the wind becomes violent, one should say: *O God, truly I ask You for the good of it and the good for which You have sent it. I seek refuge in You from the evil of it, from the evil of what is in it and from the evil for which You sent it. O God, make it a mercy, do not make it a punishment. O God, make it pollinating, not destructive. O God, truly I ask You from the good that You have commanded through it.*

When one hears the sound of thunder, one should say: *Glory be to Him Whom the thunder glorifies with praise, and [Whom] His angels [glorify] with fear. O God, do not kill us with Your anger, do not destroy us with Your punishment and, above all, give us well-being.*

When rain falls one should say, *O God, [make this a] beneficial downpour*, and supplicate for what one wishes, and say afterwards: *Rain fell upon us by the bounty of God and His mercy*. It is disliked [for one] to say, 'We have had rain due to the rising of such-and-such [a star],' or to stare into the clouds and point at the rainclouds.

وَإِذَا رَأَى حَرِيقاً أَوْ مَاجَتْ رِيحٌ مُظْلِمَةٌ يُكَبِّرُ فَإِنَّ التَّكْبِيرِ يُطْفِئُ الْحَرِيقَ وَيَجْلُو الْعَجَاجَ الأَسْوَدَ.

وَيَقُولُ عِنْدَ هَيْجَانِ الرِّيحِ: اَللّٰهُمَّ إِنِّي أَسْأَلُكَ خَيْرَهَا وَخَيْرَ مَا أُرْسِلَتْ بِهِ. وَأَعُوذُ بِكَ مِنْ شَرِّهَا وَشَرِّ مَا فِيهَا وَشَرِّ مَا أُرْسِلَتْ بِهِ. اَللّٰهُمَّ اجْعَلْهَا رَحْمَةً وَلَا تَجْعَلْهَا عَذَاباً. اَللّٰهُمَّ اجْعَلْهَا لَقَحاً لَا عَقِيماً. اَللّٰهُمَّ إِنِّي أَسْأَلُكَ مِنْ خَيْرِ مَا أَمَرْتَ بِهِ.

وَإِذَا سَمِعَ صَوْتَ الرَّعْدِ قَالَ: سُبْحَانَ الَّذِي ﴿يُسَبِّحُ الرَّعْدُ بِحَمْدِهِ وَالْمَلَائِكَةُ مِنْ خِيفَتِهِ﴾. اَللّٰهُمَّ لَا تَقْتُلْنَا بِغَضَبِكَ وَلَا تُهْلِكْنَا بِعَذَابِكَ وَعَافِنَا قَبْلَ ذٰلِكَ.

وَإِذَا نَزَلَ الْمَطَرُ قَالَ: اَللّٰهُمَّ صَيِّباً نَافِعاً، وَيَدْعُو بِمَا شَاءَ وَيَقُولُ بَعْدَهُ: مُطِرْنَا بِفَضْلِ اللهِ وَرَحْمَتِهِ. وَيُكْرَهُ أَنْ يَقُولَ: «مُطِرْنَا بِنَوْءِ كَذَا» وَأَنْ يَتْبَعَ بَصَرَهُ وَأَنْ يُشِيرَ إِلَى الْوَدَقِ.

VARIOUS REPORTED SUPPLICATIONS

O God, forgive me for my mistakes, my ignorance, my extravagance in my affairs and for what You know better than I. O God, forgive me for my seriousness, my foolhardiness, my mistakes, my resolutions and for all that I have. O God, I have submitted to You, I believe in You, I have placed my trust in You, I have turned to You in repentance and I have opposed [others] for Your sake. O God, truly I seek refuge in Your might—there is no god besides You—lest You allow me to go astray. You are the Living, the Self-Subsisting, Who does not die, while humankind and the jinn do.[W]

O God, I ask You for guidance, God-fearingness, chastity and independence.

O God, Changer of hearts, direct our hearts to obedience of You.

O God, make me balanced in word and deed. O God, rectify my religion, which is a protection for my affairs. Rectify my worldly life for me, in which is my livelihood, and rectify my Hereafter for me, in which is my return. Make life increased in every good for us and make death a relief for us from every evil. Lord, help me, and do not help [others] against me. Make me victorious, do not bring victory against me and make me victorious over whoever oppresses me. Lord, make me grateful to You, mentioning You, desiring and obeying You, humbling [myself] before You and always turning back to You. Accept my repentance, wash away my sins, answer my supplications, establish my proof, guide my heart, make firm my tongue and gently remove the sickness of my heart.

دَعَوَاتٌ مُطْلَقَةٌ مَأْثُورَةٌ

اَللّٰهُمَّ اغْفِرْ لِي خَطِيئَتِي وَجَهْلِي وَإِسْرَافِي فِي أَمْرِي وَمَا أَنْتَ أَعْلَمُ بِهِ مِنِّي. اَللّٰهُمَّ اغْفِرْ لِي جِدِّي وَهَزْلِي وَخَطِيئَتِي وَعَمَدِي وَكُلُّ ذٰلِكَ عِنْدِي. اَللّٰهُمَّ لَكَ أَسْلَمْتُ وَبِكَ آمَنْتُ وَعَلَيْكَ تَوَكَّلْتُ وَإِلَيْكَ أَنَبْتُ وَبِكَ خَاصَمْتُ. اَللّٰهُمَّ إِنِّي أَعُوذُ بِعِزَّتِكَ وَلَا إِلٰهَ إِلَّا أَنْتَ أَنْ تُضِلَّنِي. أَنْتَ الْحَيُّ الْقَيُّومُ الَّذِي لَا يَمُوتُ وَالْإِنْسُ وَالْجِنُّ يَمُوتُونَ.

اَللّٰهُمَّ إِنِّي أَسْأَلُكَ الْهُدَى وَالتُّقَى وَالْعَفَافَ وَالْغِنَى.

اَللّٰهُمَّ مُصَرِّفَ الْقُلُوبِ، صَرِّفْ قُلُوبَنَا عَلَى طَاعَتِكَ.

اَللّٰهُمَّ سَدِّدْنِي. اَللّٰهُمَّ أَصْلِحْ لِي دِينِيَ الَّذِي هُوَ عِصْمَةُ أَمْرِي، وَأَصْلِحْ لِي دُنْيَايَ الَّتِي فِيهَا مَعَاشِي وَأَصْلِحْ لِي آخِرَتِيَ الَّتِي فِيهَا مَعَادِي. وَاجْعَلِ الْحَيَاةَ زِيَادَةً لَنَا فِي كُلِّ خَيْرٍ وَاجْعَلِ الْمَوْتَ رَاحَةً لَنَا مِنْ كُلِّ شَرٍّ. رَبِّ أَعِنِّي وَلَا تُعِنْ عَلَيَّ. وَانْصُرْنِي وَلَا تَنْصُرْ عَلَيَّ وَانْصُرْنِي عَلَى مَنْ بَغَى عَلَيَّ. رَبِّ اجْعَلْنِي شَاكِراً لَكَ، ذَاكِراً لَكَ، رَاغِباً مُطَوَّعاً إِلَيْكَ، مُخْبِتاً مُنِيباً. تَقَبَّلْ تَوْبَتِي وَاغْسِلْ حَوْبَتِي وَأَجِبْ دَعْوَتِي وَثَبِّتْ حُجَّتِي وَاهْدِ قَلْبِي وَثَبِّتْ لِسَانِي وَاسْلُلْ سَخِيمَةَ قَلْبِي.

O God, truly I ask You [to aid me] in doing good things, in putting aside bad things and to love the poor. And I ask You to forgive me and to show mercy to me. If You wish [to bring] temptations or tribulations to a people, then give me death without being tempted.

O God, inspire me with guidance. I seek refuge in You from the evil of my self.

O God, truly I ask You for Your love, for the love of those who love You and for the deeds that will cause me to attain Your love. O God, make love of You more beloved to me than [my love for] myself or my family, or the love of cold water.

O God, truly I ask You for pardon and well-being, and for continued goodness in this world and the Hereafter. O God, I ask You for the good of that which Your Prophet ﷺ asked of You. I seek refuge in You from the evil from which Muḥammad ﷺ, Your Prophet, sought protection. You are the One in Whom aid is sought and it is upon You that [all] depend. There is no power and no might save in God.

O God, provide me with Your love and with the love of those whose love will benefit me with You. O God, just as You have provided me with what I love, make it a [source] of strength for me [to do] what You love. O God, whatever You have put aside from me amongst that which I love, make [the time] I would have spent on it [be spent instead on] what You love. O God, make my inner nature better than my outer one, and make my outer one righteous.

O God, I ask You for the best of that which You give to people of wealth, family and children, without being misguided or misguiding [others]. O God, make me attach great importance to thanking You, [make me] remember You abundantly, [make me] follow Your advice and preserve Your covenant.

اَللّٰهُمَّ إِنِّي أَسْأَلُكَ فِعْلَ الْخَيْرَاتِ وَتَرْكَ الْمُنْكَرَاتِ وَحُبَّ الْمَسَاكِينِ. وَأَنْ تَغْفِرْ لِي وَتَرْحَمْنِي. وَإِذَا أَرَدْتَ فِتْنَةً أَوْ بَلَاءً فِي قَوْمٍ فَتَوَفَّنِي غَيْرَ مَفْتُونٍ.

اَللّٰهُمَّ أَلْهِمْنِي رُشْدِي. وَأَعُوذُ بِكَ مِنْ شَرِّ نَفْسِي.

اَللّٰهُمَّ إِنِّي أَسْأَلُكَ حُبَّكَ وَحُبَّ مَنْ يُحِبُّكَ وَالْعَمَلَ الَّذِي يُبَلِّغُنِي حُبَّكَ. اَللّٰهُمَّ اجْعَلْ حُبَّكَ أَحَبَّ إِلَيَّ مِنْ نَفْسِي وَأَهْلِي وَمِنَ الْمَاءِ الْبَارِدِ.

اَللّٰهُمَّ إِنِّي أَسْأَلُكَ الْعَفْوَ وَالْعَافِيَةَ وَالْمُعَافَاةَ الدَائِمَةَ فِي الدُّنْيَا وَالْآخِرَةِ. اَللّٰهُمَّ إِنِّي أَسْأَلُكَ مِنْ خَيْرِ مَا سَأَلَكَ بِهِ نَبِيُّكَ ﷺ. وَأَعُوذُ بِكَ مِنْ شَرِّ مَا اسْتَعَاذَ مِنْهُ مُحَمَّدٌ نَبِيُّكَ ﷺ. وَأَنْتَ الْمُسْتَعَانُ وَعَلَيْكَ التُّكْلَانُ. وَلَا حَوْلَ وَلَا قُوَّةَ إِلَّا بِاللهِ.

اَللّٰهُمَّ ارْزُقْنِي حُبَّكَ وَحُبَّ مَنْ يَنْفَعُنِي حُبُّهُ عِنْدَكَ. اَللّٰهُمَّ كَمَا رَزَقْتَنِي مِمَّا أَحْبَبْتُ فَاجْعَلْهُ قُوَّةً لِي فِيمَا تُحِبُّ. اَللّٰهُمَّ مَا زَوَيْتَ عَنِّي مِمَّا أُحِبُّ فَاجْعَلْهُ فَرَاغاً لِي فِيمَا تُحِبُّ. اَللّٰهُمَّ اجْعَلْ سَرِيرَتِي خَيْراً مِنْ عَلَانِيَتِي، وَاجْعَلْ عَلَانِيَتِي صَالِحَةً.

اَللّٰهُمَّ إِنِّي أَسْأَلُكَ مِنْ صَالِحِ مَا تُؤْتِي النَّاسَ مِنَ الْمَالِ وَالْأَهْلِ وَالْوَلَدِ غَيْرَ الضَّالِّ وَالْمُضِلِّ. اَللّٰهُمَّ اجْعَلْنِي أُعَظِّمُ شُكْرَكَ وَأُكْثِرُ ذِكْرَكَ وَأَتْبَعُ نَصِيحَتَكَ وَأَحْفَظُ وَصِيَّتَكَ.

O God, allow me to enjoy my hearing and my sight, and make them both inheritors from me. Grant me well-being in my religion and in my Hereafter for as long as You keep me alive. Grant me victory over whoever oppresses me and [allow me] to take revenge on them.

O God, increase us and do not decrease us. Honour us and do not disgrace us. Grant us and do not deprive us. Prefer us and do not prefer [others] over us. Be pleased with us and make us pleased.

O God, make me fear You as if I could see You, forever until I meet You. Make me happy through God-fearingness of You and do not make me wretched through disobeying You. Make my choice for me through Your decree. Bless me in Your apportioning so that I do not wish to hasten what You have delayed, or to delay what You have hastened. Make my soul content, [grant me] enjoyment in my hearing and my sight, and make them both inheritors from me. Grant me victory over whoever oppresses me, show me my revenge on them and gladden me with that.

O God, expand Your provision [for me] during my old age and at the end of my life. O God, forgive me my mistakes, my insistence [in this], my levity and my seriousness. Do not bar me from the blessings of what You have given me, and do not test me through what You have denied me.

O God, abundant praise be to You as everlastingly as Your eternality. Abundant, everlasting praise be to You [that] is not impaired at the time of asking You. Abundant praise be to You [that] has no reward other than Your pleasure. Abundant praise be to You upon the blink of every eye and the breathing of every breath.

اَللّٰهُمَّ مَتِّعْنِي بِسَمْعِي وَبَصَرِي وَاجْعَلْهُمَا الوَارِثَ مِنِّي. وَعَافِنِي فِي دِينِي وَآخِرَتِي عَلَى مَا أَحْيَيْتَنِي. وَانْصُرْنِي عَلَى مَنْ ظَلَمَنِي وَخُذْ مِنْهُ بِثَأْرِي.

اَللّٰهُمَّ زِدْنَا وَلَا تَنْقُصْنَا. وَأَكْرِمْنَا وَلَا تُهِنَّا. وَأَعْطِنَا وَلَا تَحْرِمْنَا. وَآثِرْنَا وَلَا تُؤْثِرْ عَلَيْنَا. وَارْضَ عَنَّا وَأَرْضِنَا.

اَللّٰهُمَّ اجْعَلْنِي أَخْشَاكَ كَأَنِّي أَرَاكَ أَبداً حَتَّى أَلْقَاكَ. وَأَسْعِدْنِي بِتَقْوَاكَ وَلَاتَشْقِنِي بِمَعْصِيَتِكَ. وَخِرْ لِي فِي قَضَائِكَ. وَبَارِكْ لِي فِي قَدْرِكَ حَتَّى لَا أُحِبَّ تَعْجِيلَ مَا أَخَّرْتَ وَلَا تَأْخِيْرَ مَا عَجَّلْتَ. وَاجْعَلْ غِنَايَ فِي نَفْسِي وَمَتِّعْنِي بِسَمْعِي وَبَصَرِي وَاجْعَلْهُمَا الْوَارِثَ مِنِّي. وَانْصُرْنِي عَلَى مَنْ ظَلَمَنِي وَأَرِنِي فِيهِ ثَأْرِي وَأَقِرَّ بِذٰلِكَ عَيْنِي.

اَللّٰهُمَّ اجْعَلْ أَوْسَعَ رِزْقِكَ عِنْدَ كِبَرِ سِنِّي وَانْقِطَاعِ عُمْرِي. اَللّٰهُمَّ اغْفِرْ لِي خَطَئِي وَعَمَدِي وَهَزْلِي وَجِدِّي. وَلَا تَحْرِمْنِي بَرَكَةَ مَا أَعْطَيْتَنِي وَلَا تَفْتِنِّي فِيمَا حَرَّمْتَنِي.

اَللّٰهُمَّ لَكَ الْحَمْدُ حَمْداً دَائِماً مَعَ خُلُودِكَ. وَلَكَ الْحَمْدُ حَمْداً دَائِماً لَا نُسِيءَ لَهُ وَقْتَ مَسْأَلَتِكَ. وَلَكَ الْحَمْدُ حَمْداً لَا جَزَاءَ لَهُ إِلَّا رِضَاكَ. وَلَكَ الْحَمْدُ حَمْداً عِنْدَ طَرْفَةِ كُلِّ عَيْنٍ وَتَنَفُّسِ نَفْسٍ.

O God, make every difficulty easy for me by facilitating [it], for indeed making a difficulty easy is easy for You. I ask You for ease and goodness in this world and the Hereafter. O Patron of Islam and its people, strengthen me through Islam until I meet You.

O God, praise be to You; to You is the complaint and aid is sought through You. There is no power and no might save in God, the Most High, the Almighty.

O God, truly we ask You for that which is good, for abandoning that which is bad and for loving the needy. [And I ask You] to turn to me, to forgive me and show mercy to me. If you wish [to try] Your servants with a temptation, then take me to You without being tempted.

O God, make me constantly patient. O God, make me always appreciative.

O God, in my [own] eyes, make me small and in the eyes of others great.

O God, protect me through Islam while standing, protect me through Islam while sitting and protect me through Islam while lying down. And cause me not to be the target of an enemy or jealous person. I seek refuge in You from the evil of every creature that You take by its forelock. I ask You for all of the goodness that You have in Your Hand.

O God, truly I ask You for protection like that of a newborn baby. O God, accept my turning to Your religion, and protect us from [what is] behind [us] through Your mercy.

O God, guide us towards the right path.

اَللّٰهُمَّ يَسِّرْ لِي فِي تَيْسِيرِ كُلِّ عَسِيرٍ فَإِنَّ تَيْسِيرَ الْعَسِيرِ عَلَيْكَ يَسِيرٌ. أَسْأَلُكَ الْيَسِيرَ وَالْمُعَافَاةَ فِي الدُّنْيَا وَالآخِرَةِ. يَا وَلِيَّ الْإِسْلَامِ وَأَهْلِهِ مَكِّنِّي بِالْإِسْلَامِ حَتَّى أَلْقَاكَ.

اَللّٰهُمَّ لَكَ الْحَمْدُ وَلَكَ الْمُشْتَكَى وَبِكَ الْمُسْتَعَانُ. وَلَا حَوْلَ وَلَا قُوَّةَ إِلَّا بِاللهِ الْعَلِيِّ الْعَظِيمِ.

اَللّٰهُمَّ إِنَّا نَسْأَلُكَ الطَّيِّبَاتِ وَتَرْكَ الْمُنْكَرَاتِ وَحُبَّ الْمَسَاكِينِ. وَأَنْ تَتُوبَ عَلَيَّ وَتَغْفِرَ لِي وَتَرْحَمَنِي. فَإِنْ أَرَدْتَ بِعِبَادِكَ فِتْنَةً فَاقْبِضْنِي إِلَيْكَ غَيْرَ مَفْتُونٍ.

اَللّٰهُمَّ اجْعَلْنِي صَبُوراً. اَللّٰهُمَّ اجْعَلْنِي شَكُوراً.

اَللّٰهُمَّ اجْعَلْنِي فِي عَيْنِي صَغِيراً وَفِي أَعْيُنِ النَّاسِ كَبِيراً.

اَللّٰهُمَّ احْفَظْنِي بِالْإِسْلَامِ قَائِماً وَاحْفَظْنِي بِالْإِسْلَامِ قَاعِداً وَاحْفَظْنِي بِالْإِسْلَامِ رَاقِداً. وَلَا تُطْمِعْ فِيَّ عَدُوّاً وَلَا حَاسِداً. وَأَعُوذُ بِكَ مِنْ شَرِّ كُلِّ دَابَّةٍ أَنْتَ آخِذٌ بِنَاصِيَتِهَا. وَأَسْأَلُكَ مِنَ الْخَيْرِ الَّذِي بِيَدِكَ كُلِّهِ.

اَللّٰهُمَّ إِنِّي أَسْأَلُكَ وَاقِيَةً كَوَاقِيَةِ الْوَلِيدِ. اَللّٰهُمَّ اقْبَلْ تَقَلُّبِي إِلَى دِينِكَ وَاحْفَظْنَا مِنْ وَرَائِنَا بِرَحْمَتِكَ.

اَللّٰهُمَّ اهْدِنَا إِلَى سَوَاءِ السَّبِيلِ.

O God, hold me fast lest I fall and guide me lest I am misguided.

O God, just as You came between me and my heart, so too place a barrier between me and Satan and his work.

O God, provide for me from Your bounty and do not deny us our provision. Bless us in what You have provided for us, make our wealth be in our souls and make our desires be in what is Yours.

O God, purify my heart of hypocrisy, my deeds of ostentation, my tongue of lies and my eyes of treachery, for truly You know the treachery of eyes and what breasts hide. O God, to You is all praise, to You is the dominion, all good is in Your Hand and all matters return to You, both public and private. Truly You are deserving of praise and truly You have power over all things.

O God, forgive me for all of my sins that have come to pass, protect me in what remains of my life and provide me with pure deeds that will make You pleased with me.

O God, from fear of You, apportion to us what would come between me and sinning against You, come between me and sinning against You; from Your obedience, [apportion to us] that which causes us to attain Your Paradise; and from certainty, [apportion to us] that which will make the tribulations of this world seem light. O God, allow us to enjoy our hearing and our sight as long as You keep us alive, and make them inheritors from us. Grant us revenge on whoever has oppressed us and grant us victory over whoever has been hostile to us. Do not make our misfortune be in our religion, do not make this worldly life our greatest concern or the extent of our knowledge. Do not grant authority over us to anyone who does not show mercy to us.

اَللّٰهُمَّ ثَبِّتْنِي أَنْ أَزِلَّ وَاهْدِنْي أَنْ أَضِلَّ.

اَللّٰهُمَّ كَمَا حُلْتَ بَيْنِي وَبَيْنَ قَلْبِيْ فَحُلْ بَيْنِي وَبَيْنَ الشَّيْطَانِ وَعَمَلِهِ.

اَللّٰهُمَّ ارْزُقْنَا مِنْ فَضْلِكَ وَلَا تَحْرِمْنَا مِنْ رِزْقِنَا وَبَارِكْ لَنَا فِيمَا رَزَقْتَنَا وَاجْعَلْ غِنَانَا فِي أَنْفُسِنَا وَاجْعَلْ رَغْبَتَنَا فِيمَا عِنْدَكَ.

اَللّٰهُمَّ طَهِّرْ قَلْبِي مِنَ النِّفَاقِ وَعَمَلِي مِنَ الرِّيَاءِ وَلِسَانِي مِنَ الْكَذِبِ وَعَيْنِي مِنَ الْخِيَانَةِ فَإِنَّكَ تَعْلَمُ خَائِنَةَ الْأَعْيُنِ وَمَا تُخْفِي الصُّدُورُ. اَللّٰهُمَّ لَكَ الْحَمْدُ كُلُّهُ وَلَكَ الْمُلْكُ، بِيَدِكَ الْخَيْرُ وَإِلَيْكَ يَرْجِعُ الْأَمْرُ كُلُّهُ عَلَانِيَتُهُ وَسِرُّهُ. فَإِنَّكَ أَهْلٌ أَنْ تُحْمَدَ، إِنَّكَ عَلَى كُلِّ شَيْءٍ قَدِيرٌ.

اَللّٰهُمَّ اغْفِرْ لِي جَمِيعَ مَا مَضَى مِنْ ذُنُوبِي وَاعْصِمْنِي فِيمَا بَقِيَ مِنْ عُمْرِي وَارْزُقْنِي عَمَلاً زَاكِياً تَرْضَى بِهِ عَنِّي.

اَللّٰهُمَّ اقْسِمْ لَنَا مِنْ خَشْيَتِكَ مَا تَحُولُ بِهِ بَيْنِي وَبَيْنَ مَعَاصِيكَ وَمِنْ طَاعَتِكَ مَا تُبَلِّغُنَا بِهِ جَنَّتَكَ وَمِن الْيَقِينِ مَا تُهَوِّنُ بِهِ عَلَيْنَا مَصَائِبَ الدُّنْيَا. اَللّٰهُمَّ مَتِّعْنَا بِأَسْمَاعِنَا وَأَبْصَارِنَا مَا أَحْيَيْتَنَا وَاجْعَلْهُمَا الْوَارِثَ مِنَّا. وَاجْعَلْ ثَأْرَنَا عَلَى مَنْ ظَلَمَنَا وانْصُرْنَا عَلَى مَنْ عَادَانَا. وَلَا تَجْعَلْ مُصِيبَتَنَا فِي دِينِنَا وَلَا تَجْعَلِ الدُّنْيَا أَكْبَرَ هَمِّنَا وَلَا مَبْلَغَ عِلْمِنَا. وَلَا تُسَلِّطْ عَلَيْنَا مَنْ لَا يَرْحَمُنَا.

O God, to You is all praise. There is no one who can give back what You have seized, there is no guide for whoever You have misguided, no one who can misguide whoever You have guided, no one who can bring near whatever You have distanced, no one who can give whatever You have prevented and there is no one who can prevent what You have given.

O God, truly I ask You for everlasting blessing, which neither changes nor vanishes. O God, truly I ask You for blessing on the Day of Poverty (Yawm al-ʿĪla) *and for safety on the Day of Fear* (Yawm al-Khawf).

O God, truly I am seeking refuge in You from the evil of what You have given and the evil of what You have withheld.

O God, make faith beloved to us and beautify it in our hearts, and make disbelief, corruption and disobedience hateful to us. Make us amongst the rightly guided, grant us death as Muslims and have us join the righteous—not those who have been disgraced or tempted.

O God, truly I ask You for firmness in [my] affairs and the resolve [that comes] with following the right path. I ask You [to help me in] thanking You for Your blessings, in beautifully worshipping You and in being satisfied with Your decree. I ask You for a sound heart and a sincere tongue. I ask You for the good of what You know, I seek refuge in You from the evil of what You know and I seek forgiveness for what You know.

O God, truly I ask You for contentment with Your decree, for ease of life after death, for the pleasure of looking at Your Face, for passionate longing to meet You with no harm, or harm to others, and no temptation that misguides.

O God, let me experience the proof of faith when I come to die.

اَللّٰهُمَّ لَكَ الْحَمْدُ كُلُّهُ. لَا بَاسِطَ لِمَا قَبَضْتَ وَلَا هَادِيَ لِمَنْ أَضْلَلْتَ وَلَا مُضِلَّ لِمَنْ هَدَيْتَ وَلَا مُقَرِّبَ لِمَا بَاعَدْتَ وَلَا مُعْطِيَ لِمَا مَنَعْتَ وَلَا مَانِعَ لِمَا أَعْطَيْتَ.

اَللّٰهُمَّ إِنِّي أَسْأَلُكَ النَّعِيمَ الْمُقِيمَ الَّذِي لَا يَحُولُ وَلَا يَزُولُ. اَللّٰهُمَّ إِنِّي أَسْأَلُكَ النَّعِيمَ يَوْمَ الْعَيْلَةِ وَالْأَمْنَ يَوْمَ الْخَوْفِ.

اَللّٰهُمَّ إِنِّي عَائِذٌ بِكَ مِنْ شَرِّ مَا أَعْطَيْتَ وَشَرِّ مَا مَنَعْتَ.

اَللّٰهُمَّ حَبِّبْ إِلَيْنَا الْإِيمَانَ وَزَيِّنْهُ فِي قُلُوبِنَا وَكَرِّهْ إِلَيْنَا الْكُفْرَ وَالْفُسُوقَ وَالْعِصْيَانَ. وَاجْعَلْنَا مِنَ الرَّاشِدِينَ وَتَوَفَّنَا مُسْلِمِينَ وَأَلْحِقْنَا بِالصَّالِحِينَ غَيْرَ خَزَايَا وَلَا مَفْتُونِينَ.

اَللّٰهُمَّ إِنِّي أَسْأَلُكَ الثَّبَاتَ فِي الْأَمْرِ وَعَزِيمَةَ الرُّشْدِ. وَأَسْأَلُكَ شُكْرَ نِعْمَتِكَ وَحُسْنَ عِبَادَتِكَ وَالرِّضَا بِقَضَائِكَ. وَأَسْأَلُكَ قَلْباً سَلِيماً وَلِسَاناً صَادِقاً. وَأَسْأَلُكَ مِنْ خَيْرِ مَا تَعْلَمُ وَأَعُوذُ بِكَ مِنْ شَرِّ مَا تَعْلَمُ وَأَسْتَغْفِرُكَ لِمَا تَعْلَمُ.

اَللّٰهُمَّ إِنِّي أَسْأَلُكَ الرِّضَا بِالْقَضَاءِ وَبَرْدَ الْعَيْشِ بَعْدَ الْمَوْتِ وَلَذَّةَ النَّظَرِ إِلَى وَجْهِكَ وَالشَّوْقَ إِلَى لِقَائِكَ فِي غَيْرِ ضَرَّاءَ مُضِرَّةٍ وَلَا فِتْنَةٍ مُضِلَّةٍ.

اَللّٰهُمَّ لَقِّنِي حُجَّةَ الْإِيمَانِ عِنْدَ الْمَمَاتِ.

O God, truly I ask You for all good, both what is immediate and what is delayed of it, and what I know of it and what I know not.

O God, truly I ask You for Paradise and what brings it closer in terms of word and deed. I seek refuge in You from Hellfire and from what brings it closer in terms of word and deed.

O God, truly I ask You for the good for which Your servant and Your Messenger Muḥammad ﷺ asked. I seek refuge in You from the evil from which Your servant and Your Messenger Muḥammad ﷺ sought refuge, O God, and whatever decree or affair You have decreed, have its outcome be guidance for me.

O God, benefit me through what You have taught me, teach me what benefits me and provide me with knowledge that benefits me.

O God, truly I ask You for knowledge that does not dissipate, for blessing that is not exhausted and for the good company of Your Prophet Muḥammad in the highest Paradise.

O God, by Your knowledge of the unseen and Your power over creation, make me live if what remains of my life is better for me, or give me death if death is better for me. I ask You for moderation in poverty and wealth. I ask You for blessing that does not cease and for a delight of the eye that is not interrupted.

O God, adorn me with the adornment of belief and make me one of those who are rightly guiding and guided.

O God, truly I seek Your guidance to the best guidance in my affairs and I seek protection in You from the evil of my soul.

اَللّٰهُمَّ إِنِّي أَسْأَلُكَ مِنَ الْخَيْرِ كُلِّهِ، عَاجِلِهِ وَآجِلِهِ، مَا عَلِمْتُ مِنْهُ وَمَا لَمْ أَعْلَمْ.

اَللّٰهُمَّ إِنِّي أَسْأَلُكَ الْجَنَّةَ وَمَا قَرَّبَ إِلَيْهَا مِنْ قَوْلٍ أَوْعَمَلٍ. وَأَعُوذُ بِكَ مِنَ النَّارِ وَمَا قَرَّبَ إِلَيْهَا مِنْ قَوْلٍ أَوْ عَمَلٍ.

اَللّٰهُمَّ إِنِّي أَسْأَلُكَ مِنْ خَيْرِ مَا سَأَلَكَ عَبْدُكَ وَرَسُولُكَ مُحَمَّدٌ ﷺ. وَأَعُوذُ بِكَ مِنْ شَرِّ مَا اسْتَعَاذَ مِنْهُ عَبْدُكَ وَرَسُولُكَ مُحَمَّدٌ ﷺ. اَللّٰهُمَّ وَمَا قَضَيْتَ بِهِ مِنْ قَضَاءٍ أَوْ أَمْرٍ فَاجْعَلْ عَاقِبَتَهُ لِي رُشْداً.

اَللّٰهُمَّ انْفَعْنِي بِمَا عَلَّمْتَنِي وَعَلِّمْنِي مَا يَنْفَعُنِي وَارْزُقْنِي عِلْماً تَنْفَعُنِي بِهِ.

اَللّٰهُمَّ إِنِّي أَسْأَلُكَ عِلْماً لَا يَرْتَدُّ وَنَعِيماً لَا يَنْفَدُ وَمُرَافَقَةَ نَبِيِّكَ مُحَمَّدٍ فِي أَعْلَى الْخُلْدِ.

اَللّٰهُمَّ بِعِلْمِكَ الْغَيْبِ وَقُدْرَتِكَ عَلَى الْخَلْقِ، أَحْيِنِي مَا دَامَتِ الْحَيَاةُ خَيْراً لِي وَتَوَفَّنِي إِذَا كَانَتِ الْوَفَاةُ خَيْراً لِي. وَأَسْأَلُكَ الْقَصْدَ فِي الْفَقْرِ وَالْغِنَى. وَأَسْأَلُكَ نَعِيماً لَا يَبِيدُ وَقُرَّةَ عَيْنٍ لَا تَنْقَطِعُ.

اَللّٰهُمَّ زَيِّنِّي بِزِينَةِ الْإِيمَانِ وَاجْعَلْنِي مِنَ الْهُدَاةِ الْمُهْتَدِينَ.

اَللّٰهُمَّ إِنِّي أَسْتَهْدِيكَ لِأَرْشَدِ أَمْرِي وَأَسْتَجِيرُكَ مِنْ شَرِّ نَفْسِي.

O God, make me one of those who rejoice when they do good and who seek forgiveness when they do evil.

O God, make us amongst Your chosen servants of brilliant white countenance (ghurr muḥajjalīn), *the accepted delegation. O God, Lord of Muḥammad ﷺ, the unlettered Prophet, forgive my sins, remove the rage in my heart and save me from misguiding temptations for as long as You give me life.*

O God, make our outcome good in all affairs, save us from the disgrace of this worldly life and from the punishment of the Hereafter.

O God, Originator of the heavens and the earth, Knower of the unseen and the seen. Truly I take a covenant with You in the life of this world that I bear witness that there is no god but You alone—You have no partner—and that Muḥammad is Your servant and Your messenger. So truly, if You were to leave me to myself, You would bring me closer to evil and distance me from good, and truly I only have confidence in Your mercy. So make a covenant for me with You that You fulfil on the Day of Resurrection; truly, You do not break Your promise.

O God, truly I ask You for sound faith, for faith with beautiful character, for success that is followed by ultimate salvation, mercy from You and good will.

O God, truly I ask You for a balanced life and for a death [like that] of the God-fearing.

O God, I am weak, so through Your good pleasure strengthen my weakness, take me by my forelock towards what is good and make Islam the ultimate goal of my contentment. O God, I am weak, so strengthen me; I am lowly, so honour me; and I am poor, so enrich me.

اَللّٰهُمَّ اجْعَلْنِي مِنَ الَّذِينَ إِذَا أَحْسَنُوا اِسْتَبْشَرُوا وَإِذَا أَسَاءُوا اِسْتَغْفَرُوا.

اَللّٰهُمَّ اجْعَلْنَا مِنْ عِبَادِكَ الْمُنْتَجِبِينَ اَلْغُرِّ الْمُحَجَّلِينَ اَلْوَفْدِ الْمُتَقَبَّلِينَ. اَللّٰهُمَّ رَبَّ مُحَمَّدٍ ﷺ اَلنَّبِيِّ الْأُمِّيِّ اغْفِرْ ذَنْبِي وَأَذْهِبْ غَيْظَ قَلْبِي وَأَجِرْنِي مِنْ مُضِلَّاتِ الْفِتَنِ مَا أَحْيَيْتَنِي.

اَللّٰهُمَّ أَحْسِنْ عَاقِبَتَنَا فِي الْأُمُورِ كُلِّهَا وَأَجِرْنَا مِنْ خِزْيِ الدُّنْيَا وَعَذَابِ الْآخِرَةِ.

اَللّٰهُمَّ فَاطِرَ السَّمَاوَاتِ وَالْأَرْضِ، عَالِمَ الْغَيْبِ وَالشَّهَادَةِ إِنِّي أَعْهَدُ إِلَيْكَ فِي هٰذِهِ الْحَيَاةِ الدُّنْيَا أَنِّي أَشْهَدُ أَنْ لَا إِلٰهَ إِلَّا أَنْتَ وَحْدَكَ لَا شَرِيكَ لَكَ، وَأَنَّ مُحَمَّداً عَبْدُكَ وَرَسُولُكَ. فَإِنَّكَ إِنْ تَكِلْنِي إِلَى نَفْسِي تُقَرِّبْنِي مِنَ الشَّرِّ وَتُبَاعِدْنِي مِنَ الْخَيْرِ وَإِنِّي لَا أَثِقُ إِلَّا بِرَحْمَتِكَ. فَاجْعَلْ لِي عِنْدَكَ عَهْداً تُوَفِّينِيهِ يَوْمَ الْقِيَامَةِ، إِنَّكَ لَا تُخْلِفُ الْمِيعَادَ.

اَللّٰهُمَّ إِنِّي أَسْأَلُكَ صِحَّةَ الْإِيمَانِ وَإِيمَاناً بِحُسْنِ خُلُقٍ وَفَلَاحاً يَتْبَعُهُ نَجَاحٌ وَرَحْمَةٌ مِنْكَ وَرِضْوَانٌ.

اَللّٰهُمَّ إِنِّي أَسْأَلُكَ عِيشَةً سَوِيَّةً وَمِيتَةً تَقِيَّةً.

اَللّٰهُمَّ إِنِّي ضَعِيفٌ فَقَوِّ فِي رِضَاكَ ضَعْفِي وَخُذْ إِلَى الْخَيْرِ بِنَاصِيَتِي وَاجْعَلِ الْإِسْلَامَ مُنْتَهَى رِضَايَ. اَللّٰهُمَّ إِنِّي ضَعِيفٌ فَقَوِّنِي وَإِنِّي ذَلِيلٌ فَأَعِزَّنِي وَإِنِّي فَقِيرٌ فَأَغْنِنِي.

O God, truly I complain to You about the weakness of my ability, my scanty resource[s] and my insignificance among people. O Most Merciful of the merciful, You are the most merciful with me. To whom do You leave me? To an enemy who attacks me, or to a relative who controls my affairs? If you are not angry with me, then I care not. But Your [providing me with] well-being is more vast for me. I seek refuge in the light of Your noble Face—through which the darknesses are illuminated and the affairs of this worldly life and the Hereafter are rectified—lest Your anger descends upon me, or Your wrath is unleashed upon me. [May I] turn to You until You are pleased [with me]; there is no power and no might save in God.

O God, open the hearing of my heart to remembrance of You and provide me with obedience to You, with obedience to Your Messenger and with deeds according to Your Book.

O God, save me from the evil of my soul and grant me resoluteness in the matter of my being well-guided.

O God, do not leave me to myself for even the blink of an eye and do not take back the righteousness that You have given me. Truly there is no one who can take back what You have given and [on the Day of Judgement] the wealth of the wealthy will be of no benefit before You.

O God, rectify the relationships between us [and others], create harmony between our hearts, guide us towards the path of peace and deliver us from darkness unto light. Avert us from obscenities, both what is manifest of them and what is hidden.

O God, bless for us our hearing, our sight, our hearts, our souls, our progeny and turn to us; truly, You are the Ever-Relenting, the Most Merciful. Make us appreciative of Your blessings, thankful for them and accepting of them, and complete them for us.

اَللّٰهُمَّ إِنِّي أَشْكُو إِلَيْكَ ضُعْفَ قُوَّتِي وَقِلَّةَ حِيلَتِي وَهَوَانِي عَلَى النَّاسِ. يَا أَرْحَمَ الرَّاحِمِينَ أَنْتَ أَرْحَمُ بِي. إِلَى مَنْ تَكِلُنِي؟ إِلَى عَدُوٍّ يَتَجَهَّمُنِي أَوْ إِلَى قَرِيبٍ مَلَّكْتَهُ أَمْرِي؟ إِنْ لَمْ تَكُنْ غَضْبَانَ عَلَيَّ فَلَا أُبَالِي غَيْرَ أَنَّ عَافِيَتَكَ أَوْسَعُ لِي. أَعُوذُ بِنُورِ وَجْهِكَ الْكَرِيمِ الَّذِي أَشْرَقَتْ لَهُ الظُّلُمَاتُ وَصَلُحَ عَلَيْهِ أَمْرُ الدُّنْيَا وَالْآخِرَةِ إِنْ تَنْزِلْ بِي غَضَبُكَ أَوْ تَحُلَّ عَلَيَّ سَخَطُكَ. لَكَ الْعُتْبَى حَتَّى تَرْضَى عَلَيَّ، وَلَا حَوْلَ وَلَا قُوَّةَ إِلَّا بِاللهِ.

اَللّٰهُمَّ افْتَحْ مَسَامِعَ قَلْبِي لِذِكْرِكَ وَارْزُقْنِي طَاعَتَكَ وَطَاعَةَ رَسُولِكَ وَعَمَلاً بِكِتَابِكَ.

اَللّٰهُمَّ قِنِي شَرَّ نَفْسِي وَاعْزِمْ لِي عَلَى أَمْرِ رُشْدِي.

اَللّٰهُمَّ لَا تَكِلْنِي إِلَى نَفْسِي طَرْفَةَ عَيْنٍ وَلَا تَنْزِعْ مِنِّي صَالِحَ مَا أَعْطَيْتَنِي. فَإِنَّهُ لَا نَازِعَ لِمَا أَعْطَيْتَ وَلَا يَعْصِمُ ذَا الْجَدِّ مِنْكَ الْجَدُّ.

اَللّٰهُمَّ أَصْلِحْ ذَاتَ بَيْنِنَا وَأَلِّفْ بَيْنَ قُلُوبِنَا وَاهْدِنَا إِلَى سَبِيلِ السَّلَامِ وَنَجِّنَا مِنَ الظُّلُمَاتِ إِلَى النُّورِ. وَجَنِّبْنَا الْفَوَاحِشَ مَا ظَهَرَ مِنْهَا وَمَا بَطَنَ.

اَللّٰهُمَّ بَارِكْ لَنَا فِي أَسْمَاعِنَا وَأَبْصَارِنَا وَقُلُوبِنَا وَأَرْوَاحِنَا وَذُرِّيَّاتِنَا وَتُبْ عَلَيْنَا، إِنَّكَ أَنْتَ التَّوَّابُ الرَّحِيمُ. وَاجْعَلْنَا شَاكِرِينَ لِنِعَمِكَ، مُثْنِينَ بِهَا، قَابِلِينَ لَهَا وَأَتِمَّهَا عَلَيْنَا.

O God, You are not a god we have imagined, nor a Lord we have invented. There was no god before You in whom we could take refuge and protection, nor did anyone help You to create us such as would give us the right to associate [partners] with You. Blessed are You and exalted are You.

O God, I seek refuge in You from every beast whose forelock is in Your Hand. I seek refuge in You from sin, from laziness, from the punishment of Hellfire, from the torment of the grave, from the trial of wealth and from the trial of poverty. I seek refuge in You from sin and loss.

O God, cleanse me of my mistakes just as a white garment is cleansed of filth.

O God, distance me from my mistakes just as you have made the east and the west distant from one another.

O God, truly I ask You for the best [form] of imploring, the best [form] of supplication, the best [way to] salvation, the best action, the best recompense, the best life and the best death. Grant me firmness and make my scales [upon which my deeds are weighed] heavy [with good deeds]. Affirm my faith, raise my status, accept my prayer and forgive my sins. I ask You for the highest ranks of Paradise, O Most Merciful of the merciful.

O God, truly I ask You for the best of what has been done, for the best of what has been performed, for the best of what has been hidden, for the best of what has been made apparent and for the highest ranks of Paradise. Amen.

O God, truly I ask You to improve my reputation, remove my burdens, rectify my affairs, clean my heart, forgive my sins, protect my freedom from distress and illuminate my heart. I ask You for the highest ranks of Paradise, O Most Merciful of the merciful.

اَللّٰهُمَّ إِنَّكَ لَسْتَ بِإِلٰهٍ اِسْتَحْدَثْنَاهُ وَلَا بِرَبٍّ اِبْتَدَعْنَاهُ. وَلَا كَانَ لَنَا قَبْلَكَ مِنْ إِلٰهٍ نَلْجَأُ إِلَيْهِ وَنَذَرُ وَلَا أَعَانَكَ عَلَى خَلْقِنَا أَحَدٌ فَنُشْرِكَهُ فِيكَ. تَبَارَكْتَ وَتَعَالَيْتَ.

اَللّٰهُمَّ إِنِّي أَعُوذُ بِكَ مِنْ كُلِّ دَابَّةٍ نَاصِيَتُهَا بِيَدِكَ. وَأَعُوذُ بِكَ مِنَ الْمَأْثَمِ وَالْكَسَلِ وَعَذَابِ النَّارِ وَمِنْ عَذَابِ الْقَبْرِ وَمِنْ فِتْنَةِ الْغِنَى وَمِنْ فِتْنَةِ الْفَقْرِ. وَأَعُوذُ بِكَ مِنَ الْمَأْثَمِ وَالْمَغْرَمِ.

اَللّٰهُمَّ نَقِّنِي مِنْ خَطَايَايَ كَمَا نَقَّيْتَ الثَّوْبَ الْأَبْيَضَ مِنَ الدَّنَسِ.

اَللّٰهُمَّ بَاعِدْ بَيْنِي وَبَيْنَ خَطَايَايَ كَمَا بَاعَدْتَ بَيْنَ الْمَشْرِقِ وَالْمَغْرِبِ.

اَللّٰهُمَّ إِنِّي أَسْأَلُكَ خَيْرَ الْمَسْأَلَةِ وَخَيْرَ الدُّعَاءِ وَخَيْرَ النَّجَاحِ وَخَيْرَ الْعَمَلِ وَخَيْرَ الثَّوَابِ وَخَيْرَ الْحَيَاةِ وَخَيْرَ الْمَمَاتِ. وَثَبِّتْنِي وَثَقِّلْ مَوَازِينِي. وَحَقِّقْ إِيمَانِي وَارْفَعْ دَرَجَتِي وَتَقَبَّلْ صَلَاتِي وَاغْفِرْ خَطِيئَتِي. وَأَسْأَلُكَ الدَّرَجَاتِ الْعُلَا مِنَ الْجَنَّةِ يَا أَرْحَمَ الرَّاحِمِينَ.

اَللّٰهُمَّ إِنِّي أَسْأَلُكَ خَيْرَ مَا فُعِلَ وَخَيْرَ مَا عُمِلَ وَخَيْرَ مَا بُطِنَ وَخَيْرَ مَا ظُهِرَ وَالدَّرَجَاتِ الْعُلَا مِنَ الْجَنَّةِ، آمِين.

اَللّٰهُمَّ إِنِّي أَسْأَلُكَ أَنْ تَرْفَعَ ذِكْرِي وَتَضَعَ وِزْرِي وَتُصْلِحَ أَمْرِي وَتُطَهِّرَ قَلْبِي وَتَغْفِرَ ذَنْبِي وَتَحْفَظَ فَرْجِي وَتُنَوِّرَ قَلْبِي. وَأَسْأَلُكَ الدَّرَجَاتِ الْعُلَا مِنَ الْجَنَّةِ يَا أَرْحَمَ الرَّاحِمِينَ.

O God, truly I ask You for the openings, endings and compilations of goodness, for its beginning and its end, for its exterior and its interior, and for the highest ranks. Amen.

O God, truly I ask You for safe deliverance from Hellfire and to admit me into Paradise. Amen.

O God, truly I ask You to bless my soul, my hearing, my sight, my spirit, my character, my body, my family, my life, my death and my deeds. O God, accept my good works. I ask You for the highest ranks of Paradise. Amen.[X]

O God, I ask You for wealth and I seek refuge in You lest any relative with whom I have severed ties curses me.

O God, I ask You for a soul that is at peace with You, which believes in meeting You, which is satisfied with Your decree and is content with Your gifts.

O God, truly I ask You for that which merits Your mercy, for that which determines Your forgiveness, for the spoils of every righteous [deed] and for safety from every sin. O God, do not leave any one of our sins without forgiving it, or any worry without removing it, or any sorrow without comforting it, or any harm without revealing it, or any debt without repaying it, or any enemy without destroying them or any need amongst the needs of this world and the Hereafter that is for Your pleasure, without decreeing it [to be bestowed], O Most Merciful of the merciful.

O God, truly I ask You for health, chastity, trustworthiness, beautiful character and contentment with Your decree, O Most Merciful of the merciful.

اَللّٰهُمَّ إِنِّي أَسْأَلُكَ فَوَاتِحَ الْخَيْرِ وَخَوَاتِمَهُ وَجَوَامِعَهُ وَأَوَّلَهُ وَآخِرَهُ وَظَاهِرَهُ وَبَاطِنَهُ، وَالدَّرَجَاتِ الْعُلَا، آمِين.

اَللّٰهُمَّ إِنِّي أَسْأَلُكَ خَلَاصاً مِنَ النَّارِ سَالِماً وَأَدْخِلْنِي الْجَنَّةَ، آمِين.

اَللّٰهُمَّ إِنِّي أَسْأَلُكَ أَنْ تُبَارِكَ فِي نَفْسِي وَفِي سَمْعِي وَفِي بَصَرِي وَفِي رُوحِي وَفِي خُلُقِي وَفِي خَلِيقَتِي وَأَهْلِي وَمَحْيَايَ وَمَمَاتِي وَفِي عَمَلِي. اَللّٰهُمَّ وَتَقَبَّلْ حَسَنَاتِي وَأَسْأَلُكَ الدَّرَجَاتِ الْعُلَا مِنَ الْجَنَّةِ، آمِينْ.

اَللّٰهُمَّ أَسْأَلُكَ الْغِنَى وَأَعُوذُ بِكَ أَنْ تَدْعُوَ عَلَيَّ رَحِمٌ قَطَعْتُهَا.

اَللّٰهُمَّ إِنِّي أَسْأَلُكَ نَفْساً بِكَ مُطْمَئِنَّةً تُؤْمِنُ بِلِقَائِكَ وَتَرْضَى بِقَضَائِكَ وَتَقْنَعُ بِعَطَائِكَ.

اَللّٰهُمَّ إِنِّي أَسْأَلُكَ مُوجِبَاتِ رَحْمَتِكَ وَعَزَائِمَ مَغْفِرَتِكَ وَالْغَنِيمَةَ مِنْ كُلِّ بِرٍّ وَالسَّلَامَةَ مِنْ كُلِّ إِثْمٍ. اَللّٰهُمَّ لَا تَدَعْ لَنَا ذَنْباً إِلَّا غَفَرْتَهُ وَلَا هَمّاً إِلَّا فَرَّجْتَهُ وَلَا كَرْباً إِلَّا نَفَّسْتَهُ وَلَا ضُرّاً إِلَّا كَشَفْتَهُ وَلَا دَيْناً إِلَّا قَضَيْتَهُ وَلَا عَدُوّاً إِلَّا أَهْلَكْتَهُ وَلَا حَاجَةً مِنْ حَوَائِجِ الدُّنْيَا وَالْآخِرَةِ إِلَّا قَضَيْتَهَا يَا أَرْحَمَ الرَّاحِمِين.

اَللّٰهُمَّ إِنِّي أَسْأَلُكَ الصِّحَّةَ وَالْعِفَّةَ وَالْأَمَانَةَ وَحُسْنَ الْخُلُقِ وَالرِّضَى بِالْقَدْرِ يَا أَرْحَمَ الرَّاحِمِينَ.

VARIOUS REPORTED EXPRESSIONS OF SEEKING REFUGE IN GOD

O God, truly I seek refuge in You from the harm of the decree, from the struggle in tribulation, from being overtaken by wretchedness and from the malice of enemies.

O God, truly I seek refuge in You from the evil of what I know and I seek refuge in You from the evil of what I know not.

O God, truly I seek refuge in You from any knowledge that does not benefit, from a heart that is not humble, from a soul that is not satiated and from a supplication that is not heard.

O God, truly I seek refuge in You from the cessation of Your blessing, [from] an abrupt change in the well-being You grant, [from] Your sudden vengeance and [from] all of Your wrath.

O God, truly I seek refuge in You from destruction, I seek refuge in You from fire and I seek refuge in You lest Satan confound me at the time of death. I seek refuge in You lest I die [while] turning my back on Your path. I seek refuge in You lest I die from a bite [or sting].

O God, truly I seek refuge in You from a death [from] destruction. I seek refuge in You from a death [from] grief. I seek refuge in You from hunger, because it is the worst bedfellow, and I seek refuge in You from unfaithfulness, because it is the worst confidante.

O God, truly I seek refuge in You from overwhelming debt, from an overwhelming enemy, from destructive sins and from the temptation of the Antichrist.

اِسْتِعَاذَاتٌ مُطْلَقَةٌ مَأْثُورَةٌ

اَللّٰهُمَّ إِنِّي أَعُوذُ بِكَ مِنْ شَرِّ الْقَضَاءِ وَمِنْ جَهْدِ الْبَلَاءِ وَدَرْكِ الشَّقَاءِ وَشَمَاتَةِ الْأَعْدَاءِ.

اَللّٰهُمَّ إِنِّي أَعُوذُ بِكَ مِنْ شَرِّ مَا عَلِمْتُ وَأَعُوذُ بِكَ مِنْ شَرِّ مَا لَمْ أَعْلَمْ.

اَللّٰهُمَّ إِنِّي أَعُوذُ بِكَ مِنْ عِلْمٍ لَا يَنْفَعُ وَمِنْ قَلْبٍ لَا يَخْشَعُ وَمِنْ نَفْسٍ لَا تَشْبَعُ وَمِنْ دُعَاءٍ لَا يُسْمَعُ.

اَللّٰهُمَّ إِنِّي أَعُوذُ بِكَ مِنْ زَوَالِ نِعْمَتِكَ وَتَحَوُّلِ عَافِيَتِكَ وَفُجَاءَةِ نِقْمَتِكَ وَجَمِيعِ سَخَطِكَ.

اَللّٰهُمَّ إِنِّي أَعُوذُ بِكَ مِنَ الْهَدَمِ وَأَعُوذُ بِكَ مِنَ الْحَرَقِ وَأَعُوذُ بِكَ أَنْ يَتَخَبَّطَنِيَ الشَّيْطَانُ عِنْدَ الْمَوْتِ. وَأَعُوذُ بِكَ مِنْ أَنْ أَمُوتَ فِي سَبِيلِكَ مُدْبِراً. وَأَعُوذُ بِكَ أَنْ أَمُوتَ لَدِيغاً.

اَللّٰهُمَّ إِنِّي أَعُوذُ بِكَ مِنْ مَوْتِ الْهَدَمِ وَأَعُوذُ بِكَ مِنْ مَوْتِ الْغَمِّ. وَأَعُوذُ بِكَ مِنَ الْجُوعِ فَإِنَّهُ بِئْسَ الضَّجِيعُ وَأَعُوذُ بِكَ مِنَ الْخِيَانَةِ فَإِنَّهَا بِئْسَتِ الْبِطَانَةُ.

اَللّٰهُمَّ إِنِّي أَعُوذُ بِكَ مِنْ غَلَبَةِ الدَّيْنِ وَغَلَبَةِ الْعَدُوِّ وَمِنْ بَوَارِ الْإِثْمِ وَمِنْ فِتْنَةِ الْمَسِيحِ الدَّجَّالِ.

O God, truly I seek refuge in You from difficulty, hypocrisy and bad character traits.

O God, truly I seek refuge in You from the evil of my hearing, the evil of my sight, the evil of my tongue and my heart, and [from] the evil of seed.

O God, truly I seek refuge in You from that which is wrong amongst character traits, deeds and desires.

O God, truly I seek refuge in You from a day of evil, an hour of evil, a friend of evil and [from] a neighbour of evil in [one's] place of residence.

O God, truly I seek refuge in You lest I associate [a partner] with You while knowing [this] and I seek Your forgiveness for what I know not.

O God, truly I seek refuge in You, in Your noble Face and in Your almighty Name from disbelief and poverty.

O God, truly I seek refuge in You from the evil of a tumultuous torrent and fire.

O God, truly I seek refuge in You from the evil of whatever crawls on its stomach, whatever walks on two feet and whatever walks on all fours.

O God, truly I seek refuge in You from a woman who turns my hair grey before my old age. I seek refuge in You from wealth that is a punishment to me. I seek refuge in You from a companion on the way who, if he sees something good [from me], conceals it, and if he sees something bad, divulges it.

O God, truly I seek refuge in You and in the light of Your Face that illuminates the heavens and the earth.[Y]

اَللّٰهُمَّ إِنِّي أَعُوذُ بِكَ مِنَ الشِّقَاقِ وَالنِّفَاقِ وَسُوءِ الْأَخْلَاقِ.

اَللّٰهُمَّ إِنِّي أَعُوذُ بِكَ مِنْ شَرِّ سَمْعِي وَمِنْ شَرِّ بَصَرِي وَشَرِّ لِسَانِي وَقَلْبِي وَشَرِّ مَنِيِّي.

اَللّٰهُمَّ إِنِّي أَعُوذُ بِكَ مِنْ مُنْكَرَاتِ الْأَخْلَاقِ وَالْأَعْمَالِ وَالْأَهْوَاءِ.

اَللّٰهُمَّ إِنِّي أَعُوذُ بِكَ مِنْ يَوْمِ السُّوءِ وَسَاعَةِ السُّوءِ وَصَاحِبِ السُّوءِ وَجَارِ السُّوءِ فِي دَارِ الْمُقَامَةِ.

اَللّٰهُمَّ إِنِّي أَعُوذُ بِكَ أَنْ أُشْرِكَ بِكَ وَأَنَا أَعْلَمُ وَأَسْتَغْفِرُكَ لِمَا لَا أَعْلَمُ.

اَللّٰهُمَّ إِنِّي أَعُوذُ بِكَ وَبِوَجْهِكَ الْكَرِيمِ وَبِاسْمِكَ الْعَظِيمِ مِنَ الْكُفْرِ وَالْفَقْرِ.

اَللّٰهُمَّ إِنِّي أَعُوذُ بِكَ مِنْ شَرِّ الْأَعْمَيَيْنِ السَّيْلِ وَالْحَرِيقِ.

اَللّٰهُمَّ إِنِّي أَعُوذُ بِكَ مِنْ شَرِّ مَنْ يَمْشِي عَلَى بَطْنِهِ وَمَنْ يَمْشِي عَلَى رِجْلَيْنِ وَمَنْ يَمْشِي عَلَى أَرْبَعٍ.

اَللّٰهُمَّ إِنِّي أَعُوذُ بِكَ مِنْ اِمْرَأَةٍ تُشَيِّبُنِي قَبْلَ الْمَشِيبِ. وَأَعُوذ بِكَ مِنْ مَالٍ يَكُونُ عَلَيَّ عَذاباً. وَأَعُوذُ بِكَ مِنْ صَاحِبِ طَرِيقَةٍ إِنْ رَأَى حَسَنَةً دَفَنَهَا وَإِنْ رَأَى سَيِّئَةً أَفْشَاهَا.

اَللّٰهُمَّ إِنِّي أَعُوذُ بِكَ وَبِنُورِ وَجْهِكَ الَّذِي أَضَاءَتْ لَهُ السَّمَاوَاتُ وَالْأَرْضُ.

O God, truly I seek refuge in the light of Your holiness, in the greatness of Your purity and in the blessing of Your majesty from every blight or canker, and from events occurring during the night and during the day, unless it is a nocturnal event that brings good, O Most Compassionate. You are my succour and You are my joy, so I seek joy in You. You are my refuge so I seek refuge in You. O He for Whom the necks of tyrants are lowered and for Whom the necks of the Pharaohs are submissive, I seek refuge in You from Your exposing [me] to disgrace, [from] Your revealing [my] secret, [from] forgetting Your remembrance and [from] turning away from thanking You. I am under Your protection day and night, in my sleep and my repose, and [in] my journeying and my travels. Your remembrance is my outer garment and Your praise is my inner garment. There is no god but You; may Your Face be magnified and may Your glorifications be honoured. Save me from Your exposing [me] to disgrace and from the evil of Your punishment. Pitch the canopy of Your protection over me, admit me to the protection of Your guardianship and straighten me with goodness from You, O Most Merciful of the merciful.

O God, truly I seek refuge in You from inability and laziness. I seek refuge in You from mercilessness, poverty, depravity and misery. I seek refuge in You from transgression, difficulties, hypocrisy, seeking a good reputation and showing off. I seek refuge in You from deafness and muteness, [from] insanity, leprosy and evil illnesses.

O God, truly I seek refuge in You from poverty and impoverishment, and lest I oppress or am oppressed.

O God, truly I seek refuge in You from a nature that leads to greed, from greedily desiring something that should not be desired and from greedily desiring where there is nothing to be desired.

اَللّٰهُمَّ إِنِّي أَعُوذُ بِنُورِ قُدْسِكَ وَعَظَمَةِ طَهَارَتِكَ وَبَرَكَةِ جَلَالِكَ مِنْ كُلِّ آفَةٍ وَعَاهَةٍ وَمِنْ طَوَارِقِ اللَّيْلِ وَالنَّهَارِ، إِلَّا طَارِقاً يَطْرُقُ بِخَيْرٍ يَا رَحْمٰنُ. أَنْتَ غِيَاثِي وَأَنْتَ مَلَاذِي فَبِكَ أَلُوذُ وَأَنْتَ عِيَاذِي فَبِكَ أَعُوذُ. يَا مَنْ ذَلَّتْ لَهُ رِقَابُ الْجَبَابِرَةِ وَخَضَعَتْ لَهُ أَعْنَاقُ الْفَرَاعِنَةِ أَعُوذُ بِكَ مِنْ خِزْيِكَ وَكَشْفِ سِرِّكَ وَمِنْ نِسْيَانِ ذِكْرِكَ وَالْاِنْصِرَافِ عَنْ شُكْرِكَ. أَنَا فِي حِرْزِكَ لَيْلِي وَنَهَارِي وَنَوْمِي وَقَرَارِي وَظَعْنِي وَأَسْفَارِي. ذِكْرُكَ شِعَارِي وَثَنَاؤُكَ دِثَارِي. لَا إِلٰهَ إِلَّا أَنْتَ تَعْظِيماً لِوَجْهِكَ وَتَكْرِيماً لِسُبُحَاتِكَ. أَجِرْنِي مِنْ خِزْيِكَ وَمِنْ شَرِّ عِقَابِكَ. وَاضْرِبْ عَلَيَّ سُرَادِقَاتِ حِفْظِكَ وَأَدْخِلْنِي فِي حِفْظِ عِنَايَتِكَ وَعُدَّ لِي خَيْراً مِنْكَ يَا أَرْحَمَ الرَّاحِمِيْنَ.

اَللّٰهُمَّ إِنِّي أَعُوذُ بِكَ مِنَ الْعَجْزِ وَالْكَسْلِ. وَأَعُوذُ بِكَ مِنَ الْقَسْوَةِ وَالْعَيْلَةِ وَالذِّلَّةِ وَالْمَسْكَنَةِ. وَأَعُوذُ بِكَ مِنَ الْفُسُوقِ وَالشِّقَاقِ وَالنِّفَاقِ وَالسُّمْعَةِ وَالرِيَاءِ. وَأَعُوذُ بِكَ مِنَ الصَّمَمِ وَالْبُكْمِ وَالْجُنُونِ وَالْجُزَامِ وَسَيِّئِ الْأَسْقَامِ.

اَللّٰهُمَّ إِنِّي أَعُوذُ بِكَ مِنَ الْفَقْرِ وَالْعَيْلَةِ وَمِنْ أَنْ أَظْلِمَ أَوْ أُظْلَمَ.

اَللّٰهُمَّ إِنِّي أَعُوذُ بِكَ مِنْ طَبْعٍ يَهْدِي إِلَى طَمَعٍ، وَمِنْ طَمَعٍ إِلَى غَيْرِ مَطْمَعٍ وَمِنْ طَمَعٍ حَيْثُ لَا مَطْمَعَ.

THE NINETY-NINE BEAUTIFUL NAMES OF GOD

اَلْأَسْمَاءُ الْحُسْنَى

We conclude this blessed book by mentioning the ninety-nine Beautiful Names of God (*al-Asmā' al-Ḥusnā*), so we say:

He is God (*Allāh*); there is no god but He,	هُوَ اللهُ الَّذِي لَا إِلٰهَ إِلَّا هُوَ
The Most Compassionate (*al-Raḥmān*)	اَلرَّحْمٰنُ
The Most Merciful (*al-Raḥīm*)	اَلرَّحِيمُ
The King (*al-Malik*)	اَلْمَلِكُ
The Most Holy (*al-Quddūs*)	اَلْقُدُّوسُ
The Source of Peace (*al-Salām*)	اَلسَّلَامُ
The Faithful (*al-Mu'min*)	اَلْمُؤْمِنُ
The Guardian (*al-Muhaymin*)	اَلْمُهَيْمِنُ
The Eminent (*al-'Azīz*)	اَلْعَزِيزُ
The Compeller (*al-Jabbār*)	اَلْجَبَّارُ
The Proud (*al-Mutakabbir*)	اَلْمُتَكَبِّرُ
The Creator (*al-Khāliq*)	اَلْخَالِقُ

The Maker (*al-Bāriʾ*)	اَلْبَارِئُ
The Fashioner of Forms (*al-Muṣawwir*)	اَلْمُصَوِّرُ
The Ever-Forgiving (*al-Ghaffār*)	اَلْغَفَّارُ
The Dominator (*al-Qahhār*)	اَلْقَهَّارُ
The Bestower (*al-Wahhāb*)	اَلْوَهَّابُ
The Ever-Providing (*al-Razzāq*)	اَلرَّزَّاقُ
The Victorious (*al-Fattāḥ*)	اَلْفَتَّاحُ
The All-Knowing (*al-ʿAlīm*)	اَلْعَلِيمُ
The Restrainer (*al-Qābiḍ*)	اَلْقَابِضُ
The Expander (*al-Bāsiṭ*)	اَلْبَاسِطُ
The Abaser (*al-Khāfiḍ*)	اَلْخَافِضُ
The Exalter (*al-Rāfiʿ*)	اَلرَّافِعُ
The Giver of Honour (*al-Muʿizz*)	اَلْمُعِزُّ
The Giver of Dishonour (*al-Mudhill*)	اَلْمُذِلُّ
The All-Hearing (*al-Samīʿ*)	السَّمِيعُ
The All-Seeing (*al-Baṣīr*)	الْبَصِيرُ
The Judge (*al-Ḥakam*)	اَلْحَكَمُ
The Just (*al-ʿAdl*)	اَلْعَدْلُ

The Benevolent (*al-Laṭīf*)	اَللَّطِيفُ
The All-Aware (*al-Khabīr*)	اَلْخَبِيرُ
The Indulgent (*al-Ḥalīm*)	اَلْحَلِيمُ
The Almighty (*al-ʿAẓīm*)	اَلْعَظِيمُ
The All-Forgiving (*al-Ghafūr*)	اَلْغَفُورُ
The Grateful (*al-Shakūr*)	اَلشَّكُورُ
The Most High (*al-ʿAlī*)	اَلْعَلِيُّ
The Great (*al-Kabīr*)	اَلْكَبِيرُ
The Preserver (*al-Ḥafīẓ*)	اَلْحَفِيظُ
The Nourisher (*al-Muqīṭ*)	اَلْمُقِيتُ
The Reckoner (*al-Ḥasīb*)	اَلْحَسِيبُ
The Majestic (*al-Jalīl*)	اَلْجَلِيلُ
The Generous (*al-Karīm*)	اَلْكَرِيمُ
The Watchful (*al-Raqīb*)	اَلرَّقِيبُ
The Answerer (*al-Mujīb*)	اَلْمُجِيبُ
The Vast (*al-Wāsiʿ*)	اَلْوَاسِعُ
The Wise (*al-Ḥakīm*)	اَلْحَكِيمُ
The Loving (*al-Wadūd*)	اَلْوَدُودُ

The All-Glorious (*al-Majīd*)	اَلْمَجِيدُ
The Raiser of the Dead (*al-Bā'ith*)	اَلْبَاعِثُ
The Witness (*al-Shahīd*)	اَلشَّهِيدُ
The Truth (*al-Ḥaqq*)	اَلْحَقُّ
The Trustee (*al-Wakīl*)	اَلْوَكِيلُ
The Strong (*al-Qawī*)	اَلْقَوِيُّ
The Firm (*al-Matīn*)	اَلْمَتِينُ
The Patron (*al-Walī*)	اَلْوَلِيُّ
The Praised (*al-Ḥamīd*)	اَلْحَمِيدُ
The Accounter (*al-Muḥṣī*)	اَلْمُحْصِي
The Originator (*al-Mubdi'*)	اَلْمُبْدِئُ
The Restorer (*al-Mu'īd*)	اَلْمُعِيدُ
The Giver of Life (*al-Muḥyī*)	اَلْمُحْيِي
The Bringer of Death (*al-Mumīt*)	اَلـمُمِيتُ
The Ever-Living (*al-Ḥayy*)	اَلْحَيُّ
The Self-Subsisting (*al-Qayyūm*)	اَلْقَيُّومُ
The Finder (*al-Wājid*)	اَلْوَاجِدُ
The Magnificent (*al-Mājid*)	اَلْمَاجِدُ

The Unique (*al-Wāḥid*)	اَلْوَاحِدُ
The One (*al-Aḥad*)	اَلْأَحَدُ
The Utterly Independent (*al-Ṣamad*)	اَلصَّمَدُ
The All-Powerful (*al-Qādir*)	اَلْقَادِرُ
The Determiner (*al-Muqtadir*)	اَلْمُقْتَدِرُ
The Expediter (*al-Muqaddim*)	اَلْمُقَدِّمُ
The Delayer (*al-Muʾakhkhir*)	اَلْمُؤَخِّرُ
The First (*al-Awwal*)	اَلْأَوَّلُ
The Last (*al-Ākhir*)	اَلْآخِرُ
The Manifest (*al-Ẓāhir*)	اَلظَّاهِرُ
The Hidden (*al-Bāṭin*)	اَلْبَاطِنُ
The Ruler (*al-Wālī*)	اَلْوَالِي
The Exalted (*al-Mutaʿālī*)	اَلْمُتَعَالِي
The Most Kind and Righteous (*al-Barr*)	اَلْبَرُّ
The Ever-Relenting (*al-Tawwāb*)	اَلتَّوَّابُ
The Avenger (*al-Muntaqim*)	اَلْمُنْتَقِمُ
The Effacer of Sins (*al-ʿAfuww*)	اَلْعَفُوُّ
The All-Pitying (*al-Raʾūf*)	اَلرَّؤُوفُ

The King of All Sovereignty (*Mālik al-Mulk*)	مَالِكُ الْمُلْكِ
The Lord of Majesty and Generosity (*Dhū'l-Jalāl wa'l-Ikrām*)	ذُو الْجَلَالِ وَالْإِكْرَامِ
The Equitable (*al-Muqsiṭ*)	اَلْمُقْسِطُ
The Uniter (*al-Jāmiʿ*)	اَلْجَامِعُ
The Independent (*al-Ghanī*)	اَلْغَنِي
The Grantor of Sufficiency (*al-Mughnī*)	اَلْمُغْنِي
The Protector (*al-Mānīʿ*)	اَلْمَانِعُ
The Punisher (*al-Ḍārr*)	اَلضَّارُّ
The Benefactor (*al-Nāfiʿ*)	اَلنَّافِعُ
The Light (*al-Nūr*)	اَلنُّورُ
The Guide (*al-Hādī*)	اَلْهَادِي
The Absolute Cause (*al-Badīʿ*)	اَلْبَدِيعُ
The Everlasting (*al-Bāqī*)	اَلْبَاقِي
The Inheritor of All (*al-Wārith*)	اَلوَارِثُ
The Right in Guidance (*al-Rashīd*)	اَلرَّشِيدُ
The Patient (*al-Ṣabūr*)	اَلصَّبُورُ
May His Majesty be exalted, there is no god besides Him.	جَلَّ جَلَالُهُ وَلَا إِلٰهَ غَيْرُهُ

ENDNOTES

[1] Aḥmad b. ʿAbd al-Ḥalīm Ibn Taymiyya, *Minhāj al-Sunna al-nabawiyya*, Beirut: Dār al-Kutub al-ʿIlmiyya, [1321–22/1903–04] and Ibn Taymiyya, *al-Kalim al-ṭayyib*, tr. Ezzeddin Ibrahim and Denys Johnson-Davies as *The Goodly Word*, Cambridge: Islamic Texts Society, 2003.

[2] Traditionally, sleep is referred to as the 'small death'.

[3] Also commonly referred to as a *miswāk*.

[4] Aḥmad Ibn Ḥanbal, *Musnad li'l-Imām Aḥmad*, Beirut: Muʾassasat al-Risāla, 2001, *ḥadīth* no. 5814.

[5] Q.III.191.

[6] The Arabic word *qibla* refers to the direction of prayer.

[7] The term *Bayt al-Maqdis* refers to the entire precinct in Jerusalem encompassing the al-Aqsa Mosque (*Masjid al-Aqṣā*) and the Dome of the Rock (*Masjid al-Ṣakhra*).

[8] According to the Shāfiʿī school of jurisprudence (*madhhab*), the preponderant (*rājiḥ*) opinion does not restrict the interpretation of this precept to a 'running' river; see Aḥmad b. Ḥajar al-Haytamī, *Tanbīh al-akhyār*, Amman: Arwiqa li'l-Dirāsāt wa'l-Nashr, 2013, p. 56.

[9] According to the Shāfiʿī *madhhab*, the term, *al-hawāʾ* ('the air'), in this context refers to 'the wind' and is the preponderant opinion; ibid., p. 56.

[10] According to Ibn Ḥajar, this is not a restriction; rather, touching one's private parts (either front or back) with the right hand—except out of absolute necessity—is disliked (*makrūh*) from a religious standpoint, but not expressly forbidden. Ibid., p. 57.

[11] This is strange because Abū Dāʾūd and Ibn Māja narrated that the Prophet used to like to perform ablution from a brass vessel; see Ibn Ḥajar, *Tanbīh al-akhyār*, p. 58. See also Abū Dāʾūd, *Sunan*, no. 100 and Ibn Māja, *Sunan*, no. 471.

[12] When fasting, a person needs to be cautious not to take in water through the nose or mouth.

[13] Here, washing the forearms and lower legs is referred to by means of the term, *taḥjīl*. This, said of a horse, literally means 'to have white legs'. According to sayings of the Prophet and the remarks of later commentators, this meant brightening one's extremities, so that on the Day of Resurrection the Muslims may be distinguished from other communities by the radiance shining from their hands and feet.

[14] That is, performing each step successively so that no part of the body dries before washing the next; the term used for this is *muwālāt*.
[15] Instead, one should wipe the water from one's arms and hands with the opposite hand in order to avoid excessively wetting one's clothes (which is disliked, *makrūh*) or the parts of the body not involved in *wuḍū*ʾ.
[16] The Messenger of God used to perform the ablution out of a vessel. Nowadays, few Muslims know that this is the *Sunna*, and even fewer perform ablution this way. A wide-mouthed vessel is placed on the right so that after washing one's hands, one may lower a hand into the vessel to scoop out water for performing the ablution. A small-mouthed vessel is placed on the left so that one can pour the water into one's right hand (since one should always begin with the right hand).
[17] The habit of the Messenger of God was to drink while sitting, except in two cases when it was desirable (*mustaḥabb*) to drink while standing: (1) when drinking the remaining water after performing ablution and (2) when drinking water from the Zamzam well in Mecca after performing the circumambulation (*al-ṭawāf*) and then performing two *rakʿa*s of prayer behind the Standing Place of Abraham (*Maqām Ibrāhīm*).
[18] Q.xcvii.
[19] A *ṣā*ʿ is a unit of measurement equivalent to slightly less than half a kilogram, while a *mudd* is equal to half a *ṣā*ʿ; see Majd al-Dīn al-Mubārak b. Muḥammad b. Athīr, *al-Nihāya fī al-gharīb al-ḥadīth wa'l-athar*, Beirut: Dār al-Maʿrifa, 2009, vol. iv, p. 308.
[20] The words of Suyūṭī, *fī ayy waqt* ('at any time'), indicate that, according to Shāfiʿī scholars, these *sunna* prayers were in fact allowed during disliked times (*awqāt al-karāha*); see ʿUmar b. ʿAlī b. al-Mulaqqin, *Tuḥfat al-muḥtāj ilā adillat al-Minhāj*, Mecca: Dār Ḥirāʾ, 1987 and Muḥammad b. Aḥmad al-Ramlī, *Nihāyat al-muḥtāj ilā sharḥ al-Minhāj*, Beirut: Dār al-Kutub al-ʿIlmiyya, 1993. This *sunna* prayer is called the *taḥiyyat al-wuḍū*ʾ ('salutation of the ablution').
[21] This was when travelling was by caravan.
[22] The Arabic, *bayn ʿishāʾayn*, literally means 'between the two *ʿishā*ʾs;' that is, between the sunset prayer (*ṣalāt al-maghrib*) and the evening prayer (*ṣalāt al-ʿishā*ʾ).
[23] Here, the 'two declarations of faith' refer to the *kalima*: *ashhadu an lā ilāh illā Allāh wa-ashhadu anna Muḥammad ʿabduhu wa-rasūluhu* ('I bear witness that there is no god but God and I bear witness that Muḥammad is His servant and His messenger').
[24] This refutes the claims that prostration was not permitted on any material except what comes from the earth. According to Ibn Ḥajar, Shaykh al-Aḥsāʾ Abū Bakr b. Muḥammad al-Ḥanafī refuted this claim

in a treatise entitled, *Relief for the Worshippers by Textual Proof for the Ritual Prayer upon a Prayer Mat* (*Is'āf Ahl al-'Ibāda bi-naṣṣ al-ṣalāt 'alā al-sajjāda*); see Ibn Ḥajar, *Tanbīh al-akhyār*, p. 71.

25 This may be performed at any time in a mosque except at the three disliked (*makrūh*) times for the ritual prayer: (1) just before sunrise, (2) just before the sun reaches its zenith (*zawāl*) and (3) just before sunset (*maghrib*). According to Ibn Ḥajar, the two *rak'as* may be performed even if the imam is delivering the sermon (*khuṭba*) on the day of *Jum'a*; ibid., p. 73.

26 According to Ibn Ḥajar, one should intend to observe spiritual retreat (*i'tikāf*) upon entering the mosque, even if only for a moment, to obtain the immense reward granted for spiritual retreat according to one opinion; ibid.

27 This is due to its being disliked (*makrūh*). Ibn Ḥajar mentioned this issue in detail in the *Tuḥfa* as follows: 'If a louse is dead, then discarding it in the mosque is prohibited without question because it will make other things filthy. If it is alive, then according to the author [meaning Ibn Ḥajar himself] it is disliked, and according to [the great authority in the Shāfi'ī *madhhab*] Imam Ramlī, it is prohibited.' See Ibn Ḥajar al-Haytamī, *Tuḥfat al-muḥtāj bi-sharḥ al-Minhāj*, Beirut: Dār al-Fikr, 1997, vol. I, pp. 167–168; Ramlī, *Nihāyat al-muḥtāj*, vol. II, p. 50; and 'Umar Ibn al-Qaradāghī, *al-Manhal al-naḍḍākh fī ikhtilāf al-ashyākh*, Beirut: Dār al-Bashā'ir al-Islāmiyya, 1934, no. 274.

28 This precept refers to unacceptable poetry (in other words, that which does not praise Islam or encourage one to acquire noble qualities) and it is *Sunna* to say to anyone performing it, 'May God shut your mouth.' Otherwise, reciting acceptable poetry in the mosque is *Sunna*, just as Ḥassān b. Thābit used to do. He would look to 'Umar and say, 'I used to perform poetry in this mosque in front of someone who is better than you [meaning, the Messenger of God].' See Ibn Ḥajar, *Tanbīh al-akhyār*, p. 74.

29 Rather, the people who should lead the *ṣalāt* are ranked in preference as follows: (1) the ruler, (2) his general representative, (3) his special representative, (4) the local imam, and if none of them are available, then (5) the person most knowledgeable in jurisprudence (*fiqh*), (6) the best reciter and (7) the most scrupulous. ibid., p. 75.

30 A *ḥanīf* is someone who turns away from idol worship and false religion; when society is doing wrong, a *ḥanīf* does what is right. See 'Abd al-Ḥāfiẓ al-Lakhnawī, *Misbāḥ al-lugha*, Karachi: Majlis-i Nashriyat-i Islam, 1992.

31 Q.I.

32 According to a *ḥadīth* in the *Musnad* of Aḥmad Ibn Ḥanbal, 'The Messenger of God said that the Qur'ān is divided [from beginning to end]

into four divisions, [in the following order]: (1) *al-sabʿ al-ṭiwāl*, the seven long *sūras*, (2) *al-miʾūn*, 'the hundreds', meaning those *sūras* with approximately one hundred *āyās*, (3) *al-mathānī*, the *sūras* with double digits (although there are other opinions about the meaning of this name), and (4) *al-mufaṣṣalāt*, the *sūras* in which the *basmala* is repeatedly interpolated.

[33] Q.III.8.

[34] Q.CIX.

[35] Q.CXII.

[36] Q.LXIII.

[37] Q.XXXII.

[38] Q.LXXVI.

[39] Ibn Ḥajar remarked that he had never seen this demarcation given by anyone else; see *Tanbīh al-akhyār*, p. 76.

[40] According to Ibn Ḥajar, it is in fact *Sunna* 'to clasp one's right hand over the left and to rest it between one's chest and one's navel, not on one's chest. His [that is, Suyūṭi's] words, "on one's chest" (*ʿalā ṣadrihi*), is astonishing coming from him. The wisdom behind this [positioning of the hands] is that one strives to remember to guard one's heart from passing thoughts that have no connection to the ritual prayer—even if they are otherworldly—and as if someone is afraid of losing something precious, one clenches it tightly with both hands, [so too is] that type of protection [of the heart] the type of devotion that is emphatically sought after because no one receives any reward from their prayer without having presence of mind. Rather, a preponderance of scholars—amongst them Imam Ghazālī—have explicitly mentioned that, as a component of one's ritual prayer, devotion (*khushūʿ*) is a condition of its [spiritual] validity.' Ibid., p. 77.

[41] According to Ibn Ḥajar, it is *sunna* to remain silent between the opening *takbīr* and the opening supplication (*iftitāḥ*); between the opening supplication and seeking refuge in God (*taʿawwudh*); between seeking refuge in God and the *basmala*; to continue [without pause] from the *basmala* to the *Fātiḥa*, and from '*al-ḍālīn*' to '*āmīn*.' However, between the '*āmīn*' and [another] *sūra*, the imam should remain silent for a time equivalent to that taken by the followers to recite the *Fātiḥa* (this is for Shāfiʿī *madhhab*). During this interval, silence [on the part of the imam] is not good; instead, it is *sunna* for him to occupy himself with recitation. It is [also] *sunna* for the imam to remain silent between the end of the *sūra* and the *takbīr* for bowing in prayer (*rukūʿ*). There is no other time at which silence is desirable other than the aforementioned. Ibid., p. 78.

[42] Q.XXVIII.24.

[43] This is according to the Shāfiʿī *madhhab*. The adherents of the Ḥanafī

madhhab only raise their hands for one *takbīr*; namely, the opening *takbīr* (*takbīr al-taḥrīm*) to commence the ritual prayer.

[44] The editor of the Arabic edition mentions that there are numerous forms of *tashahhud* and that the one given here is the form chosen from Ibn ʿAbbās by Shāfiʿī scholars.

[45] Here, Suyūṭī's mentioning, 'In the name of God' (*tasmiya*), at the beginning of the *tashahhud* contradicts the Shāfiʿī *madhhab*, because this is not considered to be *Sunna*. See Ibn Ḥajar, *Tanbīh al-akhyār*, p. 82.

[46] The Arabic word used here, *sadl*, refers to two distinct things that are both derived from authentic *ḥadīth*s. The first usage is that which is used by Suyūṭī here, which is praying with one's arms inside of one's garment whilst bowing and prostrating in prayer. This also refers to one praying with one's clothes dangling from one's body (regardless of whether one is wearing another garment underneath it or not). Nowadays, this applies to people wearing a scarf that dangles from one's neck whilst praying. The second meaning refers to praying with one's hands down by one's sides, which is an acceptable mode of ritual prayer for the Mālikī *madhhab*, based on rigorously authentic *ḥadīth*s accepted by the Mālikī *madhhab* and the actions of the Medinan community. See Ibn Athīr, *Nihāya*, vol. II, p. 676 and Khalīl b. Isḥāq al-Jundī, *Mukhtaṣar al-Khalīl*, Cairo: ʿĪsā Ḥalabī, 2004.

[47] Ibn Ḥajar wrote, 'I have never seen any of our companions to be of this opinion, even accepting [that] there are [different] perspectives about this.' Ibid., p. 85.

[48] According to Ibn Ḥajar, scholars have explained this in order to prevent people who are praying from preoccupying themselves with a person's invalidating their ritual prayer due to some occurrence (such as passing wind). Ibid., p. 86.

[49] If dirt gets on one's forehead, one should not wipe it away during the ritual prayer; rather, they should wait until after the *salām*s at the end of the prayer; see Ḥasan b. ʿAmmār al-Shurunbulālī, *Marāqī al-falāḥ*, Beirut: Dār al-Fikr, 2005, p. 131.

[50] Q.I and Q.II.255, respectively.

[51] Q. III.18.

[52] Q.III.26–27.

[53] Q.CXII.

[54] Q.CXIII and Q.CXIV.

[55] The phrase, *ardhal al-ʿumr* ('the worst stage of life'), alludes to senility or decrepitude. See Q.XVI.70.

[56] *Ḥūr al-ʿayn* is an Arabic phrase that denotes an intense blackness of the eye, which, when contrasted with the eye's stark whiteness, is a symbol of extreme beauty. In Islamic terminology, this term refers to a special

kind of creation made by God in the next life. It is a species that is separate from the human species and it is not something that one can fully comprehend with the intellect, but which is promised by the All-Merciful God to the believers as mates.

57 In Islamic terminology, the Arabic word *waṣīla* refers to a means of gaining proximity to God.

58 Q.CXII.

59 Q.CIX.

60 Q.CXII.

61 Q.II.136.

62 Q.III.64.

63 Q.II.285.

64 Q.III.84.

65 Q.III.53.

66 Q.XXXV.24.

67 In other words, after the *sunna* prayers but before the obligatory (*farḍ*) prayer; see Ibn Ḥajar, *Tanbīh al-akhyār*, p. 87.

68 This is to remind one of the constriction of the grave and in preparation for immersing oneself in righteous deeds throughout the day; ibid., p. 88.

69 According to Ibn Ḥajar, this is based upon the fact that this is the sunrise supererogatory prayer (*ṣalāt al-ishrāq*), not the morning supererogatory prayer (*ṣalāt al-ḍuḥā*). See Ibn Ḥajar, *Tuḥfat al-muḥtāj*, vol. II, p. 259 and *Tanbīh al-akhyār*, p. 87.

70 According to Ibn Ḥajar, this is what Suyūṭī mentioned and what Ramlī agreed with; the maximum number of *rakʿa*s for the morning supererogatory prayer is twelve *rakʿa*s. See Ibn Ḥajar, *Tanbīh al-akhyār*, p. 88.

71 Q.I.

72 Q.CIX.

73 Q.CXII.

74 Q.II.255.

75 Q.CXIII and Q.CXIV.

76 See above for the definition of these terms.

77 Q.L.

78 A *rātiba* is a supererogatory prayer that the Prophet regularly prayed either before or after an obligatory prayer. It is also a daily litany of supplications, or Qurʾān recitation, normally recited at a specific time of the day.

79 'Short' here means in which short *sūra*s are recited.

80 Note that this prescription is in accordance with the Shāfiʿī *madhhab*; by contrast, Ḥanafīs do not pray two *rakʿa*s before the sunset prayer.

81 Q.CIX and Q.CXII, respectively.

[82] Q.XXXII.
[83] Q.LXVII.
[84] Q.CIX.
[85] Q.CXII.
[86] That is, not to pray five together but to divide them into three *rak'a*s followed by two, and so on.
[87] Suyūṭī's claim that praying three continuous *rak'a*s is better than three separate ones is a very weak opinion. In fact, according to several of our scholars, performing three continuous *rak'a*s is disliked (*makrūh*) because of the validity of its prohibition (the narration of Dāraquṭnī) and due to taking into consideration the opinion that continuity invalidates the ritual prayer. The reliable opinion about this issue proposes three levels: (1) the best level is to pray two *rak'a*s, conclude with the *taslīm* and then pray another single *rak'a*; (2) the middle level is to pray all three *rak'a*s continuously while not sitting for the first *tashahhud* and then finishing the third *rak'a* with the normal *tashahhud*; and (3) the lowest level is to perform three continuous *rak'a*s with two *tashahhud*s as with the evening prayer (*ṣalāt al-maghrib*). Ibn Ḥajar, *Tanbīh al-akhyār*, p. 90.
[88] Q.LXXXVII.
[89] Q.CIX.
[90] Q.CXII.
[91] Q.CXIII and Q.CXIV.
[92] Q.CII.
[93] Q.XCVII.
[94] Q.XCIX.
[95] Q.CIII.
[96] Q.CX.
[97] Q.CVIII.
[98] Q.CIX.
[99] Q.CXI.
[100] Q.CXII.
[101] This is according to the Shāfi'ī *madhhab*; however, for the Ḥanafī *madhhab*, the *qunūt* prayer is offered during the third *rak'a*—after reciting the *Fātiḥa* and a *sūra*, but before performing *rukū'*—by saying a *takbīr* and raising the hands and then folding them again.
[102] On this, Ibn Ḥajar wrote, 'Imam Suyūṭī's mentioning the *basmala* here [as part of the *du'ā' al-qunūt*] is one of his anomalous opinions (*tafarrudihi*), so pay no attention to it. How could this be correct when it is disliked (*makrūh*) due to the fact that it contains some of the *Fātiḥa* [meaning, the *basmala*], since the *basmala* is [considered to be] part of the *Fātiḥa* in the Shāfi'ī *madhhab*? Thus, transmitting the *basmala* [here in the *du'ā' al-qunūt*]

is like transmitting some of a spoken integral part (*rukn qawlī*) [meaning, of the *Fātiḥa*; in other words, transmitting part of the Qur'ān in the *du'ā' al-qunūt*].' Ibn Ḥajar, *Tanbīh al-akhyār*, p. 91. It should be noted that Ibn Ḥajar's comments here assume that the reader has some knowledge of the rulings of the Sunnī *madhhabs* regarding the recitation of the *basmala*. In brief, the Mālikī *madhhab* holds that the *basmala* is (1) not considered a verse of the Qur'ān except one instance in *Sūrat al-Naḥl*, (2) is a separator between *sūras* and (3) is not part of the *Fātiḥa*. The Ḥanafī *madhhab* holds the *basmala* to be (1) a verse of the Qur'ān, (2) to not be part of the *Fātiḥa* and (3) that it separates the *sūras*. Finally, the Shāfi'ī *madhhab* holds that the *basmala* is (1) a verse of the Qur'ān, (2) is part of the *Fātiḥa* and every other *sūra*. See 'Abd Allāh b. Abū Bakr Bā Sha'ayb, *Balābala al-sādiḥa 'alā aghṣān Sūrat al-Fātiḥa*, Beirut: Dār al-Minhāj, 2003.

[103] Q.CII.

[104] Q.CIII.

[105] Q.CIX.

[106] Q.CXII.

[107] An immense reward has been recorded in connection with this prayer; hence, some scholars have said that 'no one will hear about the immensity of its reward and not perform it save someone who takes his religion very lightly.' Ibid., p. 92.

[108] Here, Suyūṭī has used the means that God loves the most, namely, the Messenger of God, to beg for a need of his. In Arabic, this is called *tawaṣṣul* (meaning, 'seeking a means to gain proximity to God') and it is both permissible and recommended.

[109] Jalāl al-Dīn al-Suyūṭī and Jalāl al-Dīn al-Maḥallī, *Tafsīr al-Jalālayn*, Damascus, Dār Ibn Kathīr, 2005, s.v. Q.XI.56.

[110] See footnote above for an explanation of the term, *ḥanīf*.

[111] Here, 'concealment' means 'concealment from others of what a person would prefer not be known,' or 'concealment of his sins and shortcomings from being known by others.'

[112] These are the angels that are to the right and left of each person and who record good and evil deeds.

[113] Q.LIX.23.

[114] Q.XXX.17–19.

[115] Q.XXIII.115–118.

[116] Q.XL.1–3.

[117] Q.II.255.

[118] Q.II.1–4.

[119] Q.XVII.

[120] Q.CXII.

[121] Q.cxiii and Q.cxiv.

[122] These twelve *rak'as* are optional *ṣalat* prayers that protect one from Hellfire.

[123] Q.cxii.

[124] The latter refers to the Qur'ānic verse: '*Say, if the sea were ink for the Words of my Lord, it would run dry before the Words of my Lord were exhausted*' (Q.xviii.109).

[125] This is ruled as being *Sunna* and should occur on the eve of the day of *Jum'a* (in other words, on Thursday after sunset) or on the morning of *Jum'a*; see Ibn Ḥajar, *Tanbīh al-akhyār*, p. 95.

[126] Taking a bath on the day of *Jum'a* is emphasised; ibid.

[127] In other words, one should beautify oneself by trimming the moustache; ibid.

[128] To this, Ibn Ḥajar added wearing a *ṭaylasān*; ibid. A *ṭaylasān* is a piece of clothing that covered both the head and shoulders; see Hans Wehr, *Arabic-English Dictionary*, Ithaca, NY: Spoken Language Services, 1976, s.v. '*ṭailasān*.'

[129] Namely, before the sermon (*khuṭba*); ibid.

[130] According to Ibn Ḥajar, the eight *rak'as* that Suyūṭī has specified here are one of his anomalous opinions (*tafarrudihi*); ibid., p. 96.

[131] There are three distinct forms of listening in the Arabic language: (1) *sam'*, 'general listening,' (2) *istimā'*, 'focused listening' and (3) *inṣāṭ*, 'blocking everything out except the object of listening.'

[132] During the *khuṭba*, one should invoke blessings upon the Prophet with an audible voice (yet without excess) when one hears his name; ibid., p. 97.

[133] Light sleep is when a person who is sleeping can hear or recognize if someone is calling out their name, whereas heavy sleep is when one cannot; see Shurunbulālī, *Marāqī al-falāḥ*, p. 46.

[134] This practice, known as *ḥibwa*, can be seen today in Yemen and other Muslim countries. In addition to it being *Sunna,* it also offers support for one's back without the need to lean on a wall.

[135] Q.cxii.

[136] Q.cxiii and Q.cxiv.

[137] Q.i.

[138] This is for those who do not intend to remain at the mosque after the *Jum'a* prayer to pray the afternoon prayer (*ṣalāt al-'aṣr*) in congregation, as in that case, one should pray in the mosque because of the virtue related about praying therein. See Ibn Ḥajar, *Tanbīh al-akhyār*, p. 96.

[139] Q.xviii.

[140] Q.iii.

[141] Q.xi.

[142] Q.XLIV.

[143] In the Shāfiʿī *madhhab*, the imam ascends the pulpit and then says, *al-salām ʿalaykum* ('peace be upon you'), to commence the *khuṭba*, whereas in the Ḥanafī and Mālikī *madhhabs*, he does not say *salāms* to commence it.

[144] *Ḥadīths* have been related saying, 'Whoever misses three successive *Jumʿas* has committed disbelief.' Scholars have explained that this does not mean that the Muslim who has done this becomes a disbeliever if they believe that the *Jumʿa* prayer is obligatory. Rather, it means that one has acted like a disbeliever by attaching so little significance and importance to attending the *Jumʿa* prayer. As for Ibn Ḥajar, he commented, 'The warning and the threat of missing *Jumʿa* is severe; yet, *ḥadīths* like this have been related from Abū Dāʾūd and Nasāʾī.' Ibid., p. 99; see also Abū Dāʾūd, *Sunan*, no. 1053 and Nasāʾī, *Sunan*, no. 1378.

[145] The 'night' in Islam precedes the day and begins after the sunset prayer (*ṣalāt al-maghrib*); meaning, for instance, that the 'night' of the day of *Jumʿa* begins after the sunset prayer on Thursday.

[146] *Ruqya* ('protecting prayer') was a practice of the Prophet and it has continued to be practised by the sages and the learned of his community up to the present day.

[147] Meaning that as this person does supplicate and does go to pray, he is not an enemy of God and is thus worthy of God's care.

[148] Q.LVI. 89.

[149] Q.XXXVI.

[150] Q.II.255.

[151] Q.CXII.

[152] Q.CXIII and Q.CXIV.

[153] Q.I.

[154] *Laylat al-Qadr* is the night during the month of Ramaḍān when the Qurʾān was revealed and is described as being 'better than a thousand months' (Q.XCVII.3).

[155] According to a *ḥadīth*, both good and bad actions are multiplied therein.

[156] The Day of ʿArafa is the ninth day of the month of Dhū'l-Ḥijja and it is the first day of the Ḥajj pilgrimage.

[157] Abū Bakr al-Bayhaqī, *Shuʿab al-īmān*, Riyadh: Maktabat al-Rushd, 1993.

[158] Q.CXII.

[159] The Qurʾān is divided into 30 parts (*juzʾ*, pl. *ajzāʾ*) and each *juzʾ* is split into two further divisions (*ḥizb*, pl. *aḥzāb*), making one *ḥizb* equivalent to one-sixtieth of the Qurʾān.

[160] Q.L–CXIV.

[161] Q.I.

[162] Q.II.
[163] Ibn Ḥajar commented, 'Our scholars have not mentioned this.' See Ibn Ḥajar, *Tanbīh al-akhyār*, p. 103.
[164] Q.LXXV.1.
[165] Q.LXXVII.
[166] Q.LXXXVII.1.
[167] Q.XCV.1
[168] Q.LV.13.
[169] Q.XCI.7.
[170] Q.II.186.
[171] Q.III.18.
[172] Q.V.64.
[173] Q.XCIII.
[174] Q.CXIV.1.
[175] Q.II.5.
[176] Q.XVIII.1–5.
[177] Q.XXVII.59.
[178] Bayhaqī, *Shuʿab al-īmān*.
[179] It is *Sunna* to hasten to break one's fast after confirming that the sun has set; see Ibn Ḥajar, *Tanbīh al-akhyār*, p. 109.
[180] Some scholars in the Ḥanafī *madhhab* have considered it mildly disliked to fast solely on Fridays, whereas others have considered it to be recommended, even if one only fasts that day alone; see Shurunbulālī, *Marāqī al-falāḥ*, p. 234.
[181] *ʿĀshūrāʾ* is the tenth day of the month of Muḥarram and *Tāsūʿāʾ* is the ninth day. The Messenger of God said, 'If I am alive next year I will fast the ninth and the tenth.' He did not live until the next year.
[182] The 'white days' (*ayyām al-bayḍ*) are the days during the middle of the Islamic lunar month when the moon is brightest.
[183] However, during the month of Dhū'l-Ḥijja one should fast on the sixteenth and seventeenth, rather than on the thirteenth, because that day is part of the days of *tashrīq* (*ayyām al-tashrīq*) and fasting is prohibited at that time. See Ibn Ḥajar, *Tanbīh al-akhyār*, p. 111.
[184] The 'black days' (*ayyām al-sūd*) are the days of the month when the moon wanes to a sliver before eventually disappearing, and the night is at its darkest.
[185] There are four sacred months in Islam, three of them consecutive (Dhū'l-Qaʿda, Dhū'l-Ḥijja and Muḥarram), and one by itself (Rajab).
[186] According to Ibn Ḥajar, the reliable position is that if it is a necessary fast (*farḍ*), then one should say this with the intention of admonishing one's antagonist; if it is a supererogatory fast (*nafl*), then one should say

this in one's heart in order to admonish oneself. See Ibn Ḥajar, *Tanbīh al-akhyār*, p. 112.

[187] About this Ibn Ḥajar wrote, 'It is as he [Suyūṭī] said with the restriction that he mentioned, and I have dedicated a section [to this subject] in my book, *The Supreme Blessing Bestowed upon the World by the Birth of the Master of the Children of Adam* (al-Niʿma al-kubrā ʿalā al-ʿālam bi-mawlid Sayyid Wuld Ādam), which I compiled to celebrate the Prophet's birth and in which I described many of the reprehensible things that most Mawlid celebrations contain by way of reprehensible corruption—especially the Mawlid celebration that is held in Mecca on the twelfth night of Rabīʿ al-Awwal, which, according to one opinion, was the night that he was born.' Ibid., p. 113. See also Ibn Ḥajar, *al-Niʿma al-kubrā ʿalā al-ʿālam bi-mawlid Sayyid Wuld Ādam*, Istanbul: Işık Kitabevi, 1977 and Ibn Ḥajar's own summary of his position in *Tuḥfat al-akhyār bi-mawlid al-mukhtār*, Shām: al-Maṭbaʿa al-Dūmāniyya, 1283/1867.

[188] Q.cxii. This was narrated by Ibn Sunnī and Ṭabarānī in a *ḥadīth* reported by Jābir b. ʿAbd Allāh. See Ibn Ḥajar, *Tanbīh al-akhyār*, p. 114; Aḥmad b. Muḥammad Ibn al-Sunnī, *ʿAmal al-yawm wa'l-layla*, Medina: Maktabat Dār al-Zamān, 2009, p. 460; and Sulaymān b. Aḥmad al-Ṭabarānī, *al-Muʿjam al-awsaṭ*, Cairo: Dār al-Ḥaramayn, 1988, p. 6867.

[189] The word *khiwān* specifically refers to a table with no food on it, whereas *māʾida* refers to a table laden with food; Lakhnawī, *Misbāḥ al-lugha*.

[190] The reason for this is that potash is caustic.

[191] On this Ibn Ḥajar wrote, 'What might be outwardly understood from this preference for green over white is not what was intended. Rather, white is unanimously preferred because of the rigorously authentic *ḥadīth* (*ṣaḥīḥ*) saying that, "The Prophet ordered us to wear white clothes because they are the best of your clothes." Yes, on the day of the *ʿĪd* festival the 'best' non-white clothes are preferred over white clothes that are not the best in order to show the person whose green garment is [his] best, and his white garment is not his best, that it is *Sunna* on the day of the *ʿĪd* festival to wear his green garb instead of his white—not because it is green, but [because it is the] colour that happens to be the best [and the same holds for any other colour]. Yes, were someone to deduce from this that green is the best colour after white, this would not be wrong.' Ibn Ḥajar, *Tanbīh al-akhyār*, p. 121.

[192] See footnote above for a definition of *ṭaylasān*.

[193] 'It is reported that our master ʿUmar said as part of a *ḥadīth*, "Be like Maʿad (*tamaʿdadū*)." Maʿad was a forefather of the Prophet who was very ascetic and used to occasionally walk barefoot.' Aḥmad Nūr

al-Dīn al-Haythamī, *Majmaʿ al-zawāʾid wa-manbaʿ al-fawāʾid*, Beirut: Dār al-Fikr, 1993, vol. v, p. 136.

194 Ibn Ḥajar wrote: 'I say, creating a connection between these three [metals] is not good because it is misleading. It would have been correct to say [that], for men, gold rings are an outright prohibition (*nahy taḥrīm*) and the other [types of ring] are mildly offensive (*nahy tanzīh*) [and to be avoided if possible]; although the preponderant (*rājiḥ*) position in the Shāfiʿī *madhhab* is that there is no offensiveness in [this] because, according to them, the prohibition is not sound.' Ibn Ḥajar, *Tanbīh al-akhyār*, p. 126.

195 The Messenger of God used to wear a ring set with this special stone (*ʿaqīq*). It is usually found in Yemen and the Horn of Africa, and is variously translated as 'agate,' 'carnelian' and, when black, as 'onyx'.

196 The reason for this is that dyeing one's hair black is prohibited (*ḥarām*), whereas dyeing it a saffron colour is permissible because that was the *Sunna* of the Messenger of God.

197 Ibn Ḥajar wrote: 'I say, that is strange [coming] from him because our *madhhab* states that trimming the beard is disliked (*makrūh*) due to the order [of the Prophet] to allow the beard to lengthen, [as stated] in a rigorously authentic *ḥadīth* that supersedes all [else that] he mentioned.' Ibn Ḥajar, *Tanbīh al-akhyār*, p. 128.

198 According to Ibn Ḥajar, that also applied to all of the hair around one's private parts, which is common knowledge. Ibid., p. 130.

199 The reason for this is its tendency to engender pride and arrogance in one; hence, it is prohibited. Ibn Hajar wrote, 'It is prohibited to sit upon the skins of predatory animals that have hair, like tigers and cheetahs—even if they are placed on the floor in accordance with the most correct opinion (*awjah*)—because it is the custom of the haughty.' Ibid., p. 131.

200 Abu Dāʾūd narrated the *ḥadīth* of Shurayd b. Suwayd, who said, 'The Prophet passed by me while I was sitting with my left hand behind my back and leaning on the palm of my hand. He said, "Do you sit like those who have earned the wrath of God sit?"' Abu Dāʾūd, *Sunan*, no. 4747.

201 Bayhaqī narrated a *ḥadīth* on the authority of Muʿādh b. Jabal, who reported that the Prophet said, '[There are] two steps, one of which is the most beloved step for God (Great and Glorious is He), and the other is the most loathsome step for God (Great and Glorious is He). As for the step that God (Great and Glorious is He) loves, it is when a man sees a gap in the prayer rows and fills it. And as for that which God loathes, it is when a man intends to stand up: he stretches out his right leg and places his hands on it [to push himself up, and then] he plants his left leg and stands.' See Bayhaqī, *Shuʿab al-īmān*, vol. II, p. 288.

[202] Ibn Ḥajar added that one should also stand for an elder (*shaykh*), a relative or a friend; Ibn Ḥajar, *Tanbīh al-akhyār*, p. 136.
[203] If there is no choice but to share the bed with a minor, or a person of the same gender, then one must sleep under separate bedcovers and not share the same one. It is also recommended to sleep head to foot.
[204] Q.I.
[205] Q.II.255.
[206] Q.II. This usually means the last two verses (Q.II.285–286).
[207] Q.XVII. This means the last two verses (Q.XVII.110–111).
[208] Q.XVIII. This usually means the last four verses (Q.XVIII.107–110).
[209] Q.XXXII.
[210] Q.XXXVI.
[211] Q.XLIII.
[212] Q.XLIV.
[213] Q.LVI.
[214] The term *musabbiḥāt* ('those that give praise') refers to the *sūra*s of the Qur'ān that begin with *sabbaḥa* or *yusabbiḥu li'Llāh*, meaning, 'glory be to God,' or, more accurately, 'transcendent is God'. See Q.LVII, LIX, LXI, LXII and LXIV.
[215] Q.LXVII.
[216] Q.CII.
[217] Q.CXII.
[218] Q.CXIII and Q.CXIV.
[219] Q.CIX.
[220] Aḥmad Ibn Ḥanbal, *Musnad*, no. 17134. As mentioned above regarding poetry, this concerns profane poetry only.
[221] Q.III.
[222] The *ṣalāt al-layl* is also referred to as the *qiyām al-layl* or *tahajjud*.
[223] According to Ibn Ḥajar, this only applied to a person who does not fear falling asleep for the whole night (in other words, sleeping for longer than a short nap). He added that it may be easier for one to ward off drowsiness through other means than actually sleeping, such as washing the face and so on, in which case that would be recommended. He also clarified that Suyūṭī was only recommending sleep for those who were actually performing a night vigil (*qiyām al-layl*), since it was not their practice to sleep the entire night. See Ibn Ḥajar, *Tanbīh al-akhyār*, p. 145.
[224] According to Ibn Ḥajar this was recommended only if one is confident of waking up in time for the morning prayer (*ṣalāt al-fajr*); ibid.
[225] It was reported that the Prophet responded in this way to a man who had greeted him. This was narrated by Ibn al-Sunnī in his *ʿAmal al-yawm wa'l-layla* from a *ḥadīth* of Anas with a weakly authenticated chain of

transmission, just as Nawawī mentioned in his *Adhkār*. See Ibn Ḥajar, *Tanbīh al-akhyār*, p. 147. See also Aḥmad b. Muḥammad Ibn al-Sunnī, *ʿAmal al-yawm wa'l-layla*, Medina: Maktabat Dār al-Zamān, 2009, no. 235 and Muḥyī al-Dīn Yaḥya al-Nawawī, *al-Adhkār min kalām Sayyid al-Abrār*, Damascus: Dār al-Malāḥ, 1971, p. 400.

226 Q.XLIII.13–14.

227 Ibn Ḥajar clarified that the Prophet did not simply curse the person who did this, he emphatically prohibited it. See Ibn Ḥajar, *Tanbīh al-akhyār*, p. 149.

228 According to Ibn Ḥajar, if this causes mild discomfort then it is tolerated; otherwise, it is prohibited. Additionally, the prohibition is not restricted to three people on an animal; rather, the prohibition also applies to two people, or one heavy-set person (*samīn*), because they may cause the animal harm. Ibid., p. 151.

229 Q.III.83.

230 According to Ibn Ḥajar, this was tolerated when it came specifically from those who were spiritual trainers (*murabbūn*), or from other people such as a judge, elder or king who said something like this in order to teach manners by means of it. Otherwise, (if one reasons by analogy) this would be prohibited because it is backbiting, which is mentioning one's brother in a way that he dislikes—regardless of whether or not he is actually like that, or if he is present. Ibn Ḥajar added that scholars had mentioned that when a person has been insulted he should retort in such a way that will not cause others to move away from one, and which contains no untruthfulness, such as, 'O fool, O ignorant one.' See Ibn Ḥajar, *Tanbīh al-akhyār*, p. 152.

231 The word *karam* means 'the generous'.

232 Ibn Ḥajar commented about this, saying, 'Imam Suyūṭī has contradicted himself [in this passage] because in another book [of his] he says that there is no offensiveness (*karāha*) in saying this, which is correct.' Ibid.

233 Ibn Ḥajar stated that saying this (by which he meant, 'May God's blessings be upon you') was allowed; ibid., p. 154.

234 According to Ibn Ḥajar, what this meant was that if the third person was not distressed by their secret conversation on account of feeling safe with them, then it was not prohibited. Similarly, if there were four people and two of them were whispering separately while the other two of them were together, then that would not be prohibited. This would be contrary to a situation in which there happened to be six individuals, four of whom began a private discussion without the other two, and those two did not feel safe, in which case it would be prohibited. Ibid., p. 156.

235 This is corroborated by part of a *ḥadīth* that states, '[...] there are

jinn in Medina who have accepted Islam. So when you see any of them [in other words, any snake], pronounce a warning [addressed to] it for three days and if it appears after that then kill it, for it is a devil.' Muslim, *Ṣaḥīḥ*, no. 5557.

236 Muslim, *Ṣaḥiḥ*, no. 5240.

237 Q.XI.41.

238 Q.VI.91.

239 Q.CXII.

240 Q.II.255.

241 Q.II.255.

242 Q.II.285–286.

243 Q.I.

244 Q.CXIII and Q.CXIV.

245 The phrase, *umm mildam*, was an Arabic nickname for a fever.

246 Q.CXII.

247 Q.III.26–27.

248 Meaning, 'in the world and the Hereafter'.

249 Many of the righteous Muslims would mention the name 'Muḥammad'.

250 Q.LV.33.

APPENDIX

A Selection of Transliterated Prayers

A. A PRAYER UPON AWAKENING

Al-ḥamdu li'Llāhi 'Lladhī 'aḥyānā ba'da mā 'amātanā wa-'ilayhi 'n-nushūru. Al-ḥamdu li'Llāhi 'lladhī radda 'alā rūḥī wa-'āfānī fī jasadī wa-'adhina lī bi-dhikrihi. Lā 'ilāha 'illā 'Llāhu waḥdahu, lā sharīka lahu. Lahu 'l-mulku wa-lahu 'l-ḥamdu, wa-Huwa 'alā kulli shay'in qadīr[un].

B. A PRAYER UPON ENTERING THE WASHROOM

Bi'smi 'Llāhi. Allāhumma 'innī 'a'ūdhu bika mina 'l-khubuthi wa'l-khabā'ithi. Allāhumma 'innī 'a'ūdhu bika mina 'r-rijsi wa'n-najasi, al-khabīthi 'l-mukhbithi, ash-shayṭāni 'r-rajīmi.

C. A PRAYER FOR THE LESSER ABLUTION

Allāhumma 'j'alnī mina 't-tawwābīna wa'j'alnī mina 'l-mutaṭahhirīna. Subḥānaka 'Llāhumma wa-bi-ḥamdika. 'Ashhadu 'an lā 'ilāha 'illā 'Anta. 'Astaghfiruka wa-'atūbu 'ilayka. Allāhumma 'ghfir lī dhanbī, wa-wassi' lī fī dārī, wa-bārik lī fī rizqī, wa-qanni'nī bi-mā razaqtanī, wa-lā taftinnī bi-mā zawayta 'annī.

D. A PRAYER UPON LEAVING FOR THE MOSQUE

Allāhumma 'j'alnī fī qalbī nūran wa-fī lisānī nūran, wa'j'al fī sam'ī nūran wa-fī baṣarī nūran, wa'j'al min khalfī nūran wa-min 'amāmī nūran, wa'j'al min taḥtī nūran wa-min fawqī nūran. Allāhumma 'j'alnī nūran.

E. A PRAYER UPON BOWING DURING THE RITUAL PRAYER

Subḥānaka Dhī 'l-mulki wa'l-malakūti wa'l-'aẓamati. Subḥānaka, lā 'ilāha 'illā 'Anta. Subḥānaka 'Llāhumma Rabbanā, wa-bi-ḥamdika. Allāhumma 'ghfir lī, 'Anta 't-Tawwābu 'r-Raḥīmu. Subbūḥun quddūsun Rabbu 'l-malā'ikati wa'r-rūḥi. Allāhumma laka raka'tu wa-bika 'āmantu wa-laka 'aslamtu. Khasha'a laka sam'ī wa-baṣarī wa-laḥmī wa-'aẓmī wa-mā 'staqallat bihi qadamāya li'Llāhi, Rabbi 'l-'ālamīna.

F. A PRAYER FOR GUIDANCE

Allāhumma 'innī 'astakhīruka bi-'ilmika wa-'astaqdiruka bi-qudratika wa-'as'aluka min faḍlika 'l-'aẓīmi, fa-'innaka taqdiru wa-lā 'aqdiru, wa-ta'lamu wa-lā 'a'lamu, wa-'Anta 'Allāmu 'l-ghuyūbi. Allāhumma 'in kunta ta'lamu 'anna hādhā 'l-'amra khayrun lī fī dīnī wa-ma'āshī wa-'āqibati 'amrī, wa-'ājili 'amrī wa-ājilihi, fa'qdurhu lī wa-yassirhu lī, thumma bārik lī fīhi. Wa-'in kunta ta'lamu 'anna hādhā 'l-'amra sharrun lī fī dīnī wa-ma'āshī wa-'āqibati 'amrī, wa-'ājili 'amrī wa-ājilihi, fa'ṣrifhu 'annī wa'ṣrifnī 'anhu wa'qdur lī 'l-khayra ḥaythu kāna, thumma 'rḍinī bihi.

G. A SUPPLICATION FOR THE MORNING OR EVENING

Allāhumma hādhā khalqun qad jā'a fa-mā 'amiltu fīhi min sayyi'atin, fa-tajāwaz 'anhā. Wa-mā 'amiltu fīhi min ḥasanatin, fa-taqabbalhā wa-ḍā'ifhā aḍ'āfan muḍā'afatan. Allāhumma 'innaka bi-jamī'i 'aḥwālī 'Ālimun, wa-'innaka 'alā jamī'i najḥihā Qādirun. Allāhumma 'anjiḥ al-yawma (or, al-laylata) kulla ḥājatin lī, wa-lā tazidnī fī dunyāya bi-mā lā yanfa'unī min 'ākhiratī. Allāhumma 'innī 'as'aluka min fujā'ati 'l-khayri, wa-'a'ūdhu bika min fujā'ati 'sh-sharri, yā Ḥayyu, yā Qayyūmu. Bika 'astaghīthu fa-'aṣliḥ lī sha'nī kullahu wa-lā takilnī 'ilā nafsī ṭarfata 'aynin. Bi'smi 'Llāhi 'alā nafsī wa-'ahlī wa-'amanī wa-mālī. Subḥāna 'l-Maliki 'l-Quddūsi.

H. A PRAYER FOR THE DAY OF JUM'A AND THAT NIGHT

Allāhumma 'Anta Rabbī, lā 'ilāha 'illā 'Anta. Khalaqtanī wa-'anā 'abduka wa'bnu 'abdika wa'bnu 'amatika, wa-fī qabḍatika wa-nāṣiyatī bi-yadika. 'Amsaytu 'alā 'ahdika wa-wa'dika mā 'staṭa'tu. 'A'ūdhu bika min sharri mā ṣana'tu. 'Abū'u bi-ni'matika 'alayya wa-'abū'u bi-dhanbī, fa'ghfir lī dhunūbī fa-'innahu lā yaghfiru 'dh-dhunūba 'illā 'Anta.

I. A PRAYER UPON VISITING GRAVES

As-salāmu ʿalaykum dāra qawmin muʾminīna, wa-yarḥamu ʾLlāhu ʾl-mustaqdimīna minnā wa-minkum wa-ʾl-mustaʾkhirīna, wa-ʾinnā ʾin shāʾa ʾLlāhu bikum lāḥiqūna. ʾAntum lanā faraṭun wa-naḥnu lakum tabaʿun. ʾAsʾalu ʾLlāha lanā wa-lakumu ʾl-ʿāfiyata. As-salāmu ʿalaykum ʾahla ʾl-qubūri, yaghfiru ʾLlāhu lanā wa-lakum. ʾAntum lanā salafun wa-naḥnu ʿalā ʾl-ʾathri. ʾAṣabtum khayran ṭawīlan wa-sabaqtum sharran ṭawīlan. As-salāmu ʿalaykum ʾayyatuhā ʾl-arwāḥu ʾl-fāniyatu, waʾl-abdānu ʾl-bāliyatu, waʾl-ʿiẓāmu ʾn-nakhiratu ʾllatī kharajat mina ʾd-dunyā, wa-hiya biʾLlāhi muʾminatun. Allāhumma ʾadkhil ʿalayhim rawḥan minka wa-salāman minnā.

J. A PRAYER FOR THE DAY OF ʿARAFA

Allāhumma lā tajʿalnī bi-duʿāʾika Rabbi shaqiyyan wa-kun bī raʾūfan raḥīman, yā Khayra ʾl-masʾūlīna wa-yā Khayra ʾl-muʿṭīna. Allāhumma ʾjʿal fī baṣarī nūran wa-fī samʿī nūran wa-fī qalbī nūran. Allāhumma ʾshraḥ lī ṣadrī wa-yassir lī ʾamrī. Allāhumma ʾinnī ʾaʿūdhu bika min waswāsi ʾṣ-ṣudūri wa-shatāti ʾl-ʾumūri wa-fitnati ʾl-qubūri, wa-sharri mā yaliju fī ʾn-nahāri wa-sharri mā yaliju fī ʾl-layli, wa-sharri mā tahubbu bihi ʾr-riyāḥu wa-min sharri nawāʾibi ʾd-duhūri.

K. A PRAYER FOR PROSTRATION WHEN RECITING THE QURʾĀN

Allāhumma ʾjʿalhā lī ʿindaka dhukhr^{an} *wa-ʾaʿẓim bihā lī ʾajr*^{an}*. Waḍaʿ ʿannī bihā wizr*^{an} *wa-taqabbalhā minnī ka-mā qabiltahā min Dāwuda (ṣallā ʾLlāhu ʿalayhi wa-sallama). Subḥāna Rabbinā ʾin kāna waʿdu Rabbinā la-mafʿūl*^{an}*.*

L. A PRAYER UPON COMPLETING THE RECITATION OF THE ENTIRE QURʾĀN

Al-ḥamdu liʾLlāhi Rabbi ʾl-ʿālamīna. Al-ḥamdu liʾLlāhi ʾLladhī khalaqa ʾs-samawāti waʾl-arḍa wa-jaʿala ʾẓ-ẓulumāti waʾn-nūri. Thumma ʾlladhīna kafarū bi-Rabbihim yaʿdilūna—lā ʾilāha ʾillā ʾLlāhu—wa-kadhaba ʾl-ʿādilūna biʾLlāhi fa-ḍallū ḍalāl^{an} *baʿīd*^{an}*—lā ʾilāha ʾillā ʾLlāhu—wa-kadhaba ʾl-mushrikūna biʾLlāhi mina ʾl-ʿarabi waʾl-majūsi waʾl-yahūdi waʾn-naṣārā waʾṣ-ṣābiʾīna wa-mani ʾddaʿā* *li'Llāhi walad*^{an} *ʾaw ṣāḥibat*^{an} *ʾaw nidd*^{an} *ʾaw shabīh*^{an} *ʾaw mathal*^{an} *ʾaw ʿadl*^{an}*. Fa-ʾAnta Rabbunā, ʾAẓamu min ʾan tattakhidha sharīk*^{an} *fīmā khalaqta. Wa'l-ḥamdu li'Llāhi 'Lladhī lam yattakhidh ṣāḥibat*^{an} *wa-lā walad*^{an}*, wa-lam yakun lahu sharīk*^{un} *fī 'l-mulki wa-lam yakun lahu walī*^{un} *mina 'dh-dhulli wa-kabbirhu takbīr*^{an}*. Allāhu ʾAkbaru kabīr*^{an} *wa'l-ḥamdu li'Llāhi kathīr*^{an} *wa-subḥāna 'Llāhi bukrat*^{an} *wa-aṣīl*^{an}*.*

M. A PRAYER UPON BREAKING THE FAST

Allāhumma laka ṣumtu wa-ʿalā rizqika ʾafṭartu wa-ʿalayka tawakkaltu, fa-taqabbal minnī, ʾinnaka ʾAnta 's-Samīʿu 'l-ʿAlīmu. Dhahaba 'ẓ-ẓamʾu wa'btallati 'l-ʿurūqu wa-thabata 'l-ajru, ʾin shāʾa 'Llāhu. Wa'l-ḥamdu li'Llāhi 'Lladhī ʾaʿānanī fa-ṣumtu, wa-razaqanī fa-ʾafṭartu. Allāhumma ʾinnī ʾasʾaluka bi-Raḥmatika 'llatī wasiʿat kulla shayʾ^{in} *ʾan taghfir lī dhanbī.*

N. A PRAYER FOR WHEN FOOD IS SERVED

Allāhumma bārik lanā fīmā razaqtanā wa-qinā ʿadhāba 'n-Nāri.

O. A PRAYER FOR PUTTING ON CLOTHES

Allāhumma ʾinnī ʾasʾaluka min khayrihi wa-khayri mā huwa lahu, wa-ʾaʿūdhu bika min sharrihi wa-sharri mā huwa lahu. Al-ḥamdu li'Llāhi 'Lladhī kasānī hādhā wa-razaqanīhi min ghayri ḥawl^{in} *minnī wa-lā quwwat*^{in}*.*

P. A PRAYER UPON STANDING UP

Subḥānaka 'Llāhumma wa-bi-ḥamdika. ʾAshhadu ʾan lā ʾilāha ʾillā ʾAnta. ʾAstaghfiruka wa-ʾatūbu ʾilayka; tub ʿalayya wa'ghfir lī.

Q. A PRAYER UPON GOING TO SLEEP

Biʾsmi 'Llāhi 'r-Raḥmāni 'r-Raḥīmi. ʾAʿūdhu bi'Llāhi mina 'sh-shayṭāni 'r-rajīmi. Biʾsmika 'Llāhumma, ʾaḥyā wa-ʾamūtu. Biʾsmika Rabbī, waḍaʿtu janbī wa-biʾsmika ʾarfaʿuhu. ʾIn ʾamsakta nafsī fa'ghfir lahā, wa-ʾin arsaltahā fa'ḥfaẓhā bi-mā taḥfaẓu bihi 'ṣ-ṣāliḥīna. Allāhumma ʾinnī ʾaslamtu nafsī ʾilayka wa-fawwaḍtu ʾamrī ʾilayka wa-ʾaljaʾtu ẓahrī ʾilayka raghbat^{an} *wa-rahbat*^{an} *ʾilayka. Lā maljaʾa wa-lā manjā ʾillā ʾilayka. ʾĀmantu bi-Kitābika 'lladhī ʾanzalta wa-bi-Nabiyyika 'lladhī ʾarsalta.*

R. A PRAYER UPON LEAVING THE HOUSE

Bi'smi 'Llāhi. Tawakkaltu ʿalā 'Llāhi. Lā ḥawla wa-lā quwwata ʾillā bi'Llāh.

S. A PRAYER UPON STEPPING OUTSIDE

Allāhumma ʾinnī ʾaʿūdhu bika ʾan ʾaḍilla ʾaw ʾuḍalla, ʾaw ʾadhilla ʾaw ʾudhalla, ʾaw ʾaẓlima ʾaw ʾuẓlama, ʾaw ʾajhala ʾaw yujhala ʿalayya. ʾĀmantu bi'Llāhi, iʿtaṣamtu bi'Llāhi, mā shāʾa 'Llāhu. Ḥasabīya 'Llāhu wa-niʿma 'l-Wakīl.

T. A PRAYER UPON RETURNING HOME

Bi'smi 'Llāhi. Allāhumma ʾinnī ʾasʾaluka khayra 'l-mawlaji wa-khayra 'l-makhraji. Bi'smi 'Llāhi walajnā wa-bi'smi 'Llāhi kharajnā wa-ʿalā 'Llāhi tawakkalnā. Al-ḥamdu li'Llāhi 'Lladhī ʾaṭʿamanī wa-saqānī, wa'l-ḥamdu li'Llāhi 'Lladhī manna ʿalayya. ʾAsʾaluka ʾan tujīranī mina 'n-Nāri.

U. A PRAYER FOR TIMES OF NEED

Lā ʾilāha ʾillā 'Llāhu 'l-ʿAẓīmu, Rabbu 'l-ʿArshi 'l-ʿaẓīmi. Lā ʾilāha ʾillā 'Llāhu, Rabbu 's-samawāti wa-Rabbu 'l-arḍīna wa-Rabbu 'l-ʿArshi 'l-karīmi. Lā ʾilāha ʾillā 'Llāhu 'l-Ḥalīmu 'l-Karīmu. Subḥāna 'Llāhi wa-tabāraka 'Llāhu, Rabbu 'l-ʿArshi 'l-ʿaẓīmi. Wa'l-ḥamdu li'Llāhi, Rabbi 'l-ʿālamīna. Yā Ḥayyu, yā Qayyūmu, bi-Raḥmatika ʾastaghīthu. Allāhumma Raḥmataka ʾarjū; fa-lā takilnī ʾilā nafsī ṭarfata ʿayn^{in}*. Wa-ʾaṣliḥ lī shaʾnī kullahu. Lā ʾilāha ʾillā ʾAnta, Rabbī, lā ʾushriku bika shayʾ*^{an}*. Lā ʾilāha ʾillā ʾAnta. Subḥānaka, ʾinnī kuntu mina 'ẓ-ẓālimīna. Tawakkaltu ʿalā 'l-Ḥayyi 'Lladhī lā yamūtu. Wa'l-ḥamdu li'Llāhi 'Lladhī lam yattakhidh walad*^{an} *wa-lam yakun lahu sharīk*^{un} *fī 'l-mulki wa-lam yakun lahu waliy*^{un} *mina 'dh-dhulli, wa-kabbirhu takbīr*^{an}*.*

V. A PRAYER DURING ILLNESS

Lā ʾilāha ʾillā 'Llāhu wa'Llāhu ʾAkbaru. Lā ʾilāha ʾillā 'Llāhu. Lahu 'l-mulku wa-lahu 'l-ḥamdu, lā ʾilāha ʾillā 'Llāhu. Wa-lā ḥawla wa-lā quwwata ʾillā bi'Llāhi. Yuḥyī wa-yumītu, wa-Huwa Ḥayy^{un}*, lā* *yamūtu. Subḥāna ’Llāhi, Rabbi ’l-ʿibādi wa-Rabbi ’l-bilādi. Al-ḥamdu li’Llāhi ḥamd^{an} kathīr^{an} ṭayyib^{an} mubārak^{an} ʿalā kulli ḥāl^{in}. Allāhu ʾAkbaru kabīr^{an}, yā Rabbanā. Wa-Jalāluhu wa-Qudratuhu fī kulli makān^{in}. Allāhumma ʾin kunta ʾamraḍtanī li-taqbiḍa rūḥī fī maraḍī hādhā, fa’jʿal rūḥī fī ʾarwāḥi man sabaqat lahum minka ’l-ḥusnā wa-bāʿidnī mina ’n-Nāri ka-mā bāʿadta ʾūlāʾika ’lladhīna sabaqat lahum minka ’l-ḥusnā. Allāhumma ʾin kunta katabta ʿalayya fīhi ’l-mawta, fa’ghfir lī wa-ʾakhrijnī min dhunūbī wa-ʾaskinnī Jannata ʿAdn^{in}. Lā ʾilāha ʾillā ’Llāhu ’l-Ḥalīmu ’l-Karīmu. Subḥāna ’Llāhi wa-tabāraka ’Llāhu, Rabbu ’l-ʿArshi ’l-ʿaẓīmi, wa’l-ḥamdu li’Llāhi, Rabbi ’l-ʿālamīna. Allāhumma ʾinnī ʾasʾaluka taʿjīla ʿāfiyatika wa-ṣabr^{an} ʿalā balāʾika wa-khurūj^{an} mina ’d-dunyā ʾilā Raḥmatika.*

W. A PLEA FOR FORGIVENESS

Allāhumma ’ghfir lī khaṭīʾatī wa-jahlī wa-isrāfī fī ʾamrī wa-mā ʾAnta ʾaʿlamu bihi minnī. Allāhumma ’ghfir lī jiddī wa-hazlī wa-khaṭīʾatī wa-ʿamadī wa-kullu dhālika ʿindī. Allāhumma laka ʾaslamtu wa-bika ʾāmantu wa-ʿalayka tawakkaltu wa-ʾilayka ʾanabtu wa-bika khāṣamtu. Allāhumma ʾinnī ʾaʿūdhu bi-ʿIzzatika—wa-lā ʾilāha ʾillā ʾAnta—ʾan tuḍillanī. ʾAnta ’l-Ḥayyu ’l-Qayyūmu, Alladhī lā yamūtu wa’l-insu wa’l-jinnu yamūtūna.

X. A Plea for Blessing

Allāhumma ʾinnī ʾasʾaluka ʾan tubārika fī nafsī wa-fī samʿī wa-fī baṣarī wa-fī rūḥī wa-fī khuluqī, wa-fī khalīqatī wa-ʾahlī wa-maḥyāya wa-mamātī, wa-fī ʿamalī, Allāhumma, wa-taqabbal ḥasanātī. Wa-ʾasʾaluka ’d-darajāti ’l-ʿulā mina ’l-Jannati. Āmīn.

Y. A Plea for Refuge

Allāhumma ʾinnī ʾaʿūdhu bika wa-bi-nūri Wajhika ’lladhī ʾaḍāʾat lahu ’s-samawātu wa’l-arḍu.

GLOSSARY

ʿ*amal*: work or action. Specifically, the external works prescribed by the *Sharīʿa*. Also, customary practice, such as the ʿ*amal* of Medina.

basmala: saying the formula, *bi-ism Allāh*. Also referred to as the *tasmiya*.

duʿāʾ: prayer of supplication.

farḍ: obligatory. One of the five legal categories (*aḥkām khamsa*) of actions regulated by the *Sharīʿa*. These are prescribed actions that must be performed. Performing them is rewarded and omitting them is punished.

ghusl: purificatory bath. The greater [major] ablution.

Ḥajj: pilgrimage to Mecca, ʿArafāt and Minā. One of the five pillars (*arkān*) of Islam and an obligatory duty to be performed once in a lifetime by all adult Muslims of sound mind and the means to do so.

ḥaram: forbidden. One of the five legal categories of actions regulated by the *Sharīʿa*. Performing these actions is punishable by God.

iqāma: the call to commence the prayer.

istighfār: an appeal for pardon.

iʿtikāf: maintaining a period of spiritual retreat in the mosque. This practice may be performed at any time, but is most common during the last ten days of Ramaḍān.

khatm: the recitation of the entirety of the Qurʾān from beginning to end. Also known as *khatma*.

Laylat al-Qadr: Night of Power. It is the night during the month of Ramaḍān when the Qurʾān was revealed and is described as being 'better than a thousand months' (Q.xcvii.1).

madhhab: school of jurisprudence. The four schools recognised by Sunnī Muslims are the Ḥanafī, Ḥanbalī, Mālikī and Shāfiʿī *madhhabs*.

makrūh: disliked. One of the five legal categories of actions regulated by the *Sharīʿa*. Although these actions are not punishable, they are considered to be reprehensible from a legal point of view.

muʾakkada: emphasized. Usually found in the phrase, *sunna muʾakkada*. This designates a category of practices that are, strictly speaking, supererogatory (*nāfila*) and not obligatory (*farḍ*), but which have actually become part of regular practice.

muʿawwadhatān: the last two chapters of the Qurʾān. *Sūrat al-falaq* and *Sūrat al-nās*.

mubāh: indifferent. One of the five legal categories of actions regulated by the *Sharīʿa*. Neither reward nor punishment are stipulated for these actions.

mubālagha: doing one's utmost. Doing what exceeds the usual or ordinary.

mustaḥabb: desireable. One of the five legal categories of actions regulated by the *Sharīʿa*. Actions in this category are also referred to as *sunna* in the sense of 'ordained custom' and as *mandūb* (recommended). The performance of these actions is rewarded, but omitting them is not punished.

nāfila: (pl. *nawāfil*) a supererogatory work. Most commonly used to designate supererogatory prayer.

qiyām al-layl: night vigil. This is a supererogatory, *sunna* prayer performed late at night or during the early hours of the morning. Also known as *tahajjud* and, during the month of Ramaḍān, as *tarāwīḥ*.

rakʿa: (pl. *rakʿāt*) unit of prayer.

rātiba: (pl. *rawātib*) fixed supererogatory prayer. These are specific supererogatory prayers performed either before or after particular obligatory (*farḍ*) prayers. They differ from other supererogatory (*nawāfil*) prayers in that the Prophet performed them on a regular basis.

ṣalāt: ritual prayer. One of the five pillars (*arkān*) of Islam and an obligatory duty to be performed by all Muslims, either communally or individually, at five set times during the day.

ṣawm: fasting.

shahāda: the declaration of faith (*lā ilāh illā Allāh wa-Muḥammad rasūl Allāh*).

sujūd: prostration.

sunna: (pl. *sunan*) norm or custom. Specifically used to designate the customary practice of the Prophet (in the present volume, given as *Sunna*). Also used to refer to a legal category of actions with the connotation of 'ordained custom' (in the present volume, given as *sunna*).

taʿawwudh: the expression of seeking refuge in God (*aʿūdhu bi'Llāh*).

taḥiyyat al-masjid: salutation of the mosque.

taḥiyyat al-wuḍūʾ: salutation of the ablution.

tahlīl: saying the formula, *lā ilāh illā Allāh*.

taḥmīd: saying the formula, *al-ḥamd li-Llāh*. Also referred to as the *ḥamdala*.

ṭahūr: ritual purification.

takbīr: saying the formula, *Allāh Akbar*.

tasbīh: saying the formula, *subḥān Allāh*. The glorification of God. Also referred to as the *sabḥala*.

tashahhud: the recitation of the *shahāda*, especially in the *ṣalāt*.

taslīm: praying for peace. Especially used to designate saying the formula, *al-salām ʿalaykum wa-raḥmat Allāh wa-barakātuhu*, at the end of the *ṣalāt*.

taṣliya: the invocation of God's blessing upon the Prophet Muḥammad.

waḍūʾ: the water for the ablution.

waẓīfa: (pl. *waẓāʾif*) daily practice.

witr: the odd-numbered prayer at the end of the day.

wird: litany. Personal supererogatory devotions performed at specific times of the day.

wuḍūʾ: ablution. The lesser [minor] ablution.

BIBLIOGRAPHY

Bā Shaʿayb, ʿAbd Allāh b. Abū Bakr, *Balābala al-sādiḥa ʿalā aghṣān Sūrat al-Fātiḥa*, Beirut: Dār al-Minhāj, 2003.

Bayhaqī, Abū Bakr al-, *Shuʿab al-īmān*, Riyadh: Maktabat al-Rushd, 1993.

Haythamī, Aḥmad Nūr al-Dīn al-, *Majmaʿ al-zawāʾid wa-manbaʿ al-fawāʾid*, Beirut: Dār al-Fikr, 1993.

Ibn Abī al-Dunyā, ʿAbd Allāh b. Muḥammad, *al-Tahajjud wa-qiyām al-layl*, ed. Masʿad ʿAbd al-Ḥamīd al-Saʿdanī, Cairo: Maktabat al-Qurʾān, 1994.

Ibn Athīr, Majd al-Dīn al-Mubārak b. Muḥammad, *al-Nihāya fī al-gharīb al-ḥadīth wa'l-athar*, Beirut: Dār al-Maʿrifa, 2009.

Ibn Ḥanbal, Aḥmad, *Musnad li'l-Imām Aḥmad*, Beirut: Muʾassasat al-Risāla, 2001.

Ibn Ḥajar al-Haytamī, Aḥmad, *Tuḥfat al-akhyār bi-mawlid al-Mukhtār*, Shām: al-Maṭbaʿa al-Dūmāniyya, 1283/1867.

———, *al-Niʿma al-kubrā ʿalā al-ʿālam bi-mawlid Sayyid Wuld Ādam*, Istanbul: Işık Kitabevi, 1977.

———, *Tanbīh al-akhyār*, Amman: Arwiqa li'l-Dirāsāt wa'l-Nashr, 2013.

———, *Tuḥfat al-muḥtāj bi-sharḥ al-Minhāj*, Beirut: Dār al-Fikr, 1997.

Ibn Iyās, Muḥammad b. Aḥmad, *Badāʾiʿ al-zuhūr fī waqāʾiʿ al-duhūr*, ed. Paul Kahle and Muṣṭafā Muḥammad, Istanbul: Staatsdruckerei, 1931.

Ibn al-Mulaqqin, ʿUmar b. ʿAlī, *Tuḥfat al-muḥtāj ilā adillat al-Minhāj*, Mecca: Dār Ḥirāʾ, 1987.

Ibn al-Qaradāghī, ʿUmar, *al-Manhal al-naḍḍākh fī ikhtilāf al-ashyākh*, Beirut: Dār al-Bashāʾir al-Islāmiyya, 1934.

Ibn al-Sunnī, Aḥmad b. Muḥammad, *ʿAmal al-yawm wa'l-layla*, Medina: Maktabat Dār al-Zamān, 2009.

Ibn Taymiyya, Aḥmad b. ʿAbd al-Ḥalīm, *al-Kalim al-ṭayyib*, tr. Ezzedin

Ibrahim and Denys Johnson-Davies as *The Goodly Word*, Cambridge: Islamic Texts Society, 2003.

———, *Minhāj al-Sunna al-Nabawiyya*, Beirut: Dār al-Kutub al-ʿIlmiyya, 1321–22/1903–04.

Khalīl b. Isḥāq al-Jundī, *Mukhtaṣar al-Khalīl*, Cairo: ʿĪsā Ḥalabī, 2004.

Kramers, J. H., et al., *Encyclopaedia of Islam*, 11 vols., new edn. (*EI²*), Leiden: E. J. Brill, 1954–2002.

Lakhnawī, ʿAbd al-Ḥāfiẓ al-, *Misbāḥ al-lugha*, Karachi: Majlis-i Nashriyat-i Islam, 1992.

Nasāʾī, Aḥmad b. Shuʿayb al-, *ʿAmal al-yawm waʾl-layla*, ed. Fārūq Hamāda, Beirut: Muʾassasat al-Risāla, 1987.

Nawawī, Muḥyī al-Dīn Yaḥya al-, *al-Adhkār min kalām Sayyid al-Abrār*, Damascus: Dār al-Malāḥ, 1971.

Ramlī, Muḥammad b. Aḥmad al-, *Nihāyat al-muḥtāj ilā sharḥ al-Minhāj*, Beirut: Dār al-Kutub al-ʿIlmiyya, 1993.

Saleh, M. J., 'Al-Suyūṭī and his work: their place in Islamic scholarship from Mamluk times to the present,' *Mamlūk Studies Review*, vol. v, 2000, pp. 73–89.

Sartain, E. M., 'Jalal ad-Din as-Suyuti's relations with the people of Takrur,' *Journal of Semitic Studies*, vol. XVI, no. 2, 1971, pp. 193–198.

———, *Jalāl al-Dīn al-Suyūṭī*, University of Cambridge Oriental Publications, nos. 23–24, Cambridge: Cambridge University Press, 1975.

Shādhilī, ʿAbd al-Qādir al-, *Bahjat al-ʿābidīn bi-tarjamat Ḥāfiẓ al-ʿAṣr Jalāl al-Dīn al-Suyūṭī*, ed. ʿAbd Allāh Nabhān, Damascus: Majmaʿ al-Lugha al-ʿArabiyya, 1998.

Shaʿrānī, ʿAbd al-Wahhāb al-, *al-Ṭabaqāt al-ṣughrā*, ed. ʿAbd al-Qādir Aḥmad ʿAṭā, Cairo: Maktabat al-Qāhira, 1970.

Shurunbulālī, Ḥasan b. ʿAmmār al-, *Marāqī al-falāḥ*, Beirut: Dār al-Fikr, 2005.

Suyūṭī, Jalāl al-Dīn al-, *ʿAmal al-yawm waʾl-layla*, ed. ʿAbd al-Raḥmān Āl ʿAbd al-Qādir, Cairo: Maktabat wa-Maṭbaʿat Muṣṭafā al-Bābī al-Ḥalabī wa-Awlādihi, 1946.

———, *Dāʿī al-falāḥ fī adhkār al-masāʾ waʾl-ṣabāḥ*, ed. Aḥmad ʿAbd

Allāh Bājūr, Cairo: Dār al-Miṣriyya al-Lubnāniyya, 1994.

———, *Taʾyīd al-ḥaqīqa al-ʿaliyya wa-tashyīd al-ṭarīqa al-Shādhiliyya*, ed. ʿAbd Allāh al-Ghumārī, Cairo: al-Maṭbaʿa al-Islāmiyya, 1352/1934.

———, *Waẓāʾif al-yawm wa'l-layla*, ed. Muṣṭafā ʿAbd al-Qādir ʿAṭā, Beirut: Dār al-Kutub al-ʿIlmiyya, 1407/1987.

Suyūṭī, Jalāl al-Dīn al-, and Jalāl al-Dīn al-Maḥallī, *Tafsīr al-Jalālayn*, Damascus, Dār Ibn Kathīr, 2005.

Ṭabarānī, Sulaymān b. Aḥmad al-, *al-Muʿjam al-awsaṭ*, Cairo: Dār al-Ḥaramayn, 1988.

Wehr, Hans, *Arabic-English Dictionary*, Ithaca, NY: Spoken Language Services, 1976.